Also by Matt Margolis

The Worst President in History: The Legacy of Barack Obama

THE SCANDALOUS PRESIDENCY OF BARACK OBAMA

MATT MARGOLIS

A BOMBARDIER BOOKS BOOK
An Imprint of Post Hill Press

The Scandalous Presidency of Barack Obama
© 2018 by Matt Margolis
All Rights Reserved

ISBN: 978-1-68261-581-2
ISBN (eBook): 978-1-68261-582-9

Cover Design by Cody Corcoran

Post Hill Press
New York • Nashville
posthillpress.com

Published in the United States of America

To my wife, Beth,
whose loving support made this book possible.

Contents

Introduction

On November 20, 2016, while speaking at a news conference on the last foreign tour of his presidency in Lima, Peru, Barack Obama claimed, "I'm extremely proud of the fact that over eight years we have not had the kinds of scandals that have plagued other administrations."[1] He would echo this claim weeks later in an interview on *60 Minutes*, telling host Steve Kroft, "I'm proud of the fact that, with two weeks to go, we're probably the first administration in modern history that hasn't had a major scandal in the White House. In that sense, we changed some things."[2]

He actually said those things.

It's true that Obama often distanced himself from controversies as they arose in his administration by claiming he heard about them on the news. However, given the volume of scandals from which he distanced himself, such claims are hard to swallow.

Yet the mainstream press frequently echoed his dubious sentiments. Obama's top advisor Valerie Jarrett told CNN's Fareed Zakaria, "The president prides himself on the fact that his administration hasn't had a scandal."[3] A few days before Obama left office, White House Chief of Staff Denis McDonough told CNN's Jake Tapper that he was most proud of the fact that the Obama administration was "historically free of scandal."[4]

This should surprise no one. The press made a habit of pressing the same "scandal-free" talking point throughout Obama's two terms. Rana Foroohar, managing editor of *TIME* magazine, said on MSNBC back in May 2013, "...the president has been very rightfully proud of the lack of scandal in his administration so far."[5] The same day, Steve Inskeep, host of NPR's *Morning Edition* said, "this administration has been described—I don't even know how many times—as remarkably scandal-free."[6]

Here are a few other examples of this remarkable consistency of narrative among the press. *The New York Times* columnist David Brooks wrote, "The Obama administration has been remarkably scandal-free."[7] In a May 2016 column in *The Week*, Paul Waldman marginalized Obama's scandals as "piddling little scandalettes," later claiming, "as far as we know, whether you like Barack Obama or not, his hands are pretty clean."[8] *USA Today*'s editorial board wrote, "Obama has been a largely classy, mature, and personally scandal-free presence in the White House."[9] Joe Klein wrote in *TIME* magazine, "There would be little melodrama and absolutely no hint of scandal during his time in office."[10] Tom Brokaw, reacting to Obama's farewell address a month later on MSNBC, said, "He's been scandal free, frankly, in the White House. We haven't had that what for a while."[11] *The View*'s Joy Behar said, "President Obama, for eight years, was completely scandal-free." This patently absurd claim was actually met with applause. According to Behar, "The worst thing he did was smoke a cigarette and put his feet up on his desk."[12]

The media could not have been more consistent with their "scandal-free" messaging if the press operated right out of the Oval Office. Even when *The Washington Post* fact checker Glenn Kessler addressed these claims of a scandal-free administration, a bumbling litany of nuances and excuses for various "controversies" resulted in "no rating" for a four-Pinocchio lie. He claims that "scandals are in the eye of the beholder."[13]

Liberal media bias is well documented, but with Barack Obama, something worse is happening. In 2007, Ezra Klein, blogger and columnist for *The Washington Post*, founded JournoList.[14] The private, invitation-only online forum of several hundred left-wing journalists, academics, and activists served as a conduit for collusion. According to records obtained by *The Daily Caller*, while Obama was running for president in 2008, "employees of news organizations including *Time*, *Politico*, the *Huffington Post*, the *Baltimore Sun*, the *Guardian*, *Salon* and the *New Republic* participated in outpourings of anger over how Obama was treated in the media and, in some cases, plotted to fix the damage."[15]

Members of this group trashed conservative figures, but they also collaborated to protect candidate Obama when stories, such as his association with anti-American pastor Reverend Jeremiah Wright, threatened his campaign. If they failed to kill or bury a story, they tried to smear his critics. Jonathan Strong, a contributor at *The Daily Caller*, reported, "In one instance, Spencer Ackerman of the *Washington Independent* urged his colleagues to deflect attention from Obama's relationship with Wright by changing the subject. 'Pick one of Obama's conservative critics,' Ackerman wrote, 'Fred Barnes, Karl Rove, who cares—and call them racists.'"[16] Tucker Carlson, the cofounder and former editor-in-chief of *The Daily Caller*, said, "Again and again, we discovered members of JournoList working to coordinate talking points on behalf of Democratic politicians, principally Barack Obama. That is not journalism, and those who engage in it are not journalists. They should stop pretending to be."[17]

JournoList may have disbanded in 2010, but organized left-wing collusion to protect Obama continued unabated, and wasn't limited to the media. Academia also played a role in covering up the scandalous Obama years. When *TIME* magazine asked ten historians to weigh in on Obama's legacy, their comments often sounded much more like propaganda than analysis. Presidential historian Doris Kearns Goodwin said Obama would be remembered "for his dignity, grace, and the lack of scandal." James Grossman, executive director of the American Historical Association, said Obama was "virtually scandal free." Timothy Naftali, Clinical Associate Professor of History and Public Service at New York University, said Obama would "leave office scandal-free." Nikhil Pal Singh, Associate Professor in the Departments of Social and Cultural Analysis and History at New York University, said Obama "avoided scandal."[18] Edna Greene Medford, a Professor of History of Howard University and the academic advisor of C-SPAN's 2017 Presidential Historians Survey, said she was surprised that Obama ranked as 12th best president in the survey . . . not because 12th was absurdly high, but because she thought Obama should have ranked *higher*. Amongst other reasons, she said, "I am especially surprised that he was ranked at 7th in moral authority (despite heading a scandal-free administration)."[19] Are these so-called experts in history ignorant of the recent past, or co-conspirators in whitewashing Obama's record?

When I coauthored *The Worst President in History: The Legacy of Barack Obama,* I warned you this was coming. After all, even before Obama took the oath of office on January 20, 2009, greatness of messianic proportions was bestowed upon him and his presidency. Americans learned the hard way that "hope and change" weren't all they were cracked up to be. Obama couldn't possibly live up to such premature canonization, so his allies constantly made excuses. The media turned a blind eye, and academics are now covering his tracks for posterity. While the impact of his policies will be debated for years, no one can pretend that the Obama years weren't plagued from the beginning by controversy and scandal—unless, that is, they're either ignorant or dishonest.

Obama was one who liked to feign ignorance in order to distance himself from his scandals. When a scandal broke, Obama's default response was to claim he had learned about it from the media at the same time the rest of country did. That's not a rejection of the scandalous nature of any given outrage; it's an *admission* that the outrage was warranted. Only Obama could get away with spinning his responses as proof of the lack of scandal in his administration.

Is the media so left-biased that spying on journalists or waging war on whistleblowers is seen as problematic only when conducted by a Republican? What do historians think there is to gain by downplaying the significance of Fast and Furious, the IRS scandal, or the Benghazi cover-up? Why are they protecting Obama from us instead of protecting us from Obama? If we refuse to recognize teachable moments in history as they happen just because they reflect poorly on the political savior du jour, we will learn nothing from our mistakes, and are, thus, doomed to repeat them.

While it may be cliché to do so, it's worth quoting George Orwell here. In his classic dystopian novel, *1984*, he wrote "Who controls the past controls the future. Who controls the present controls the past." Today, historians control the past and "journalists" control the present. If they're both getting it so terribly wrong, then it is safe to say that the facts surrounding the scandals, that so many pretend never happened, will be lost to the memory hole. If people like you don't expose the truth about Obama's scandal-ridden administration, we're going to wake up, one day, in a world that thinks he's Santa Claus—a savior as fictional as a fairy tale.

Of course, Kessler's point about scandals being in the eye of the beholder forces us to more carefully define our terms. In one sense, he's right. In 2016, polls showed that the Hillary Clinton email scandal was a much bigger deal for conservatives than it was for liberals.[20] The eye of the beholder may be biased, but journalists should be focused on reporting the objective facts. They're not, and that's why I wrote this book.

In *The Worst President in History: The Legacy of Barack Obama*, Mark Noonan and I detailed the many failings of his presidency, but we also noted that history will be the ultimate judge of Obama's legacy. While we are confident that our assessment, and the plethora of facts to back it up, will stand the test of time, it will take years before Obama's presidency can be more objectively assessed by the masses. We wrote that book because we saw so clearly that the media wasn't speaking truth to power and that academia was a willing accomplice in a massive cover up to protect Obama's presidency from proper scrutiny. While that book covered all aspects of his presidency, this book will focus specifically on the scandals and controversies that marred Obama eight years in office, putting an end to the fallacy of a scandal-free administration.

Years of political polarization has resulted in a political climate where corruption and scandal are selectively tolerated—where party identification, not the facts, determines one's perception of guilt or innocence. This is by no means limited to the political left, but the media outlets with the loudest megaphones are all working as one to turn a false narrative about Obama's sterling record into historical "fact." Knowing this, Obama heard from the "watchdogs" of the press: do as you please. And he did. As the following pages will show, Obama's eight years in office were constantly tainted by scandal and controversy, not even his presidential transition or his return to the private sector were immune.

Many of the scandals and controversies covered in this book could have entire books devoted to them individually (and some of them do) in order to cover *everything* there is to know about each of them. This book is meant to be a resource covering the most significant scandals and controversies, and the most salient details you need to respond with the next time someone tells you that Barack Obama had a scandal-free presidency. They might not like to hear the facts, but they *need* to. Leftists, I have noticed, tend to self-segregate ideologically and don't like having their beliefs questioned. So, they may call you a racist for daring to question the conventional wisdom as reported by the media, but don't be discouraged because they won't stop. Obama's supporters in the media, academia, and the grassroots of the Democratic Party are invested in the idea that his presidency was an unparalleled success, and that he was the archetype of presidential ethics. Nothing could be further from the truth, as the following pages prove, but if they repeat their lies often enough, perhaps others will believe them.

It is up to conservatives and ethically consistent liberals who approach this book with an open mind to digest the facts and use them to debunk the myths of friends and family members with unflinching Obama messianism. My message is this: let this book be your reference in that next argument at the dinner table or debate on social media. Each and every little crack in the impenetrable wall of their citadel of denial takes us one step closer to the day when we all wake up and begin standing for truth and moral rectitude.

The BlagoGate Scandal

Obama's corrupt administration began before he took office. On December 9, 2008, just over a month after Obama's historic victory, Illinois Governor Rod Blagojevich was arrested at his home following a years-long corruption investigation.[1] In the state of Illinois, the governor has the power to fill a U.S. Senate vacancy; Blagojevich was charged with attempting to sell it. In transcripts of tapped phone conversations, Blagojevich called the position "a [expletive] valuable thing. You just don't give it away for nothing."[2] What did the Governor want in exchange for the seat? The criminal complaint claimed he was interested in several positions, including a position in Obama's cabinet, or an ambassadorship. If Obama failed to meet his demands, Blagojevich considered appointing himself.[3]

Obama distanced himself from Blagojevich when the corruption charges came to light. He claimed he was "appalled and disappointed" and denied any involvement in the scandal. "I have never spoken with the governor on this subject. I am confident that no representative of mine would have any part in any deals related to this seat."[4]

There was just one problem with that claim. It turned out that Valerie Jarrett, Obama's top advisor, was interested in his vacant seat, and is referred to in the criminal complaint as "Senate Candidate 1."

> Later on November 3, 2008, ROD BLAGOJEVICH spoke with Advisor A. By this time, media reports indicated that Senate Candidate 1, an advisor to the President-elect, was interested in the Senate seat if it became vacant, and was likely to be supported by the President-elect. During the call, ROD BLAGOJEVICH stated, "unless I get something

real good for [Senate Candidate 1], shit, I'll just send myself, you know what I'm saying."[5]

According to the complaint, Blagojevich offered to appoint Jarrett "in exchange for the position of Secretary of Health and Human Services in the President-elect's cabinet."[6] Four days after the presidential election, CNN reported that a "Democratic source close to Barack Obama" had confirmed that Valerie Jarrett was "Obama's choice to replace him in the Senate."[7] But Jarrett ultimately followed Obama to the White House as an advisor.

To nip the brewing scandal in the bud, the Obama Transition "investigated" his connection to Blagojevich. Astonishingly, no improper contact was discovered![8] In a written statement, Dan Pfeiffer, communications director of the Obama Transition, 'cleared' the president-elect. The Obama Transition's internal review "affirmed the public statements of the president-elect that he had no contact with the governor or his staff, and that the president-elect's staff was not involved in inappropriate discussions with the governor or his staff over the selection of his successor as U.S. senator."[9] Did anyone really expect that Obama's transition team would conclude that Obama talked to Blagojevich about his Senate seat and violated federal law? Was Pfeiffer really going to say, "Yes, Obama's guilty, but we *hope* this doesn't *change* anything"? Of course not. However, their findings contradict both the criminal complaint against Blagojevich and numerous documents obtained by Judicial Watch through a Freedom of Information Act (FOIA) request.

Judicial Watch president Tom Fitton explained, "Not only was Team Obama aware of Blagojevich's scheme but they seemingly participated in illegal negotiations with Blagojevich and his representatives."[10] One of the documents was a letter from president-elect Obama to Governor Blagojevich, dated December 2, 2008—just one week before Blagojevich's arrest—thanking him for meeting him the day before.[11]

What did they discuss at this meeting? KHQA, a CBS affiliate based out of Quincy, Illinois, published two stories about the meeting between Obama and Blagojevich, both acknowledging that the two met to discuss Obama's Senate seat. KHQA withdrew both stories without explanation.[12] Obama's senior advisor, David Axelrod, confirmed that Blagojevich and Obama met and that the Senate was discussed when asked about it on Fox Chicago Sunday on November 28, 2008. "I know he's talked to the governor. And, you know, he's—there are a whole range of names, many of which have surfaced. And he's—I think he has a fondness for a lot of them."[13] Axelrod would later claim he "misspoke" in a statement released shortly after Blagojevich's arrest. "I was mistaken when I told an interviewer last month that the president-elect has spoken directly to Governor Blagojevich about the Senate vacancy."[14]

Testimony during the trial also debunked the internal Obama team's investigation. Barack Obama and his chief of staff Rahm Emanuel came up frequently during Blagojevich's trial.[15] In May 2010, Blagojevich's top aide, John Harris, testified that Obama knew he wanted a job in his administration in exchange for appointing an Obama-approved candidate. "The president understands that the governor would be willing to make the appointment of Valerie Jarrett as long as he gets what he's asked for."[16] When Jarrett withdrew from consideration, a list of "acceptable" candidates to fill Obama's seat in the United States Senate was supplied by Obama.[17] Harris's testimony matched secret FBI recordings of conversations between him and Blagojevich. Governor Blagojevich also wanted Obama to testify, since he had "direct knowledge to allegations made in the indictment" and his public statements "contradict other witness statements..."[18]

More damning testimony came from Tom Balanoff, a powerful union official in Chicago, and Obama's emissary to the governor regarding his Senate seat. He claimed that Obama called him the night before the election to talk about what he was looking for in his successor in the U.S. Senate. He said he wouldn't publicly support anyone, but that Valerie Jarrett would fit his criteria. Balanoff then relayed this information to Governor Blagojevich.[19] The Obama Transition team's internal investigation failed to mention this conversation. Yet, the media treated it as if it were a thorough and honest investigation, sufficient to put the issue to rest.

What do we know? Obama was interested in who replaced him in the Senate, provided a list of acceptable candidates to the governor and met with him about the seat, and used an intermediary to discuss the quid pro quo. All of this is public record. Obama's statements also contradicted sworn testimony in Blagojevich's trial. How was this not a bigger story?

When the media wasn't trying to distance Blagojevich from Obama, they were trying to turn the scandal into a positive story for the new president. CBS correspondent Chip Reid dubbed GOP attempts to link Obama and Blagojevich a "tough sell." He added, "Barack Obama and Rod Blagojevich have both been leaders in Illinois Democratic politics for years, but long-time observers say that's about as far as the connection goes."[20] George Stephanopoulos not only accepted Axelrod's claim that he misspoke without question, but he called Blagojevich Obama's "best character witness."[21] NBC's Chuck Todd bizarrely claimed, "there's clearly no evidence that anything was going on, and if anything, the quotes from Blagojevich in that amazing indictment are the most exculpatory thing there for the President-elect."[22] Others suggested the scandal was insignificant. "What's the big deal here?" asked PBS's Jim Lehrer.[23] If you have to ask, you have no business being in the media.

In retrospect, this scandal served notice to the American people that Obama's tenure would be rotten to the core and that the press would cover the stench. With a zealous investigation, he'd have resigned in disgrace, ending his presidency before it began. Instead, the media tipped its hand. Obama had the freedom to push the boundaries of ethical governance and the media would cover for him. Establishment "journalists" were anxious for Obama to take office unencumbered by scandal so he could deliver on all that "hope and change" he spoke of during the campaign. Far from acting as America's watchdog, the press became Obama's lapdog.

The Audacity of Opacity

Remember when Barack Obama was running for president, and he promised that his administration would be the most transparent and open administration? As the pages of this book show, there's a reason Obama's promise for transparency was as much of a sham as his Nobel Peace Prize. If you believe he sincerely intended to open up the government to public scrutiny, his actions are even more galling. For the record, I don't.

From the start, the grandiose platitudes of the campaign proved empty. Obama played the part of a president who desired transparency. On day one of his presidency he issued a memorandum instructing federal agencies "to usher in a new era of open government."[1] How did he do following his own instructions? Prior to entering the White House, Obama promised that all bills would be posted online for the American public to read for five days prior to signing them into law. It took him nine days to abandon that promise when he signed the *Lilly Ledbetter Fair Pay Act* less than a day after it arrived on his desk.[2]

Failing to live up to a relatively minor campaign promise was just the first in a long string of decisions made by the most opaque and guarded administration in American history to undermine all attempts to hold government accountable. Here are several other instances of obfuscation. Remember, this is far from an exhaustive survey.

Obama gets praise for his policy of voluntarily releasing White House visitor logs, but he fought hard to keep them secret, only revising the policy after a lawsuit from Citizens for Responsibility and Ethics in Washington (CREW).[3] After that "change," the White House conducted many meetings with lobbyists *off* White House grounds to keep his associations secret.[4] It took losing a lawsuit from Judicial Watch to force the administration to release all visitor logs.[5]

As a candidate for president, Obama promised to protect whistleblowers. As president, he waged war against them. The Obama administration used the 1917 Espionage Act to go after whistleblowers who spoke with the media three times more than all past presidents... *combined!*[6] In a rare moment of honesty, his promise to offer increased whistleblower protections was deleted off his transition website change. gov in the summer of 2013.[7]

Transparency on health care reform also met an untimely demise at the hands of an ethics death panel. Remember when Obamacare negotiations were supposed to be televised on C-SPAN to demonstrate true openness with the voters? Obama said, "I'm going to have all the negotiations around a big table. We'll have doctors and nurses and hospital administrators. Insurance companies, drug companies—they'll get a seat at the table, they just won't be able to buy every chair. But what we will do is, we'll have the negotiations televised on C-SPAN..."[8] That never happened. The bill was instead drafted by a panel of Obama-appointed experts behind closed doors[9] and then rammed through both houses of Congress using parliamentary tricks to stop Americans from knowing anything about the plan.[10] Perhaps that explains why we had to pass the bill to find out what was in it.

Did you know the Obama White House had a policy of banning photojournalists from certain events? The media, despite its glowing coverage of Obama, was not amused. In lieu of a hashtag campaign on Twitter, the White House Correspondents Association and nearly forty leading media outlets and organizations sent a letter to the White House to protest their policy. They believed the Obama policy set "a troubling precedent with a direct and adverse impact on the public's ability to independently monitor and see what its government is doing," and "raised constitutional concerns."[11]

Early in Obama's administration—less than four months in—White House Counsel sent a memo to all federal agencies instructing them to delay, censor, or prevent the release of any documents involving or referencing any communication with the White House requested under the Freedom of Information Act. According to one FOIA officer, the Obama

White House also kept a "Nixonian list" of FOIA requesters. "They not only want to know what is sent out from the government, but also who's doing the asking."[12] If a president is that paranoid, something is very wrong. It should have been widely discussed when the *Washington Times* broke the story in the summer of 2014, but it met with crickets outside the conservative blogosphere.

And, speaking of FOIA requests, the Obama administration spent a record amount of money—our tax dollars, no less—fighting FOIA lawsuits to prevent the release of documents. An Associated Press analysis concluded that the Obama administration also "set records for outright denial of access to files, refusing to quickly consider requests described as especially newsworthy, and forcing people to pay for records who had asked the government to waive search and copy fees."[13] Your tax dollars at work preventing you from exercising your rights as defined under federal law?

While Obama thinks he deserves credit for signing bipartisan FOIA reform in the summer of 2016, he was actually a strong *opponent* of those reforms. That's according to documents obtained by the Freedom of the Press Foundation, a nonprofit group that had to sue Obama's Department of Justice for stonewalling their FOIA requests. Those documents show the Obama administration actively undermining bipartisan efforts to reform FOIA and make government more transparent.[14] When given the chance to codify his stated ideal of a transparent government into law, with rare, bipartisan support in Congress, Obama balked.

When it really mattered, Obama fought to keep his administration anything but transparent. He fought (and won) the right "to keep secret a memo that outlines the supposed legal authority for the Federal Bureau of Investigation to collect Americans' telephone and financial records without a subpoena or court order."[15] Even *The New York Times* editorial board lambasted Obama over that one.

In 2012, *Bloomberg News* gave the Obama administration a transparency test, and found that "Nineteen of 20 cabinet-level agencies disobeyed the law requiring the disclosure of public information."[16] A major study by the Committee to Protect Journalists released in 2013 called the Obama White House the most secretive since Nixon. "The administration's war on leaks and other efforts to control information are the most aggressive I've seen since the Nixon administration when I was one of the editors involved in *The Washington Post*'s investigation of Watergate," wrote Leonard Downie Jr.[17] A 2014 Associated Press analysis reached a similar conclusion, determining that the Obama administration grew increasingly secretive over the years.[18] According to analysis from Reporters Without Borders (RWB), the United States' ranking on the World Press Freedom Index plummeted from 20th out of 180 countries when Obama took office,[19] to 41th place in 2016, after hitting a low point in 2015 coming in at 49th overall.[20]

James Risen, the Pulitzer Prize-winning reporter for *The New York Times* who was pressured by the Obama administration to reveal his confidential sources in a leak investigation, called the Obama administration "The greatest enemy of press freedom in a generation."[21] *The New York Times* executive editor Jill Abramson called the Obama White House, "the most secretive White House that I have ever been involved in covering."[22]

The Washington Post was also critical of Obama's record on transparency and secrecy, noting that *WaPo* reporters had only been given an opportunity to interview Obama during his first year in office. "Think about that. The Post is, after all, perhaps the leading news outlet on national government and politics, with no in-depth, on-the-record access to the president of the United States for almost all of his two terms," wrote columnist Margaret Sullivan in May 2016. "I couldn't get anyone in the White House press office to address this, despite repeated attempts by phone and email—which possibly proves my point."[23]

Sullivan showed that Obama gave an unprecedented number of interviews, but his strategy was to avoid hostile cross-examination and dictate the terms of his media appearances. According to a study from retired Towson University professor Martha Joynt Kumar, access to Obama was strictly controlled, as were terms and topics of all interviews. Press conferences and question and answer sessions with the media were limited.[24] Rather than face a potentially combative press corps that would be unwilling to tolerate a list of demands by Obama for an interview, he focused on smaller media outlets more willing to accept those demands for access. Take his interview with YouTube celebrity GloZell Green, famous for a video of herself immersed in a bathtub filled with milk and cereal...and *eating* it.[25] I watched the infamous bathtub video as part of my research for this book. There are literally no words to describe it, and no legitimate justification for Obama to debase the office of the presidency by granting an amateur YouTube attention-seeker like GloZell an interview.

While Obama lauded transparency in public, he avoided transparency like the plague behind the scenes. Even so, he pushed the "most transparent administration" mythology throughout his presidency. It wasn't enough for Obama to pretend that he was a true advocate for government transparency; he actually *demanded* credit for it. In what can only be described as a pathetic attempt to rewrite Obama's scandalous record on transparency, press secretary Josh Earnest wrote a letter to the editor that appeared in *The New York Times* on August 31, 2016, claiming Obama improved government transparency and journalists should recognize and acknowledge that.[26] Forty journalism and open-government groups responded with a letter explaining how transparency had actually gotten *worse*.[27]

What do you get when you cross the least accessible White House in history with a submissive, fawning press? A transparent scandal that's invisible to the average American.

The New Black Panther Scandal

On Election Day 2008, members of the New Black Panther Party stood outside a Philadelphia polling place wearing military garb making racial remarks and discouraging people from voting. The incident was captured on video and uploaded to YouTube, gaining national attention. A voter intimidation case against the New Black Panther Party began weeks before Obama took office.[1] And that's where this open-and-shut case turned in one of the earliest Obama administration scandals.

The case continued under the Obama administration. Between the video evidence and eyewitness accounts, it was a slam dunk. In fact, the New Black Panthers never showed up in court to defend themselves, establishing their likely conviction by default. But then, in May 2009, the Justice Department made the controversial decision to drop the case. Despite the video evidence of the men using racial slurs, with one of them brandishing a weapon, and witness reports of voters turning away from the poll because of their intimidating presence, the Justice Department claimed the incident was minor and blown out of proportion. They said career attorneys had determined there was no merit to the case.[2] Their excuses were as implausible as the pitch for Obamacare.

Many believed Obama's Justice Department was refusing to prosecute minorities for civil rights abuses. As Virginia Congressman Frank Wolf asked, "If showing a weapon, making threatening statements and wearing paramilitary uniforms in front of polling station doors does not constitute voter intimidation, at what threshold of activity would these laws be enforceable?"[3] For the Obama administration, the answer—apparently—was "only when the victims aren't white."

Around the same time this scandal was growing, Obama got himself in the middle of another race-based controversy by speaking publicly about the arrest of Harvard professor Henry Louis Gates, Jr. at his home. He implied that the officers who were responding to a neighbor's 911 call about a possible break-in in progress had suspected the professor based solely on his race. He called together the professor, the police officer and, of course, the press, to hold a "beer summit" to open a dialogue about race relations in law enforcement.[4]

But, the scandal at the Justice Department was far more serious. The U.S. Commission on Civil Rights looked into the allegations against the Justice Department. Republicans in Congress demanded answers. The new "open and transparent" Obama administration was having none of it, however. If you'll pardon my echoing of Obama here, they "acted stupidly." They refused to respond to requests from the commission and congressional inquiries.[5] Obviously, they had nothing to hide, right? Months of stonewalling later, the commission voted to formally investigate the Justice Department's actions.[6]

And the obstruction continued. The Justice Department instructed federal attorneys J. Christian Adams and Christopher Coates, who were subpoenaed by the commission, not to cooperate with the investigation. Adams and Coates had both worked on the case against the New Black Panthers and wanted it to move forward.[7] Coates was removed from his position at the Department of Justice and sent to a U.S. Attorney's office in South Carolina.[8] Adams later resigned from his position at the Justice Department "because of the corrupt nature of the dismissal, statements falsely characterizing the case and, most of all, indefensible orders for the career attorneys not to comply with lawful subpoenas investigating the dismissal."[9]

Adams asserts that "the dismissal of the Black Panther case was motivated by a lawless hostility toward equal enforcement of the law."[10] He is not alone in this assessment. According to Adams, others in the department agree with him. "The department abetted wrongdoers and abandoned law-abiding citizens victimized by the New Black Panthers," he added.[11] When Adams appeared before the Civil Rights Commission in July 2010, he testified "I was told by voting section management that cases are not going to be brought against black defendants on [behalf] of white victims."[12] Adams mentioned deputy assistant Attorney General Julie Fernandes, an Obama appointee, by name, saying she'd told him that the Obama administration was only interested in pursuing civil rights case where the victims were minorities.[13] Assistant Attorney General for Civil Rights Tom Perez refused to confirm or deny whether she made the statements. Christopher Coates, after originally being blocked from testifying by the Justice Department, echoed a similar story when he spoke before the commission. "I had people who told me point-blank that [they] didn't come to the voting rights section to sue African American people."[14] Equal justice under the law was not an ideal of the Obama administration.

Both Adams and Coates also accused Tom Perez of lying under oath when he testified to the commission about the case. According to documents obtained by Judicial Watch via a FOIA lawsuit, they were right. The Justice Department had been claiming—for over a year, to both Congress and the commission—that career attorneys, not political appointees, had been responsible for dismissing the case. Perez had testified under oath to this point, but according to internal emails, high ranking political appointees were regularly discussing the case. *The Washington Times* even reported in 2009 that Associate Attorney General Thomas J. Perrelli, the third-ranking official in the Justice Department at the time, "was consulted and ultimately approved" the decision to drop the case.[15] Attorney General Eric Holder was also being updated on the case, bringing the corruption straight to Obama's cabinet.[16]

So, Perez lied under oath. No big deal, right? Obama was pleased. Perez later became Labor Secretary in 2013, serving until the end of Obama's presidency. As of this writing, he is the chairman of the Democratic National Committee. Lying under oath pays if you're an Obama crony. Considering the Democrats already have a president who was impeached for lying under oath, and a former chairman who resigned in disgrace after rigging the 2016 Democratic presidential primaries for that president's wife, having a party chairman who lied under oath (and got away with it) is small potatoes.

Not only were senior officials at the Justice Department involved but, according to an analysis by *The Washington Times,* there was also evidence of *coordination* with the White House.

Flagrant Justice Department stonewalling of numerous outside inquiries concerning the case already had deepened the suspicion that high-level political interference was involved. Now a new analysis shows that the top Justice political appointee positively identified as having approved the controversial decisions, Associate Attorney General Thomas J. Perrelli, had a strange habit of consulting key White House lawyers in person at exactly the times the key Black Panther decisions were being made—but very rarely visiting the White House when Black Panther matters were not pressing.[17]

On January 27, 2011, the U.S. Commission on Civil Rights released their final, damning report on the New Black Panther Party intimidation case. It not only detailed the merits of the case, but also the Obama administration's involvement in the decision to drop it, the stonewalling of the investigation by the Justice Department (including not allow key witnesses in the department to testify) and unambiguous evidence of a racial double standard in the Civil Rights Division.[18] Despite all the damning evidence, an internal Justice Department investigation concluded that politics played no role in the dismissal of the Black Panther case.[19] Gee, who didn't see that coming?

What we had here was an explosive scandal involving accusations of systemic racial bias in the Department of Justice, stonewalling investigations, lying under oath, and evidence of White House involvement. Calling it a scandal is an understatement. Surely the media covered the story with gusto, right?

Not. Even. Close.

There was no coverage of the scandal at ABC, CBS, or NBC. In the summer of 2010, more than a year after the controversy began, *The Washington Post*'s ombudsman skewered the paper for ignoring the scandal while other papers like *The Washington Times* and even *The New York Times* had covered it.[20] Around the same time, CBS anchorman Bob Schieffer interviewed Eric Holder, but never asked him about the scandal, claiming, after the fact, that he didn't know about it during the interview.[21] Even more ridiculous was a claim by MSNBC's Keith Olbermann that the decision not to prosecute the New Black Panther Party "was not made by Obama, nor the Obama administration, nor the Attorney General, Mr. Holder. It was made during the administration of President

George W. Bush."[22] Perhaps Schieffer was ignorant of the scandal (which I doubt) since the media gave it little attention, but Olbermann's claim was a verifiable lie. As I've already documented, the decision to drop the case happened *after* Obama took office and was made by Obama appointees.

Soon after the release of the Commission on Civil Rights' final Interim Report on the scandal, several commissioners' terms expired, and the vacancies filled by Obama's appointees.[23] The commission's investigation was as good as dead.

In 2012, the New Black Panthers once again returned to polling places in Philadelphia to intimidate potential voters. With Barack Obama and Eric Holder protecting them from being held accountable, what was stopping them? So much for that post-racial presidency we were promised. Like the rest of the media narrative surrounding Obama's term in office, reality bore little resemblance.

The Walpin Firing Scandal

Most people probably don't know who Gerald Walpin was, or why he's important in the grand scheme of Obama's scandals. He was the Inspector General for the Corporation for National and Community Service (CNCS), appointed by George W. Bush and confirmed by the U.S. Senate in December 2006 by voice vote. Walpin, a conservative, had a long and distinguished career in the private and public sectors and had worked to convict Democrats *and* Republicans for wrongdoing.[1] When Obama nominated Sonia Sotomayor to the Supreme Court, the White House distributed a talking points memo to support her nomination citing Walpin's past support of Sotomayor's nomination to the Second Circuit in 1998.[2] Twelve days after the White House distributed this memo citing Walpin to bolster Obama's nomination of Sotomayor, Obama fired Walpin without explanation or warning. One reporter for *The Daily Beast* said that the firing: "might be President Obama's first scandal since taking office."[3] It wasn't the *first*, obviously, but it would prove to be quite the scandal.

Gerald Walpin had been investigating Sacramento Mayor Kevin Johnson, a former NBA basketball star and Obama supporter, for misusing federal grant money from AmeriCorps. The program was created by the National and Community Service Trust Act of 1993 and has grown to over 80,000 members since its inception. Participants get benefits such as student loan deferment, living allowances, health benefits, career opportunities and training, and so forth.[4] The program has done some good, but has also been plagued by waste and corruption.

What did Walpin do to merit being fired by Obama? He found that Johnson gave $850,000 of AmeriCorps grant money to a nonprofit organization he founded called St. HOPE Academy. That grant money was used to pay AmeriCorps volunteers for political activity, to wash his car, and to run his personal errands.

Because of the investigation, Walpin recommended criminal charges and Johnson was barred from receiving any federal money. He referred the case to the local U.S. Attorney's office. Prosecutors chose not to file charges against St. HOPE, but a settlement agreement was reached: about half the $850,000 grant money it received from AmeriCorps had to be paid back in exchange for restoring its eligibility to receive future grants.[5] Johnson called the settlement agreement "excessive." Walpin disagreed. He said the settlement was lenient, and that the U.S. Attorney's office had given into political pressure.

White House lawyer Norman Eisen then informed Walpin that he had an hour to resign or be fired. He refused to resign and Obama informed Congress that Walpin was fired. His only explanation was: "It is vital that I have the fullest confidence in the appointees serving as Inspectors General. That is no longer the case with regard to this Inspector General."[6]

Obama's justification was vague, and his actions were illegal. The president has the power to fire inspectors general, but he must give them thirty days' notice, and Congress must receive a letter explaining the firing, according to the Inspector General Reform Act of 2008. Obama was aware of this since he was a cosponsor of the legislation while in the U.S. Senate.[7]

The day Obama terminated Walpin, Rick Maya, the executive director of St. HOPE, resigned from his position. In his resignation letter, Maya accused Johnson and other St. HOPE board members of obstructing the investigation into their spending practices, and said emails under federal subpoena had been deleted. The allegations not only gave more credence to Walpin's claims, but also prompted a new FBI investigation.[8]

A Republican-led investigation began almost immediately, as did a White House smear campaign against Walpin to justify his firing. Obama's excuse wasn't even cutting it for some Democrats, so he responded with a letter the leaders of the Senate committee overseeing AmeriCorps. In it, he accused Walpin of, among other things, being "confused, disoriented and unable to answer questions," and exhibiting "behavior that led the board to question his capacity to serve" during a CNCS board meeting a month earlier. He also asserted that Walpin's dismissal was the result of a "unanimous request from the AmeriCorps board of directors." Walpin told Glenn Beck he was amazed at these claims since, a mere two days before he was fired, they asked him to go to San Francisco to give a speech.[9]

The Republican investigation of Walpin's illegal dismissal concluded that all the accusations against Walpin came *after* his firing, and were likely part of a cover-up of Obama's illegal actions. The Obama White House never sought the opinion of the board until *after* the firing, providing them with talking points on the matter in case the media asked any questions. Documents previously withheld by the White House, released only hours after Senator Charles Grassley and Rep. Darrell Issa released the report on their findings, corroborated the report. The only person with any "substantive input" on Walpin's removal was the board chairman, Alan Solomont, an Obama supporter and big-time Democrat donor. The board's vice-chairman, Stephen Goldsmith, was contacted before the firing, but after the decision to fire Walpin had already been made. As *Hot Air*'s Ed Morrissey noted, "The White House not only deliberately misled Congress on Walpin's firing, they also withheld these new documents until *after* Grassley and Issa made their initial report on the investigation..."[10]

The report also found that "concerns about Walpin's fitness to serve as IG lacked merit," and that White House lawyer Norman Eisen's statements to Congress were "explicitly contradicted by witness testimony." Walpin's investigation also unearthed an apparent cover-up of sexual abuse allegations against Johnson by three female St. HOPE Academy students. One student was offered hush money but refused to accept it.[11]

This all begs the question: How did Johnson avoid prosecution? Well, acting U.S. Attorney Lawrence Brown "was actively seeking a Presidential appointment as the U.S. Attorney at the same time he was negotiating a lenient settlement agreement with Kevin Johnson, excluding the Inspector General from the negotiations, and filing a complaint against Walpin with the Integrity Committee," according to an update and supplement to Senator Grassley and Rep. Issa's initial report on the firing.[12]

Walpin was cleared of all the charges made against him; the smear campaign against him failed and Brown never got the appointment.

Nevertheless, Obama broke the law to protect a donor and ally who had misused federal grant money and sexually abused three students, then he and his appointees misled Congress in an attempt to cover it up. Is that not a scandal?

According to the media, it wasn't. Analysis from the Media Research Center shows that, except for the Fox News Channel, and a few reports on CNN, the media was silent.[13] Tom Brokaw featured a laudatory profile of Johnson, including his founding of St. HOPE, in a documentary called "American Character Along Highway 50" that aired in January 2010.[14] Somehow, Tom Brokaw's "search of the American character" lead him to Johnson despite Johnson's misuse of AmeriCorps grants, the obstruction of the investigation, the FBI investigation of that obstruction, and the allegations of sexual misconduct. Why? Because protecting Obama meant protecting Johnson too.

Members of the media had a duty to be government watchdogs—like Gerald Walpin—and expose corruption and abuse of power. Walpin did his job. The only crime he committed was going after Johnson, Obama's friend and donor. And Johnson knew he could rely on the president because he knew the press wouldn't hold Obama accountable for abusing the power and resources of the government to help a friend and donor.

The Sestak Job Offer Scandal

In 2016, the Obama administration got in some hot water over reports that hundreds of thousands of tax dollars were sent to an Israeli group with ties to Obama's campaign in an attempt to oust Prime Minister Benjamin Netanyahu.[1] Many found this shocking but the truth is, Barack Obama was in the business of trying to manipulate elections as early as his first term, and much closer to home. He urged New York Governor David Paterson not to run for reelection over concerns of his unpopularity impacting congressional elections in New York State in 2010.[2] He also attempted to persuade Illinois Attorney General Lisa Madigan and Cook County Sheriff Tom Dart to run for his old Senate seat.[3] Yes, this is the same Senate seat at the center of the Blagojevich scandal. There is nothing wrong with persuading someone to run for office or drop out of the race, but Obama crossed a legal line when he got involved in the 2010 U.S. Senate election in Pennsylvania.

In 2009, Senator Arlen Specter, after having spent nearly thirty years in the Senate as Republican, announced he would run for reelection in 2010 as a Democrat. Specter's career in politics began as a registered Democrat, but in 1965 he switched to the Republican Party.[4] Specter had been a moderate Republican and had often sided with Senate Democrats. His announcement came just weeks after Pat Toomey, the former president of the Club For Growth, entered the race to challenge Specter for the Republican nomination.

The White House had been trying to convince Specter to switch parties for weeks, but he was reluctant. As poll after poll piled up showing him trailing Toomey, he saw the writing on the wall. "I'm not prepared to have my 29-year record in the United States Senate decided by the Pennsylvania

19

Republican primary electorate," Specter said at a press conference, "not prepared to have that record decided by that jury." Specter saw that his career as a Republican was all but over, however, as a *Democrat* with Obama's support, he saw a chance at survival. Obama saw a potential sixtieth vote in the Senate that would leave the Republican Party powerless to stall his agenda. In exchange for switching parties, Obama promised his full support. He would campaign for Specter and help him fundraise.[5]

They didn't count on interference from Joe Sestak, Navy veteran and two-term Democrat congressman from Pennsylvania's traditionally Republican 7th congressional district. Sestak had been eying a run for the U.S. Senate prior to Specter's switch and didn't appreciate Obama and the Democrat establishment backing Specter.

In February 2010, Sestak revealed during a radio interview with veteran journalist Larry Kane that he'd been offered a job the previous summer by the Obama administration to put an end to his campaign. When asked by Kane, "Were you ever offered a federal job to get out of this race?" Sestak answered, "Yes," and confirmed the job was offered "by the White House."[6] Sestak's allegation was very serious. In fact, he had just accused the Obama White House of committing a federal crime.

The cat was out of the bag and Rep. Darrell Issa (R-CA), ranking Republican of the House Committee on Oversight and Government Reform, opened a probe. The White House offered zero cooperation. Issa's attempts to sort out this scandal met with endless deflections. Obama spokesman Robert Gibbs refused to confirm or deny that any job offer was made, claiming to have no information and promising to investigate further. On March 16, 2010, he told reporters, "I've talked to several people in the White House; I've talked to people that have talked to others in the White House. I'm told that whatever conversations have been had are not problematic. I think Congressman Sestak has discussed that this is—whatever happened is in the past, and he's focused on his primary election."[7] Issa was displeased by the White House investigating itself, saying "that the White House is allowing its communications staff to carry out investigative tasks ordinarily conducted by legal professionals in the Counsel's office. Such slipshodness has all the makings of a cover-up."[8]

While the White House was stonewalling, legal experts were weighing in. They were split along party lines as to whether anything illegal occurred.

Hans von Spakovsky, a former Justice Department attorney, said "I don't know if I would use the word bribery, but offering a federal job in exchange for a political favor [...] is against federal law." However, Melanie Sloan, the executive director of the left-wing ethics watchdog group Citizens for Responsibility and Ethics in Washington (CREW), disagreed, saying, "I don't think there is any issue. I don't see the crime." Others avoided judgment without the benefit of more information–which neither the White House nor Sestak was interested in providing. An investigation was necessary and, while the Obama administration stonewalled, Republicans requested a special counsel be appointed to investigate the allegations. That request was rejected by Obama's Justice Department.[9] Rep. Issa was outraged: "The attorney general's refusal to take action in the face of such felonious allegations undermines any claim to transparency and integrity that this administration asserts."[10]

The Obama administration was anything but transparent on the brewing scandal. Despite their claims of no wrongdoing, months of White House stonewalling looked like a cover-up. Even left-wing journalist David Corn acknowledged in a *Mother Jones* column that the White House looked suspect. "The issue, though, is whether any conversation of this sort—if it indeed occurred—would have violated the law."[11]

And the conversation *did indeed* occur. After months of stonewalling, the White House disclosed their version of what happened on Memorial Day weekend in a memo from White House counsel Robert F. Bauer. Sestak had just defeated Specter ten days prior, pulling off a stunning upset after spending most of the campaign behind in the polls. The memo acknowledged the illicit offer, but still denied any wrongdoing on part of the White House. "We have concluded that allegations of improper conduct rest on factual errors and lack a basis in the law."[12] The memo also revealed that Obama's Chief of Staff Rahm Emanuel sent former President Bill Clinton to discuss a trade with Sestak. He would drop out of the race in exchange for an unpaid yet influential, position on a presidential advisory board. This would "avoid a divisive Senate primary, allow him to retain his seat in the House, and provide him with an opportunity for additional service to the public in a high-level advisory capacity for which he was highly qualified."[13]

For mainstream media, this was enough. They were willing to let the White House be its own judge and jury and treated their verdict as gospel; the matter was now closed and any attempts to discuss or perpetuate the story were partisan scandalmongering. House Republicans requested an FBI investigation, prompting CBS reporter Brian Montopoli to accuse the GOP of "trying to keep the Joe Sestak affair alive despite today's White House memo denying wrongdoing."[14] Did he imagine that the Obama White House would admit to committing a federal crime?

After three months of ignoring the scandal, the media kept right on sweeping it under the rug with a White House broom. In their eyes, the story didn't merit coverage. According to the Media Research Center, "The Sestak job-offer scandal drew only nine stories or mentions on the three networks. NBC offered only one evening anchor brief. CBS featured an evening anchor brief, a morning anchor brief, and a Saturday night interview where analyst John Dickerson dismissed the scandal. ABC did the most with five offerings: three stories or discussions on World News, and two on Good Morning America. All nine segments were contained within the Memorial Day weekend."[15]

Even as contradictions in Sestak's story and the White House story raised more questions, the media was silent. "During the following week, the White House narrative fell apart, since Sestak could not serve on these advisory boards as a member of Congress. Press Secretary Robert Gibbs obfuscated and dodged reporters when peppered with questions, which led to some newspaper and cable coverage, but ABC, CBS, and NBC all blacked out the story as it crumbled."[16] Just like that, Obama got another free pass even after the White House confirmed Sestak's version of events.

Between Sestak's initial accusation, the months of stonewalling, the White House admission, and the contradictions in the White House brief, the media was sitting on an explosive story. There were countless questions still unanswered, including the extent of Obama's involvement, and the specific details of the job with which Obama tried to bribe Sestak. The best excuse Obama's defenders offered was that this kind horse-trading was "politics as usual." That's an interesting appeal given that these same left-wing operatives won the 2008 election by accusing George W. Bush and Congressional Republicans of trapping America in "politics as usual."

Judicial Watch listed at least four federal laws that Obama may have broken: 18 USC 210: Offer to procure appointive public office; 18 USC 211: Acceptance of solicitation to obtain appointive public office; 18 USC 595: Interference by administrative employees by Federal, State or Territorial Governments; and 18 USC 600: Promise of employment or other benefit for political activity.[17] Alas, once Sestak lost the election to conservative firebrand Pat Toomey, Republicans lost interest in pursuing an investigation. Perhaps they'd have had more stomach for a fight if the media wasn't tag-teaming with the guilty party. We'll never know. But we do know that, once again, Obama played a role in dirty, illegal political chicanery and got away with it.

The Obamacare Fraud

Obamacare may have been Obama's signature achievement, but it was also rife with controversy and scandal. Nancy Pelosi's infamous remark that "we have to pass the bill so that you can find out what's in it," perfectly encapsulates the most scandalous aspect of the legislation. It was a huge fraud. The bill gained support only through the endless repetition of myths and blatant lies by Obama and liberals in Congress.

The controversy surrounding the Affordable Care Act began long before the bill reached Obama's desk. Obama's first lie was easy to spot. He claimed he wanted his healthcare bill to be bipartisan. To the surprise of no one, there was nothing bipartisan about it, not the process of drafting it, not the debate in Congress, and certainly not the methods used to pass the bill. The trouble began as early as one month into "negotiations." Minority Whip Eric Cantor warned that Obama stopped engaging with Republicans on the health care bill in May 2009. "No matter what the cry is from the White House, no matter what the president claims, they have not engaged with us," he said.[1]

With Republicans kicked out of the process and the public unconvinced about the proposed plan, the next step was to negotiate the major details of the legislation *in secret*. Obama had promised, during his presidential campaign, to broadcast the final negotiations on C-SPAN. Instead, House Speaker Nancy Pelosi declared in January 2010, "The House and Senate plan to put together the final healthcare reform bill behind closed doors according to an agreement by top Democrats." Obama, according to Press Secretary Robert Gibbs, was in full agreement and wanted to "get a bill to his desk as quickly as possible," his promise of transparency and bipartisanship be damned.[2]

And then Republican Scott Brown won a special election for the U.S. Senate seat vacated by the late Ted Kennedy in a stunning upset in Massachusetts, breaking the Democrats' filibuster-proof majority. Scott Brown had campaigned on a pledge to be the "41st vote," and the election was seen as a referendum on Obama's plans for health care reform. Without their 60-vote safeguard, Senate Democrats were reluctant to hold a second vote and risk a filibuster. To overcome this hurdle, they abused a Senate rule called reconciliation, designed to reduce spending by allowing the Senate to pass cuts with a simple majority vote. There were no more hearings and debate ended in a midnight, closed-door, party-line vote, all for a bill that would increase spending, not reduce it. The *Wall Street Journal* editorialized, "What we are about to witness is an extraordinary abuse of traditional Senate rules to pass a bill merely because they think it's good for the rest of us, and because they fear their chance to build a European welfare state may never come again."[3]

Not all Democrats were on board when the debate started in the House of Representatives. It took deception to ensure Obamacare's passage. A coalition of pro-life Democrats had refused to vote for Obamacare because of language that would allow for taxpayer-funded abortions. To get around this, Obama promised to issue an executive order—*after* the final House bill passed—that would prevent taxpayer money from being used to fund abortions. This promised satisfied the pro-life Democrats, who would now vote for Obamacare and pave the way for its passage. Obama then abandoned his promise—violating his own executive order—and the Department of Health and Human Services issued a mandate requiring coverage of contraception and abortion-inducing drugs. Adding insult to injury, the requirement had no exemption for religious groups.[4] Former congressman Bart Stupak, who negotiated the executive order with Obama, realized he'd been lied to. "I am perplexed and disappointed that, having negotiated the executive order with the President, not only does that HHS mandate violate the executive order, but it also violates statutory law. I think it is illegal," he said at Democrats for Life forum at the 2012 Democratic convention.[5]

After abusing reconciliation and lying to pro-life Democrats to get their votes, Obamacare passed without a single Republican vote. Obama signed the bill into law on March 23, 2010. We finally had Nancy Pelosi's permission to see what was in it...and that's when things got ugly.

The employer mandate—by law—was to go into effect on January 1, 2014. As the midterm elections loomed, approval ratings for Obamacare had dropped to around 40 percent in *Real Clear Politics*' polling averages,[6] in part because the rollout of the public insurance marketplace—Health-Care.gov—was a disaster, and in part because people realized that they might lose their employer-provided plans and have to pay more for their ACA-compliant replacements. Hoping to avoid an electoral slaughter aided by dissatisfaction with the ACA, the Obama administration did what you'd expect them to do. In July 2013, Obama unilaterally delayed implementing the employer mandate until after the 2014 midterm elections.[7]

Before Obamacare's first open enrollment period, Obama had already amended or delayed Obamacare 19 times, according to the Congressional Research Service.[8] A study by the Galen Institute published in January 2016 found over seventy significant changes to Obamacare. By their count, "at least 43 of the changes to the Affordable Care Act have been made unilaterally by the Obama administration, 24 have passed Congress and been signed into law by President Obama, and three were made by the Supreme Court, which had to rewrite the law to uphold it." The changes may have been to delay the law's negative impacts, but Obama had no authority to change the law without Congress.[9] One major delay, announced in March 2014, allowed insurers to continue offering health plans that *didn't* comply with Obamacare's standards to delay more health plan cancellations until after the 2014 midterms.[10] Those were the health plans that Obama said you could keep if you liked them. Obamacare was just so good that Obama didn't want Democrats to take the blame.

As I mentioned above, the Obamacare rollout, beginning on October 1, 2013, was a complete disaster. Millions of Americans went to HealthCare.gov and got 404 errors or intolerable loading times. Website problems kept people from accessing the site and getting their plans. Only six people succeeded in signing up for Obamacare on launch day. *No joke. Six people.* That's according to an internal Obama administration memo.[11] In the first week, less than 0.5 percent of visitors could complete enrollment.[12] The irony here, is that this was a preventable catastrophe.

The Obama administration had been warned that the site couldn't handle the expected traffic it would receive.[13] They also knew the site had major security flaws before the launch and went ahead with it anyway, putting the private data of anyone who signed up on the site at risk.[14] This would be hilarious if it weren't costing people their privacy, their money, and their valuable time.

There's one more fun fact that you should know about Healthcare.gov: the company that the government contracted to build it, CGI Federal, was given the green light without ever facing competition or presenting a viable development plan.[15] You might be asking yourself, "Why would they take such a risk on something so central to their collective legacy as the governing party?" Guess who was one of the leading figures at CGI Federal? It was a major Democrat fundraiser and a classmate and friend of Michelle Obama named Toni Townes-Whitley.[16]

After the failed rollout, Obama needed a win on healthcare. If the results of the launch didn't qualify, the Obama administration had no problems creating the illusion of a win. They projected at least 7 million sign ups at the end of open enrollment. And, believe me, they made sure they got at least 7 million—by fudging the numbers.

Of course, saying they fudged the numbers is both an understatement and an insult to chocolate confectioneries. On April 1, 2014, the end of Obamacare's first open enrollment, Obama announced that 7.1 million Americans had signed up on the Obamacare exchanges. Included in his announcement was the declaration that "the Affordable Care Act is here to stay."[17] It turned out it was appropriate that he made that announcement on April Fools' Day. While health insurers only count people as being enrolled in a health plan when they've submitted a payment, the Obama administration was using their own broad definition for what counted as an enrollee. According to *The Washington Post*, the Obama administration counted those "who have purchased a plan as well as those who have a plan sitting in their online shopping cart but have not yet paid."[18] Guy Benson of *Townhall* called the enrollment numbers "incomplete to the point of deception." In addition to the incredibly loose definition of what makes an enrollee an *enrollee*, there were also a significant number of duplicates after problems with the HealthCare.gov website caused large numbers of enrolled people to create new accounts and re-enroll, sometimes more than once. "That's why the administration's enrollment statistics are useless in the aggregate." Benson wrote. "They just manufactured the largest-sounding number possible and heralded it as exciting proof that the 'law is working' and the 'debate is over.'"[19] The RAND Corporation put the real number of enrollees at 3.9 million. Only 36 percent of those enrollees, about 1.4 million, were previously uninsured.[20] Another study, this one by McKinsey & Company, found that "of the people signing up for new ACA plans in 2014, only 22 percent were previously uninsured individuals who have paid for coverage and therefore enrolled in health insurance."[21] Obama and members of his administration knew they were touting bad enrollment numbers, but pushed them anyway because they were desperate to declare Obama's signature legislation a success.

And that's just part of the story. Don't forget that people who liked their existing health care plans were supposed to be able to keep them. Obama made this promise *repeatedly* while making the case for Obamacare. At least thirty-seven times, without caveat, Obama promised: "if you like your health care plan, you can keep it." When people started getting cancellation notices the Obama administration tried to shift blame from the law to the insurance companies, but to no avail. Eventually, Obama changed his script and "If you like your health care plan, you can keep it, period" became "you can keep it if it hasn't changed since the law passed." It was a big enough lie that the left-wing fact checking site *PolitiFact* crowned, "If you like your health care plan, you can keep it" the Lie of the Year for 2013.[22] At least that was an accolade Obama truly deserved, unlike his Nobel Peace Prize. Obama's policy advisors knew people would lose their plans, but Obama kept lying to the American people anyway, to sell Obamacare to the people.[23] In fact, the Obama administration knew, back in 2010, that *millions* could lose their plans despite Obama's repeated promises to the contrary.[24]

So, how many people lost their plans? Six years after Obamacare was became law, a net nine million people had lost their private health plans because of the law, *The Weekly Standard* reported.[25] The bottom line is that Obama lied, and that lie probably got him reelected. According to a poll taken after the botched Obamacare rollout, if voters had known they'd lose their health care plans because of Obamacare, Mitt Romney would have defeated Obama in 2012.[26]

As the years passed, things didn't improve with Obamacare either. Like many others, I'm still waiting for the $2,500 decrease in premiums Obama promised. Of course, Obama knew that number was malarkey, just like many of the other promises he made about his healthcare plan. They were fairy tales meant to sell the idea to the public with no intention of delivering. For example, Obamacare established a series of nonprofit health care co-ops intended to provide more choices for Americans, but they proved to be unsustainable. As of this writing, nineteen of the original twenty-three co-ops have failed, leaving just four in operation for 2018.[27] That, combined with huge, unprecedented premium increases—25 percent from 2016 to 2017—have many saying Obamacare is in a "death spiral."[28]

From the passage of Obamacare to its launch to its current dreadful state, the law has been blemished by controversy, deception, and incompetence. Through it all, the mainstream media did its part to keep public opinion of the law as positive as possible. Media Research President Brent Bozell likened the media's coverage of Obamacare to a cover-up.[29] Perhaps the best example of this is the media blackout of the viral video that showed Obamacare architect Jonathan Gruber admitting that deceiving the public was key to making Obamacare pass. "Lack of transparency is a huge political advantage," Gruber said during a discussion of Obamacare at University of Pennsylvania on October 17, 2014. "And, basically, call it the stupidity of the American voter, or whatever, but basically that was really, really critical in getting the thing to pass." The media, including big newspapers, mostly ignored the video and this shockingly candid remark about Obamacare. Those that covered it downplayed Gruber's role in the crafting of Obamacare.[30] What benefit is there to covering up the very real faults of a bill impacting a huge chunk of the economy? Was protecting Obama's legacy really worth it? The American people will still have to figure out how to make ends meet after they pay their higher premiums, regardless of whether Obama or the complicit media concede that Obamacare was a scandalous disaster.

The BP Oil Spill Response and Cover-Up

In the summer of 2010, the Deepwater Horizon offshore oil rig exploded, sending vast quantities of oil spilling into the Gulf of Mexico. This was one of the worst environmental disasters of the twenty-first century. Just as Americans judged George W. Bush by his handling of Hurricane Katrina—some might say unfairly judged—Obama knew his response would be scrutinized. Unfortunately for the Gulf Coast, he was not up to the task. He formed the National Commission on the Deepwater Horizon Oil Spill to oversee the administration's cleanup efforts; that body repeatedly faulted Obama for underestimating the magnitude of the spill and for slowing the federal response.

Obama is not the first president to oversee a federal disaster recovery effort that didn't live up to expectations, but that isn't what earned this event a place in my book. The reason I wrote about the spill is the Obama administration's repeated lies to the American public about the severity of the spill and the cleanup efforts. Obama wanted us to believe he was in charge and handling the situation with precision, but the facts on the ground told another story. The aforementioned Commission reported that "the federal government created the impression that it was either not fully competent to handle the spill or *not fully candid* with the American people about the scope of the problem."[1] Ouch.

One example of Obama's dishonesty is his mischaracterization of the resources he made available to emergency managers. Republicans on the House Oversight and Government Reform Committee noted that the White House had claimed one hundred forty skimmers were cleaning up oil in the Gulf when only thirty-one were actually deployed. They found that Obama was more concerned with public relations than actual cleanup and resource management.[2] This becomes obvious when you compare reports from credentialed scientists with public comments by Obama and his supporters. While BP officials and government scientists believed the flow rate of the oil spill could be as high as 110,000 barrels per day, the Obama administration was claiming—for over a month— that the flow rate was 5,000 barrels per day. Three months after the spill, Carol Browner, Obama's energy adviser, claimed that scientists had found that more than 75 percent of the oil was gone—when the government's own data suggested otherwise.[3] Browner also claimed data on the cleanup had been peer-reviewed, even though it hadn't.[4]

Misleading the public is a serious ethical breach, and the Obama administration's lowball estimates raised lots of questions. One watchdog group, Public Employees for Environmental Responsibility, which represents whistleblower government scientists, sued the Obama admin- istration after they stonewalled FOIA requests to find out why the Obama administration was making such lowball claims.[5] In 2012, we found out why. The White House didn't just mislead the public about the spill; the White House, according to emails released following the lawsuit, had *pressured* government scientists to underestimate the size of it.[6]

Next, the White House tweaked an Interior Department report to give the false impression that an independent panel of scientists and engi- neers had supported Obama's six-month drilling moratorium in the wake of the Deepwater Horizon explosion. The Interior Department Inspector General said scientists and experts were concerned that the Executive Summary of the report, "was worded in a manner that implied that the experts peer reviewed and supported this policy decision, when...they had neither reviewed nor supported such a policy decision and had never been asked to do so." Those changes, the Inspector General determined, were made by the White House—specifically the office of Carol Browner.[7]

Three days after the oil spill, the Netherlands had offered the Obama administration the use of high-tech skimmers able to handle the spill at no charge...and Obama rebuffed them. Why? The Dutch skimmers did not meet overzealous EPA standards. Twelve other governments also offered their help and were turned away. When the Obama administration relented, they wasted time retrofitting the equipment onto American ships and training U.S. crews to use the equipment, rather than letting experienced Dutch teams begin cleanup immediately. The delay had one cause: Obama needed to appease the labor unions insisting that American crews do the work.[8] Even though Obama had described the oil spill as "the worst environmental disaster America has ever faced,"[9] he wasn't above letting government regulations and political loyalties impede the cleanup, environment be damned.

Unfortunately, the media was as concerned about Obama's image as Obama himself was. Browner's lies about the cleanup and misleading edit of the Interior Department report were buried by *The Washington Post* and ignored by *The New York Times*.[10] MSNBC worked hard to defend Obama. *Morning Joe* host Joe Scarborough gave his efforts glowing reviews.[11] Chris Matthews and Andrea Mitchell seemed relieved that Obama's firing of General Stanley McChrystal might improve his poll numbers after they took a beating from Obama's response to the oil spill.[12] In an interview with Barack Obama on NBC *Nightly News*, Brian Williams seemed to lament characterizations that the BP oil spill cleanup was "Obama's Katrina."[13] He also expressed disappointment that Obama's handling of the oil spill seemed to damage his approval ratings. "[Obama] had to own it and now he's getting tagged with how he's reacting to it," he lamented.[14] Americans clearly saw a deficit of leadership, but the media insisted on being his personal cheering section with cries of adulation.

The Slush Fund Scandal

What would you say if I told you that a sitting president of the United States used the Justice Department to force large corporations to hand over hundreds of millions of dollars to groups engaged in boosting his own political party? If you're a liberal, my guess is that you pictured an evil Republican cutting backroom deals with powerful allies whose agendas you don't support. You couldn't imagine a Democrat—certainly not Barack Obama—involved in such things. But he was, and instead of criticizing him, you either praised his efforts or turned a blind eye, because you thought he was striking a blow against a part of the economy you hated, and anything done in the name of social justice is fair and good. The corporations Obama extorted were, rightly, reviled for their role in the 2008 economic collapse. But, Obama seemed less interested in having them compensate their victims and more interested in taking advantage of the situation to direct large sums of that money towards politically allied groups.

To understand this scandal—and it's a doozy—let me take you back to the 1990s when Clinton administration regulations encouraged lenders to offer mortgages to people who would otherwise be unable to afford them. The theory was that encouraging home ownership—even to people who couldn't afford it—was a way to boost home construction and grow the economy and that moving people from renting to owning their homes was a crucial step in lifting them out of poverty. Obama believed it, too; he also believed the banks had racist standards for mortgage approval. As a civil rights lawyer in Chicago, he sued Citibank in a landmark 1995 civil suit on behalf of one hundred eighty-six African-American clients for alleged mortgage lending discrimination, pushing banks to give mortgages to minorities with no regard to whether they had the means to make their payments. It turns out they didn't. By 2012, only nineteen of the complainants in that case still owned a home.[1]

Obama was more than happy to get paid to accuse a big bank of discrimination, but he sang a different tune after the subprime mortgage crisis. Obama went from accusing banks of discriminating when they denied mortgages to calling them greedy for *approving* them. "Instead of saving their pennies to buy their dream house, many Americans found they could take out loans that, by traditional standards, their incomes just could not support," Obama said in a speech in 2009. "Others were tricked into signing these subprime loans by lenders who were trying to make a quick profit."[2] I can think of nearly two-hundred people who were tricked by *Obama*, not by lenders.

In 2009, Obama launched the Financial Fraud Enforcement Task Force (FFETF) "to hold accountable those who helped bring about the last financial crisis, and to prevent another crisis from happening."[3] Attorney General Eric Holder chaired the task force, so it shouldn't surprise you that something dishonorable and illegal came of their efforts. Anyone familiar with Obama's record knows his disdain for checks and balances; he'll get what he wants. This time, he acted under the auspices of the Department of Justice mandate to protect Americans from predatory or discriminatory lending practices. His administration sued big banks, and negotiated huge settlements meant to compensate the victims. Then they steered hundreds of millions of dollars of those settlement funds to third-party political activists that boosted Democratic politicians and causes, but that claimed to offer services to help the victims. Groups like National Council of La Raza, ACORN, the National Community Reinvestment Coalition and the National Urban League and others that share Obama's ideology got millions of dollars out of this shady scheme.[4]

Senator Chuck Grassley, the ranking Republican on the Senate Finance Committee, got word of the scheme and investigated the Department of Justice. He said, "While these settlements may appear reasonable on their face, I am concerned that this change in policy has the potential to divert compensation intended for victims to third party interest groups that were not wronged by the defendant." DOJ Civil Rights Division official Bob Driscoll suggested that "steering settlement funds to favored advocacy groups is at odds with both civil rights laws and common sense. If Congress wants to fund certain advocacy groups or set up grants for agencies to award in order to promote non-discrimination, it can. But allowing the Civil Rights Division to steer a defendant's money to its ideological allies is offensive."[5]

As Ed Morrissey of *Hot Air* noted, "while the practice existed before the Obama administration, it flourished under Attorneys General Eric Holder and Loretta Lynch."[6] When the Department of Justice negotiated billion dollar settlements with big banks for predatory lending, the deals allowed them to reduce their penalties by donating to groups approved by the Obama administration. "Not only was this an inappropriate politicization of the DoJ and of attorney-client interests, it was also a big incentive to sue people so as to pay off constituencies," Morrissey added.[7] That groups enjoying the terms of the DOJ settlements weren't victimized by the banks or parties to the case did not matter. That some of the groups had their funding cut by Congress didn't matter either. Obama had Democratic operatives to pay off. "Advocates for big government and progressive power are using the Justice Department to extort money from corporations," Judicial Watch's Tom Fitton said of the scheme. "It's a shakedown. It's corrupt, pure and simple."[8]

This practice is unconstitutional. "When the Justice Department negotiates settlements that send money to third parties instead of to the United States Treasury or to the primary victims of the challenged conduct without legislative authority, they violate separation of powers by effectively using executive-branch enforcement authority to create legislative spending power." Explained Theodore Frank of the Competitive Enterprise Institute (CEI) in testimony to the House Judiciary Committee in February 2015. "The spending may evade laws and regulations limiting or controlling federal spending, or create or fund programs that Congress never would have agreed to spend," he added.[9]

Obama isn't known for being a stickler for the limits of the Constitution and justified his tactics by claiming the donations were voluntary by the banks, and were not funds that would have otherwise gone to the Treasury for disbursement. Of course, if the banks did not make the donations, they had to pay twice as much in settlements or violate their plea agreements.[10] Sounds like a shakedown to me.

Citigroup had to pay at least $50 million to Democrat-friendly groups as part of its $7 billion settlement, and Bank of America had to pay at least $80 million out of its record $16.6 billion settlement. Naturally, there was no cap on how much they could "donate" to the pre-approved groups to reduce their penalties.[11]

Think this can't get any worse? Well, it does. The Obama administration incentivized banks to pay out to these liberal groups instead of the actual victims. "When it came to paying down settlement obligations, dollar-for-dollar credit was given for donations to legal plaintiffs in the cases, but dollars 'donated' to third parties were worth double," explained Ian Tuttle, Thomas L. Rhodes Fellow at the National Review Institute. "So, third-party organizations—that, again, had *no legal connection* to the case being adjudicated—would compete against victims for settlement money, and companies had a strong financial incentive to pay them, instead of the actual victims."[12]

To put an end to the slush fund scheme, Rep. Bob Goodlatte (R-VA) introduced *The Stop Settlement Slush Funds Act of 2016*. "When DOJ recovers money from parties who have broken the law, those funds should be going to victims, or to the Treasury so that Congress can ensure accountability for how the funds are spent. These funds should not be funneled to the president's pet liberal groups," he said in a statement. According to the Office of Management and Budget, the Obama administration opposed the legislation because it was "unnecessary and would harm the public interest," and Obama would veto the legislation if it came to his desk.[13]

This story has a happy ending though. On June 7, 2017, Attorney General Jeff Sessions declared that the Justice Department would no longer allow payments to outside groups as part of settlement agreements. "When the federal government settles a case against a corporate wrongdoer, any settlement funds should go first to the victims and then to the American people—not to bankroll third-party special interest groups or the political friends of whoever is in power," he said in a statement. "With this directive, we are ending this practice and ensuring that settlement funds are only used to compensate victims, redress harm, and punish and deter unlawful conduct."[14] It was a rare victory against Obama-era corruption that, according to investigators, funneled $3 billion to Obama-friendly groups before being stopped by the Trump administration.[15]

If you haven't heard about it, it's not your fault—the media didn't bring this scandal to light. As of this writing, the mainstream press still had not given any coverage at all to it.[16] They went out of their way to criticize Sessions for his decision.[17] They continue their longstanding practice of ignoring an Obama scandal until it becomes convenient to speak of it, usually as part of the larger media canard that Republicans are unfairly attacking Obama and Democrats for political gain and hurting society as a result.

Fast and Furious

Operation Fast and Furious was the largest covert gun-walking operation by the Bureau of Alcohol, Tobacco, Firearms, and Explosives (ATF) under Project Gunrunner. The mission was to track the flow of firearms from the United States into Mexico and aid authorities in arresting Mexican drug cartel leaders. Fast and Furious launched in 2009 and delivered about 2,000 firearms across the border—most of which disappeared. Border Patrol agent Brian Terry and Immigration and Customs Enforcement (ICE) agent Jaime Zapata were both shot and killed with guns connected to Fast and Furious; an untold number of Mexican civilians also died. The Mexican government reported that at least one hundred and fifty Mexicans were killed or wounded with Fast and Furious weapons.[1] Despite the innocent bloodshed caused by Fast and Furious, the scheme captured zero drug cartel leaders. Katie Pavlich, who wrote the definitive book on Operation Fast and Furious, called it "the deadliest and most sinister scandal in American history." She continued, "it's worse than Iran-Contra and makes Watergate look like a high school prank gone wrong."[2]

There were significant differences in how Reagan and Obama treated their respective scandals. "Where the Reagan administration insisted on accountability, the Obama administration has moved to cover up its scandal."[3] Accountability in the Reagan administration led to congressional hearings, a presidential commission, and fourteen indictments of administration officials. Despite not being directly involved in Iran-Contra, Reagan accepted responsibility for it. In contrast, Obama denied, covered up, and stonewalled the investigation of Operation Fast and Furious. He even tried to shift blame onto George W. Bush, like he did with most of his failings.[4]

Katie Pavlich doesn't buy the explanation that the purpose of Fast and Furious was to take down a major drug cartel. "If so, it certainly failed, and it is hard to see how it could have succeeded," she wrote in her book, *Fast And Furious: Barack Obama's Bloodiest Scandal and Its Shameless Cover-Up*. "While the guns walked during Fast and Furious could be traced to crime scenes (only after a crime, not before), there was never going to be any way to trace them to cartel kingpins. If the point was to gain evidence to arrest the straw buyers, they could have been arrested well before they walked guns across the border."

So what could Fast and Furious *really* have accomplished? "The only thing Operation Fast and Furious could do was link American gun shop-sold guns to Mexican crimes—even if these sales were in fact forced by the ATF," said Pavlich.[5] "Was Fast and Furious designed to help build a case for new gun control measures that could not otherwise pass Congress? Did the Obama administration and its political appointees put their zeal for their own political agenda ahead of public safety? The evidence suggests the answer is yes."[6] Documents obtained by CBS News, in December 2011, showed that ATF officials used Fast and Furious to help make the case for Obama's gun control agenda.[7] It didn't matter that innocent people died, shot by guns the Obama administration let into Mexico, just as long as there was a way to take advantage of the situation to advance partisan politics.

The first phase of Obama's refusal to accept responsibility for Fast and Furious was denial. After ATF whistleblowers brought the connection between Brian Terry's murder and Fast and Furious to Congress, the DOJ sent a letter to Senator Chuck Grassley (R-IA), in February 2011, denying that the ATF had ever walked guns into Mexico. This was absurd and debunked soon after. But, it still took the DOJ nine months to retract the letter.[8] As for Obama, he claimed he was ignorant of the operation, telling reporters, "I heard on the news about this story, that, uh, Fast and Furious."[9] This was far from the last time Obama made that sham excuse when a scandal threatened his presidency.

On May 3, 2011, Attorney General Holder took a page out of Obama's *How To Play Dumb* playbook when he testified before the House Judiciary Committee that he'd heard about Operation Fast and Furious only recently. "I'm not sure of the exact date," he claimed, "but I probably heard about Fast and Furious for the first time over the last few weeks." However, documents obtained by CBS News investigative reporter Sharyl Attkisson that October revealed that Holder was briefed on the program at least as far back as July 2010, ten months before the hearing. After being caught lying to Congress, Holder backtracked, claiming he had misunderstood the question he was answering, that he knew *of* Fast and Furious, but not the details of the plot.[10]

But playing dumb wasn't enough. Once you're caught lying to Congress, you need a Plan B; for Democrats, that meant stonewalling to delay any further investigation. The operation was a total failure that killed a Border Patrol agent and an ICE agent, but that didn't stop them from accusing Republicans of playing politics for daring to hold an investigation. House Democrats conducted their own "investigation." Wonder of wonders, they absolved the Obama administration of any wrongdoing! "Contrary to repeated claims by some, the committee has obtained no evidence that Operation Fast and Furious was a politically motivated operation conceived and directed by high-level Obama administration political appointees at the Department of Justice," wrote Elijah E. Cummings (D-MD) in the report.[11]

The problem for Democrats was that the report contradicted known information. According to Pavlich, Democrats on the House Oversight Committee were "officially trying to cover for Attorney General Eric Holder" prior to his testifying before Congress a couple days after they issued their report. "New emails released last Friday in a late night document dump show Attorney General Eric Holder was briefed about Brian Terry's death just hours after he was murdered in the early morning hours on December 15, 2010. Later in the day, Holder's deputy chief of staff at the time, Monty Wilkinson, was told directly by former Arizona U.S. Attorney Dennis Burke that the guns found at the murder scene were part of Operation Fast and Furious."[12] So, Holder lied to Congress about when he knew about Fast and Furious, there was evidence that the operation promoted Obama's gun control agenda by design, and innocent people died. Were Republicans playing politics? I think they protest too much.

Sharyl Attkisson pursued the story aggressively, much to the Obama administration's disdain. Judicial Watch got documents that showed the DOJ and the White House hoped to silence Attkisson's reporting on the scandal. On October 4, 2011, Attorney General Holder's top press aide, Tracy Schmaler, emailed White House Deputy Press Secretary Eric Schultz, saying, "I'm also calling Sharyl's editor and reaching out to Schieffer. She's out of control". Schultz responded, "Good. Her piece was really bad for the AG." Schultz also revealed plans to undermine Rep. Darrell Issa, who was leading the investigation. The email chain, according to Judicial Watch president Tom Fitton, "implicates both the Obama White House and the Department of Justice in an effort to secretly undermine a congressional investigation and to suppress critical media reporting of the Obama administration."[13] On *The Laura Ingraham Show*, Attkisson revealed that both Schmaler and Schultz yelled at her over her damaging story that exposed Attorney General Holder's lies to Congress. He "literally screamed at me and cussed at me" about it.[14]

Despite the Obama administration's attempts to kill the bad coverage, the investigation continued, and the Obama administration continued to stonewall. They refused to turn over subpoenaed documents and stopped witnesses from testifying.[15] When these efforts got them into trouble, they denied that they intended to mislead investigators. "There's no attempt at any kind of cover-up," Holder told Congress in February 2012. "We're not going to be hiding behind any kind of privileges or anything."[16] Guess what? They hid behind Obama's executive privilege. In response to a request from Attorney General Holder, on June 20, 2012, Obama asserted that documents related to Fast and Furious requested by Congress in their investigation fell under executive privilege and would not be released.[17]

In response to the unprecedented stonewalling, the House of Representatives voted on June 28, 2012, to hold Attorney General Holder in contempt of Congress. It was the first time in history an Attorney General was held in both civil and criminal contempt of Congress. While there was bipartisan support for both measures, many Democrats walked out in protest and there were charges of racism against Republicans for daring to think Holder should have cooperated with an investigation into a failed operation that resulted in two deaths at home and dozens abroad.[18]

There was a Department of Justice inspector general investigation of Fast and Furious, which Attorney General Holder personally requested. That fact alone raised red flags. ATF whistleblowers predicted it would absolve DOJ leadership and blame the operation on rogue employees.[19]

And, they were right. The Inspector General investigation concluded, in September 2012, that DOJ officials misled Congress about Fast and Furious when they claimed they "did not knowingly permit straw buyers to take guns into Mexico,"[20] but that Attorney General Holder was unaware of the operation. From the report:

> We determined that Attorney General Holder did not learn about Operation Fast and Furious until late January or early February 2011 and was not aware of allegations of "gun-walking" in the investigation until February. We found no evidence that Department or ATF staff informed the Attorney General about Operation Wide Receiver or Operation Fast and Furious prior to 2011.[21]

The watchdogs were also the suspects, and the result was a fraudulent investigation. Shocking, I know. It is a fact that Attorney General Holder got briefed on Fast and Furious in the summer of 2010, much earlier than he claimed under oath before Congress. He also knew the murder of Brian Terry involved Fast and Furious guns within hours.[22] Yet, the liberal media still claimed the IG report exonerated Holder.

The congressional investigation continued—as did the stonewalling until, in January 2016, a federal judge rejected Obama's claim of executive privilege over Fast and Furious documents and, three months later, the White House withdrew Obama's executive privilege claim, making the documents available to Congress.[23] The House Committee on Oversight and Government Reform released their final report on the matter in February 2017. In it, they determined that Attorney General Holder played a major role in covering up the scandal and obstructing Congress.

> Documents obtained by Congress demonstrate the Department's failure to adequately supervise field offices or to focus on fixing the problems brought to light in the controversy over Operation Fast and Furious. Instead, senior leaders of the Department, including Attorney General Eric Holder, were disproportionately fixated on countering the congressional investigation, massaging the media, and protecting the Department's public image.[24]

They added, "Holder was most active at times of heightened congressional scrutiny or media attention. Emails sent to the Attorney General regarding ongoing media and congressional matters ranged from the mundane to the strategic stonewalling of Congress." Holder and other DOJ officials also showed "disdain" for congressional oversight. "With support and direction from senior leaders, staff in DOJ's Office of Legislative Affairs consistently deployed tactics to delay and withhold information from Congress."[25] Perhaps the most shameful thing in the report is how the DOJ treated slain Border Patrol Agent Brian Terry's family. The DOJ, according to the report, "viewed the Terry family as a public relations nuisance and failed to provide the family with answers regarding Brian's murder."[26] The report also determined the DOJ investigation, which had cleared Attorney General Holder of being a part of the cover-up, "was largely a sham, and it prioritized politics and spin over public safety."[27]

It wasn't just the Obama administration that covered up the scandal; the media did their part. This was a big scandal to cover, but this was an Obama scandal, so they didn't dig too far. According to analysis from the Media Research Center, coverage on ABC and NBC was rare. CBS News, however, did great reporting, thanks to the efforts of Sharyl Attkisson, who, as I mentioned earlier, became an enemy of the Obama administration.[28] Remember how the DOJ and the White House wanted to pull the plug on Sharyl Attkisson's investigative reporting? Well, according to Attkisson, the higher-ups at CBS News axed her coverage of the story. "They felt, fairly early on, that this story was over when I felt as though we had barely begun to scratch the surface," Attkisson said during an appearance on *The O'Reilly Factor*.[29] Sounds like the Obama administration pressured a media organization to stop criticizing the attorney general, doesn't it?

Print media wasn't much better. *The Washington Post* and *The New York Times* treated the scandal like other left-wing publications did—as a right-wing conspiracy theory. MSNBC's Rachel Maddow called media coverage of the scandal the result of "the insane paranoid message from the NRA." Chris Matthew's didn't think the scandal merited an investigation, and the only people who did were "another strain of the crazy far right."[30] An MSNBC panel spun the scandal as a good thing for Obama, and a bad thing for Republicans for pursuing the truth.[31]

Because of Operation Fast and Furious, an operation that had little chance of bringing drug cartel leaders to justice, the administration has blood on its hands. The so-called transparent Obama administration was not only aware of the operation, they did everything in their power to cover up that advance knowledge. Many played dumb. Attorney General Eric Holder lied to Congress and got away with it. The White House and the Department of Justice even tried to kill damaging coverage in connection with the scandal. Relations with Mexico also suffered, thanks to the scandal.[32] What more does it take for the media to recognize and document a scandal? I'm sure that, if this were the fault of George W. Bush, we'd never hear the end of it.

The Solyndra Scandal

It would take an encyclopedia with multiple volumes to account for every government loan disbursed to a company that later failed. One such company was Solyndra—a solar power manufacturer based in California that received a $535 million loan guarantee from the Department of Energy. The loan was part of an $80 billion initiative under Obama's economic stimulus to invest in renewable energy; in fact, it was the first loan issued.[1] It later collapsed and filed for bankruptcy, taking a half a billion tax dollars with it to the void. What happened? Why does this matter?

See, Obama wanted Solyndra to be an example of both the promise of a green energy economy and the success of the stimulus itself. Obama praised the company as an example of future of America's economy, and a success story of his economic policy. "The true engine of economic growth will always be companies like Solyndra, will always be America's businesses," he said in May 2010 at Solyndra's new facility in Fremont, California—built with federal loan money. "Less than a year ago, we were standing on what was an empty lot. But through the Recovery Act, this company received a loan to expand its operations. This new factory is the result of those loans."[2]

If this was just an unwise investment that failed due to misplaced optimism, I wouldn't have bothered covering it in this book, but Solyndra was a special case. The administration approved the loan despite concerns from a Department of Energy employee who reviewed the loan that the company would run out of money by September 2011.[3] The DOE employee who made that prediction *nailed it*; that very month, Solyndra filed for bankruptcy and 1,100 employees lost their jobs.[4] The White

House had all the information it needed to spot this bad investment before it wasted our tax dollars on it. Why would the White House push for a loan of more than half a billion dollars to a startup that DOE officials knew was heading towards bankruptcy and then make it the poster child of the success of the Stimulus?

Dig a little deeper and you find that Democrats have a habit of supporting companies run by powerful Democrats, including Solyndra. The company's leading representatives in the loan application process were donors to the Democratic Party and one of Solyndra's largest investors, billionaire George Kaiser, was a fundraising bundler for Obama in 2008.[5] In fact, according to author and investigative journalist Peter Schweizer, 80 percent of the renewable energy companies that received Department of Energy loans were "run by or primarily owned by Obama financial backers—individuals who were bundlers, members of Obama's National Finance Committee, or large donors to the Democratic Party."[6] White House visitor logs showed Kaiser made four visits to the White House in two days—*just before* Solyndra got the DOE green energy loan. Kaiser visited the White House 16 times between March 2009 and April 2011, often to speak with Obama's Chief of Staff Rahm Emanuel and top adviser Valerie Jarrett.[7]

After the scandal broke, Obama's rosy optimism about Solyndra turned overnight; he needed someone to blame. Guess who he picked? Yep, he tried to pass the buck to George W. Bush. Jonathan Silver, Executive Director of the U.S. Department of Energy's Loan Programs, claimed, "by the time the Obama administration took office in late January 2009, the loan programs staff had already established a goal of, and timeline for, issuing the company a conditional loan guarantee commitment in March 2009." But, the Bush administration rejected Solyndra's loan request two weeks before Obama took office. In fact, the Energy Department's credit committee *unanimously* voted to deny them a loan.[8] Nice try. Silver later resigned from his position because of the scandal as questions over the vetting process for loan applicants intensified.[9]

Before Solyndra collapsed—as the 2010 midterm elections approached—the Obama administration covered up the company's financial woes. Solyndra planned to lay off workers in October of that year, but the Obama administration urged them to delay those layoffs until after the midterm elections to protect the Democratic majority in Congress. Obama had been aggressively touting Solyndra as a success story; job losses would damage his claims that the stimulus was working. Solyndra bowed to the pressure and the layoffs weren't announced until *the day after* the elections. *The Washington Post* added that, even though Solyndra wasn't meeting the key terms of the loan, the Energy Department continued to give Solyndra their loan installments.[10] The Democrats may have lost the House in the 2010 midterm elections, but Solyndra still played ball with the Obama administration's demands and reaped a taxpayer-funded reward. An Energy Department Inspector General investigation, with help from the FBI, determined that Solyndra executives "repeatedly misled federal officials and omitted information about the firm's financial prospects."[11]

Solyndra was not the only bad investment made by the Obama administration in renewable energy companies. In January 2012, a CBS News Investigation by Sharyl Attkisson identified "eleven green energy companies beside Solyndra that, together, got billions of tax dollars and then declared bankruptcy or are suffering other serious financial issues."[12] By October, the number of failing or bankrupt green energy firms jumped to 34, according to the Heritage Foundation, though other estimates had it as high as fifty. Of the $80 billion earmarked in Obama's stimulus for green energy companies, at least 10 percent went to companies that filed for bankruptcy or were in dire financial straits.[13]

Why were there so many bad or risky investments? If you guessed politics played a role, you'd be right. Internal DOE emails uncovered during an investigation showed that Obama was personally involved in approving loans for green energy projects in Nevada in order help Harry Reid's 2010 reelection campaign. DOE officials were concerned about Obama's desire to fast track loan approvals considering tax dollars were at risk.[14] Other emails released during the investigation showed that George Kaiser, the billionaire Solyndra investor and Obama bundler, worried that his connections to both Solyndra and Obama might be controversial. He advised associates on how to get more federal assistance for the failing Solyndra.[15] These emails contradicted public statements by Obama, who said, "And these are decisions, by the way, that are made by the Department of Energy, they have nothing to do with politics."

I guess you could say, "Obama lied. Green energy firms died."

Given the American public's loathing for cronyism and government waste, the media must have been interested, right? As *National Review*'s Rich Lowry observed, "President Bush was flayed for the Enron bankruptcy, based on his tenuous ties to the firm. If the same media rules applied, Solyndra would be Obama's Enron, given his active promotion of the company and his lavish funding of it."[16]

But, according to analysis from the Media Research Center, the media did everything they could to prevent Solyndra from becoming Obama's Enron. "In the six weeks after Solyndra filed for bankruptcy in 2011, the evening newscasts ran just eight stories (four full reports, plus brief mentions in four additional stories)." News coverage in 2012—the same year Obama was running for reelection—was even worse: a few brief mentions of the scandal between the big three networks resulted in the cumulative evening news coverage of 1 minute and 43 seconds for the entire year.[17] The three networks ignored the revelation that the Obama administration had urged Solyndra to postpone layoffs until after the midterm elections and that they continued to give them loan money despite their bleak financial prospects and violating the terms of the loan.[18] I'm sure that this was a simple oversight.

The GSA Scandal

When conservatives talk about reckless spending under Obama, they usually mean the enormous debt accrued or the unwise choices made when distributing stimulus money. This next scandal, though, is an example of unlawful spending that occurred on Obama's watch, and the lengths to which his administration went to cover it up.

On April 2, 2012, a GSA Inspector General audit exposed lavish spending at a 2010 training conference in Las Vegas that cost taxpayers $823,000 for 300 GSA employees. The conference featured a clown, a mind reader, and a reception costing $31,208. Six scouting trips for the conference cost $130,000, and a party in the suite of Public Buildings Service chief Robert Peck cost $2,000, amongst many other extravagances. Those expenses violated federal limits on conference spending.[1]

After the IG report became public, videos of the conference surfaced and made the scandal even worse. One video featured a GSA employee playing the ukulele and singing about excessive government spending during a talent show at the conference. The employee sang, "Spend BA 61 all on fun. ATF can't touch GS-15 guns! Cause I buy everything your field office can't afford. Every GS-5 would get a top hat award. Donate my vacation, love to the nation, I'll never be under OIG investigation," to the tune of "Billionaire" by Travis McCoy.[2]

Oops.

Several GSA officials resigned, were put on administrative leave, or were fired hours before the release of the audit; they knew they were about to feel the wrath of the taxpayers. GSA Administrator Martha Johnson, an Obama appointee who had promised to run the agency as ethically as possible, resigned. Johnson's top adviser Stephen Leeds, and Robert Peck were also "forced out."[3]

Western Regional Commissioner Jeffrey Neely, the organizer of the conference, was placed on administrative leave when photos surfaced showing him in a hot tub at the resort during a scouting trip for the conference. Emails released during a congressional investigation of the conference showed Neely had even invited his friends to live it up with him on the taxpayers' dime.[4] Since he wasn't fired, he was still making $179,000 a year and getting a $9,000 annual bonus.[5] Neely didn't resign until May 24, 2012, after a congressional inquiry discovered he was charging personal expenses to a government account, making him the target of bipartisan criticism.[6] He was indicted in September 2014, and plead guilty in March 2015, to submitting false expense claims in connection to the infamous GSA conference in Las Vegas.[7]

In true Obama fashion, the administration's response to the scandal was to blame Bush by pointing out that GSA costs were rising before Obama took office. One White House official tried to spin the scandal as a positive for the Obama administration. "At least we have taken bold, swift, forceful action to hold those responsible accountable and put in place protections to make sure this never happened again."[8] According to Obama advisor David Axelrod, "On the GSA issue, he [Obama] was I think it's fair to say apoplectic."[9] This is the same Obama who spent as much as $90 million in taxpayer dollars on vacations over eight years in office.[10]

Rep. John Mica (R-FL), the chairman of the committee investigating the scandal, accused the White House of a cover-up. "People from the White House knew about it, did nothing, kept it quiet," he said on CNN a couple weeks after the scandal broke. "We have hundreds of pages of testimony and some of that will come out in today's hearing and in fact people did let the White House know and the White House did not choose to intervene or to take action early on."[11] GSA Chief of Staff Mike Robertson testified that the White House counsel's office knew of the ongoing investigation into the GSA's excessive spending nine months before the scandal broke, but did nothing. After the hearing, Robertson, a former Obama staffer when Obama was in the Senate, later walked his testimony back, claiming he mentioned the investigation in passing to a

White House staffer.[12] While both sides of the aisle expressed outraged by the scandal, congressional Democrats weren't willing to acknowledge that the cover-up involved the White House, and the White House denied being a part of it.[13]

Not only were Democrats unwilling to accept responsibility for the waste at the GSA—they tried to stop anyone from investigating. According to the GSA Inspector General, political operatives in the Obama administration improperly stripped government watchdog group Judicial Watch of "media" status, forced them to pay higher fees for Freedom of Information Act requests, and delayed the release of records. Determined to keep a lid on the situation, the GSA denied Judicial Watch's subsequent appeal. The same person who denied the first request—a White House political appointee—denied the appeal, violating GSA procedures. "Why are White House liaisons involved in our FOIA request?" asked Tom Fitton, the president of Judicial Watch.[14] Of course, we all know the answer to that.

A top GSA administrator also attempted to keep the GSA Inspector General's audit under wraps months before the report was released. "Is there something we can do to prevent another potential embarrassing episode from unfolding and keep this report from being made public?" wrote Ruth Cox, the GSA regional administrator who worked on Obama's presidential transition team, in an email to a colleague in Washington, D.C. The GSA excused her emails by saying she wrote them before the release of the report and before "having any knowledge of the findings."[15] It's ironic that the second excuse makes the quoted email look worse. Having not seen the report, Ms. Cox was already in damage control mode. How is that exculpatory?

The Vegas conference wasn't the only example of wasteful spending at the GSA. Documents obtained through a FOIA request by Fox News showed similar excessive spending at as many as 77 other GSA conferences. One conference held in Crystal City, Virginia, in 2010 was allegedly part of a team building exercise featuring employees drumming together for hours. It turned out to be an excuse to hand out $1,000 bonuses for 3,700 GSA employees. Several GSA conferences had no record of spending, making it impossible to reconcile those costs. "The lack of accountability is so bad that it's impossible to fire anyone," according to Tom Schatz of

Citizens Against Government Waste. "It takes a hot-tub scandal to get rid of people at these agencies."[16]

So, how did the media respond to the scandal? ABC and CBS waited days after the IG audit was released to report on it.[17] NBC didn't touch it until two weeks after.[18] Reports didn't connect the scandal to Obama or his appointees. They offered his supposed outrage over the lavish spending as fact, without any irony. Melanie Sloan of the left-leaning watchdog group Citizens for Responsibility and Ethics in Washington (CREW) dismissed the investigations as redundant and wasteful. "Surely there are far better uses for Congress' time than 'investigating' $823,000 in waste, an amount aptly characterized by NPR's On the Media as 'less than a rounding error in the budget of the executive branch.'"[19] CBS News parroted those talking points, questioning whether investigating the GSA's wasteful spending amounted to "its own form of government waste"? Perhaps a better question would be, "does ignoring a cover-up amount to a cover-up of a cover-up?"[20]

The Benghazi Attack
and Cover-Up

On September 11, 2012, a group with connections to al Qaeda attacked the U.S. consulate in Benghazi, Libya. Four Americans, including U.S. Ambassador Christopher Stevens, died. The timing couldn't have been worse for Barack Obama or Hillary Clinton. During an AFL-CIO Labor Day rally in Detroit just before this act of terror, Vice President Joe Biden said, "I've got a little bumper sticker for you: Osama bin Laden is dead and General Motors is alive."[1] Most of Obama's signature policies were unpopular among the American people, but the attack on bin Laden was a rare victory, so it became a central theme of his reelection campaign. To ensure that the attack didn't undercut his dubious claim that he had crippled al Qaeda, Obama and his appointees engaged in a wide-reaching cover-up, misleading Americans about the attack for weeks and denying their duplicity thereafter.

Obama's reelection wasn't the administration's only concern; then Secretary of State Hillary Clinton's political prospects were also threatened. She was the driving force behind the Obama administration's decision to intervene in the Libyan civil war and our involvement tore the country apart and left it wide open for terrorism.[2] If the public saw the attack as further evidence that their policy in Libya was failing and making us less safe, *both* Obama and Clinton were in trouble. The deception, therefore, began immediately.

In defense of her policy, Clinton's first public statement on the attack blamed a little-known YouTube video called *Innocence of Muslims* for the events in Benghazi, saying, "Some have sought to justify this vicious behavior as a response to inflammatory material posted on the Internet."[3] Two days after the attack, she blamed the video again: "I also want to take a moment to address the video circulating on the internet that has led to these protests in a number of countries. Let me state very clearly—and I hope it is obvious—that the United States Government had absolutely nothing to do with this video. We absolutely reject its content and message."[4] The lie became plain-old despicable when Secretary Clinton spoke at the ceremony for the transfer of the remains of the four dead Americans, "We've seen rage and violence directed at American embassies over an awful internet video that we had nothing to do with."[5]

The rest of Obama's representatives quickly picked up the false talking point. Not long after Clinton's first claims that the attack in Benghazi was in response to a YouTube video, Obama spokesman Jay Carney said, "We have no information to suggest that it was a pre-planned attack. The unrest we've seen around the region has been in reaction to a video that Muslims, many Muslims find offensive."[6] U.N. Ambassador Susan Rice hit the Sunday talk shows that weekend to repeat the lie. "The best information and the best assessment we have today is that this was not a pre-planned, pre-meditated attack. What happened initially was that it was a spontaneous reaction to what had just transpired in Cairo as a consequence of the video," she said on *Fox News Sunday*.[7] On NBC's *Meet the Press*, she parroted, "This is a response to a hateful and offensive video that was widely disseminated throughout the Arab and Muslim world. It's not dissimilar, but perhaps on a slightly larger scale, than what we have seen in the past with the [Salman Rushdie's novel] [*The*] *Satanic Verses*, with the [2006 Danish newspaper] cartoon of the Prophet Muhammad."[8]

Obama himself repeated the lie many times. During his weekly radio address a few days after the attack, he alluded to the video as being the cause. "We reject the denigration of any religion—including Islam," he said. A few days after that, now a full week after the attack, Obama was on *The Late Show with David Letterman* and, where Letterman asked him about it, he replied, "Here's what happened....You had a video that was released by somebody who lives here, sort of a shadowy character who—who made an extremely offensive video directed at—at Mohammed and Islam." He referenced the video again later. "As offensive as this video was, and obviously, we've denounced it and the United States government had nothing to do with it, that's never an excuse for violence."[9]

The Obama administration's explanation for the Benghazi attack was as honest as an email from a Nigerian prince. The absurd blame-the-video strategy fell apart and the official story "evolved." During a September 25 appearance on *The View*, cohost Joy Behar expressed some confusion to Obama about what the official cause of the attack was. She asked, "It was reported that people just went crazy and wild because of this anti-Muslim movie, or anti-Mohammed, I guess, movie. But then I heard Hillary Clinton say it was an act of terrorism. Is it? What do you say?" While Hillary had called it terrorism at this point, Obama, now a month and half away from the election, was unwilling to call the attack what it really was, a pre-planned *terrorist* attack. "Well, we're still doing an investigation," he told her. [10]

Once Obama was reelected, the focus of his administration was the defense of Hillary Clinton. In January 2013, Hillary testified for six hours before the Senate Foreign Relations Committee, during which she shrugged off suggestions that the Obama administration had misled the public about the cause of the attack. "Was it because of a protest, or was it because of guys out for a walk one night who decided they'd go kill some Americans? What difference, at this point, does it make?"[11]

What difference does it make? If it didn't matter what caused the attack, why did she, Ambassador Rice, President Obama, and others claim the attack was caused by the video even though they all knew the video had *nothing* to do with the attack?

And let me be clear: they knew from the beginning the attack was pre-planned by an al Qaeda-linked group. A little over a week after Obama won reelection, former CIA Director David Petraeus testified to Congress behind closed doors that the Obama administration knew the attack was an act of terrorism committed by an al Qaeda-linked group early on. [12]

On April 29, 2014, Judicial Watch released stunning evidence proving that White House public relations helped craft the Benghazi talking points for administration officials in the wake of the attack. One of these documents was a recently declassified email "showing then White House Deputy Strategic Communications Adviser Ben Rhodes and other

Obama administration public relations officials attempting to orchestrate a campaign to 'reinforce' President Obama and to portray the Benghazi consulate terrorist attack as being 'rooted in an internet video, and not a failure of policy.'"[13]

Other emails proved that the administration knew the attack was well-planned and not a spontaneous demonstration—contradicting the talking points used by the administration. What exactly happened to those talking points? How were they so wrong? They were heavily edited by then CIA deputy director Mike Morell because they were "unsuitable."[14] Most of the correspondence referred to the event as an attack and not a demonstration.[15]

To Judicial Watch president Tom Fitton, these documents were a smoking gun. "Now we know the Obama White House's chief concern about the Benghazi attack was making sure that President Obama looked good," he said in a statement. "And these documents undermine the Obama administration's narrative that it thought the Benghazi attack had something to do with protests or an internet video."[16] In May 2015, Judicial Watch released more documents from the Defense Department and State Department that showed that the Obama administration knew within a day of the attack that it was planned at least ten days in advance by an al Qaeda and Muslim Brotherhood-linked group. Yet they still pushed the nonsense story about the YouTube video long afterwards.[17] A month later, even more State Department documents appeared, showing just how much effort went into the "blame the video" strategy. The released materials revealed that "the Obama administration engaged domestic and foreign Islamist groups and foreign nationals to push the internet video narrative."[18]

According to notes and emails produced by the Select Committee on Benghazi investigation, Hillary knew an al Qaeda-linked group was responsible almost immediately. In a conversation with Egyptian prime minister Hesham Kandil a day after the attack, Hillary told him that there had not been a protest in Libya and the internet video was unrelated to the attack. "It was a planned attack–not a protest," she said, according to a record of the conversation. "Based on the information we saw today we believe the group that claimed responsibility for this was affiliated with al Qaeda." She also told her daughter, Chelsea, in an email the night of the attack that it had been an al Qaeda-like group responsible.[19] Yet, she still pushed the bogus "internet video" story publicly, and shamelessly, to the family members of those killed in the attacks.

Competent management from the State Department could have prevented the loss of American life. The Senate Intelligence Committee found that safety conditions in the area had been deteriorating for months but the State Department didn't increase security.[20] Ambassador Stevens even made repeated requests for security to no avail.[21] In one cable from August 16, 2012, less than a month before the attack, Stevens specifically stated that the consulate could not withstand a coordinated attack.[22] A House Armed Services Committee report released in February 2014 also faulted the White House for dropping the ball in Libya. Among the report's key findings, the White House "failed to comprehend or ignored the dramatically deteriorating security situation in Libya." The Defense Department also knew it was terrorist attack "nearly from the outset."[23]

As with any investigation into corrupt Obama administration actions, the stonewalling was legendary. After the attack, the administration put Benghazi survivors under a federal gag order, thus preventing them from discussing, or even testifying about, the attack.[24] Hillary Clinton stone-walled a congressional investigation by not turning over emails that were under subpoena from her private server.[25]

Congressional Democrats did their part to protect Hillary from what they claimed was a partisan witch hunt. "This committee's thorough, fact-centered investigation has been repeatedly stonewalled by the Obama administration, Ranking Member Elijah Cummings, and Committee Democrats," said Rep. Trey Gowdy, the chairman of the Select Committee on Benghazi in May 2016. "Not only have they failed to identify a single administration witness worth talking to or a single document worth accessing in the past two years, they have affirmatively delayed the identification of witnesses and the production of unquestionably relevant documents. Committee Democrats have not lifted a finger to help the Select Committee speed up its investigation and release a report."[26]

The Senate Intelligence Committee's report on the attack also blasted the White House and the FBI for their lack of cooperation with their investigation. "Important questions remain unanswered as a direct result of the Obama administration's failure to provide the Committee with access to necessary documents and witnesses," the report said. "We have also learned that the Federal Bureau of Investigation has developed significant information about the attacks and the suspected attackers that is not being shared with Congress, even where doing so would not in any way impact an ongoing investigation."[27] How can there be accountability in the executive branch if the executive branch wields such power to cover for itself?

With the presidential election of 2016 on the horizon, the media worked tirelessly to protect Hillary Clinton and Barack Obama from being tainted by the Benghazi cover-up scandal and framed the various investigations and coverage of the scandal as partisan. Andrea Mitchell of *NBC Nightly News* dismissed the hearings as having "an obvious political undercurrent." The Associated Press downplayed a May 2013 hearing featuring testimony from whistleblowers by labelling it a partisan "GOP hearing." The *Huffington Post* didn't cover any hearings, but had ample criticism for Fox News's coverage of the scandal.[28]

When, thanks to a FOIA request, the State Department released emails showing the White House knew the attack was premeditated, contrary to their past public statements, ABC *World News* gave it "a dismissive 20 seconds of lip service."[29] Former CBS investigative reporter Sharyl Attkisson accused her former network of hiding a clip of Obama refusing to call the Benghazi attack an act of terrorism "in order to help him get re-elected."[30] Brent Bozell, the president of the Media Research Center, called the mainstream media "Accessories to the Benghazi cover-up" for not covering explosive and damaging developments in the scandal.[31]

Patricia Smith, the mother of the slain Sean Smith, spoke at the Republican National Convention and declared, "I blame Hillary Clinton personally for the death of my son." She accused Hillary of lying to her about the cause of the attack. Even I was stunned at the brutality and fervor of the media effort to discredit the grieving mother.[32]

What happened in Benghazi, Libya, on September 11, 2012, was tragic and preventable. Rather than hold the perpetrators accountable— or accept responsibility for the failure of their policy in Libya and, perhaps, learn something—the Obama administration was more concerned with protecting Obama and his heir apparent to the White House. No act was too low or *deplorable* for them in their zeal to shield themselves from the fallout of a bad policy and a worse execution of that policy.

EPA Transparency Scandals

Since Richard Nixon signed an executive order creating the Environmental Protection Agency in 1970, it has wielded increasing power over domestic policy and become a major source of corruption and waste. Under Barack Obama, the EPA was a magnet for scandal and controversy on an unprecedented scale. Under a Republican administration, any one of the half-dozen major scandals that have rocked the agency in the last eight years would have been a blow to the president, but, somehow, under Obama, they were each dismissed. I'll give you a few examples that show how secretive and dishonest the EPA was.

You had to be living under a rock to miss the Hillary Clinton email scandal of 2015–2016—more on that later—but did you know that it was not the first email-related scandal of Obama's presidency? Soon after the 2012 election, we learned that Obama's EPA administrator Lisa Jackson had been using secret email accounts to conduct official EPA business. Christopher Horner, a senior fellow at the Competitive Enterprise Institute, documented this blatant corruption in his book *The Liberal War on Transparency*. Two whistleblowers—former EPA officials—gave Horner the name of one of her email aliases: Richard Windsor.[1] When the news broke, congressional Republicans launched an investigation; using private emails to conduct official business violates federal law unless those emails are properly archived and tracked. The obvious reason to use an alias or a private email account is to avoid transparency.[2]

Jackson must have thought the best way to make the story go away was to resign her post, which she did on December 27, 2012.[3] After leaving the EPA, Lisa Jackson joined the Clinton Foundation, continuing a grand tradition of corrupt government officials moving over to corrupt PACs and "charities" that act as organizing arms for the Democratic Party. As of this writing, she still sits on the Board of Directors for the Clinton Foundation.[4] Richard Windsor didn't join her on the board. Perhaps he was just too busy receiving accolades at the EPA. "Richard Windsor" was more than an alias, you see. The fictional identity received certificates for completing technology training, and—no joke—won an award for being a "scholar of ethical behavior" three years in a row from 2010 to 2012.[5] You can't make this stuff up.

The story didn't end with her departure. The CEI and congressional Republicans continued to dig, and the EPA responded with classic Obama-style stonewalling. In January 2013, the EPA agreed to release 3,000 Richard Windsor emails, thanks to a FOIA request made by the CEI. Instead, they released mostly mundane emails to and from Jackson on her government account.[6]

The more Congress and the CEI learned, the more the EPA's excuses for using the aliases fell apart. According to the EPA, using a secondary email was common practice. Jackson's contact information was published on the EPA website, resulting in a flood of external emails and thus necessitating a secondary address so the official business would not get lost in the noise. This may be true, but, for most EPA employees, secondary emails stayed attached to the administrator's real name. Jackson's "Richard Windsor" account was not.

In emails released in May 2013, Jackson didn't use the Richard Windsor account only to communicate with staff, but also with people outside of government—including environmental activists and individuals who would later serve in the Obama administration. When responding to an email on the Windsor account, Jackson pretended to be Windsor rather than reveal her true identity.[7] Two months later, Americans also learned that Jackson used the Windsor account to communicate with a lobbyist and used a private email address to conduct business with environmental lobbies. "There's no ambiguity here," according to Christopher Horner. "This reflects a clear intention to violate law and policy."[8]

There was also an EPA Inspector General investigation, but that turned out to be a complete sham. The investigation concluded there was *no evidence* that senior EPA officials, including Lisa Jackson, had used aliases and private email accounts to evade federal transparency laws. I guess all of those emails didn't count as evidence. How did they come to such a biased conclusion? Arthur Elkins, Jr., the EPA Inspector General, acknowledged that the investigation was "based only on discussions with these senior officials," prompting criticism from attorneys representing the CEI. "It's kind of comical that he's come out and said that he's relying on the very people who are accused of violating federal open government laws to tell him whether there's any problem," said CEI attorney Hans Bader.[9]

As for the congressional investigation, the White House intervened. In November 2013, the EPA, after discussions with the White House, suddenly stopped releasing emails to Congress. Curiously, one of the previously released emails "suggests that the White House may have played a role in EPA withholding information from Congress," according to Oversight Chairman Darrell Issa (R-CA).[10] Emails trickled out very slowly thereafter. In late 2014, released emails included evidence of collusion between the EPA and environmental lobbying groups:

> The report, which details what the Energy & Environment Legal Institute terms "collusion" between the Environmental Protection Agency and eco-friendly groups, is also a study in the way E&E used open records laws to force transparency on a secretive agency.
>
> Chris Horner, the report's author, said the emails show EPA officials aren't acting as impartial regulators but as committed environmentalists whose minds are already made up on a number of the big issues that come before the agency. Mr. Horner said it was the equivalent of the EPA collaborating with oil companies.
>
> "These emails reveal the realities of how the Obama EPA operates, and candid admissions among themselves and pressure group allies about their shared agenda and its impacts," Mr. Horner said. "The emails' content also explains why the administration so furiously opposes efforts to obtain the oft-promised transparency: These realities wouldn't possibly sit well with the broader public."[11]

Emails offered in the report, according to Horner, "inarguably present impermissible conflicts of interest and a clear pattern of improper collusion, improper influence, and a lack of real opportunity for others to have input into, or equal opportunity to comment on, EPA's rule-making processes. The minds of senior Obama EPA appointees, implementing a costly and admittedly (among themselves, in email) ideological agenda, were closed."[12]

The EPA did everything it could to make sure the public would have to wait for a really long time to see any more of the toxic sludge collecting in its email accounts. They only released new emails at a pace of *100 per month*—the fastest the EPA claimed it could process. Apparently, we should question the agency's competence as well as its ideological biases and ethical failings. At that pace, it would take 100 years to release all the emails.[13]

This stonewalling prompted the CEI to file *another* lawsuit against the EPA in March 2015. According to the CEI, the EPA also refused to process other FOIA requests by the group until they finished processing the Windsor emails. "What are they trying to hide?" Horner asked. "If previously uncovered Windsor emails are any indication, it ranges from the embarrassing to the unlawful."[14]

The same month, a U.S. District Court judge condemned the EPA for destroying emails sought by a 2012 FOIA request by conservative radio host Mark Levin's Landmark Legal Foundation. In his decision, Judge Royce C. Lamberth called the EPA "offensively unapologetic" for their discriminatory handling of FOIA requests. "Either EPA intentionally sought to evade Landmark's lawful FOIA request so the agency could destroy responsive documents, or EPA demonstrated apathy and carelessness toward Landmark's request."[15] Given what we know about Obama's EPA—and, frankly, his entire administration—I'm leaning towards the former.

Lamberth's ruling also stated, "This court would implore the executive branch to take greater responsibility in ensuring that all EPA FOIA requests—regardless of the political affiliation of the requester—are treated with equal respect and conscientiousness."[16] I doubt Obama and his agency heads noticed or cared. Contrary to being the most open and transparent in history, Horner believes the Obama White House was "one of the most secretive administrations ever."[17]

Obama's EPA was notorious for a lack of transparency; while they were fighting to keep the Windsor emails out of the public eye, in May 2013, another scandal broke after documents obtained by the CEI showed that the EPA was discriminating against conservative groups that filed FOIA requests with the agency.[18]

According to the documents, the EPA granted fee waivers to 75 of 82 FOIA requests by green groups for a 92 percent approval rate. But it denied or ignored 21 of 26 fee waivers requests by conservative groups for an 81 percent denial rate. Every denial was overturned on appeal. This, according to Christopher Horner, is proof the EPA was discriminating.[19] "That these denials are ritually overturned on appeal, not after I presented any new evidence or made any new point, but simply restated what was a detailed and heavily sourced legal document to begin with, reaffirms the illegitimacy of these hurdles EPA places in the way of those who cause it problems." Horner added, "This demonstrates a clear pattern of favoritism for allied groups and a concerted campaign to make life more difficult for those deemed unfriendly. The left hand of big government reaches out to its far-left hand at every turn. Argue against more of the same, however, and prepare to be treated as if you have fewer rights."[20] Senator David Vitter (R-LA) called this new scandal "no different than the IRS disaster."[21]

Even after Lisa Jackson's departure from the EPA, this aversion to transparency continued. The CEI filed another lawsuit in 2013 accusing the EPA of using text messages to conduct official business in another attempt to avoid transparency laws. The EPA told a judge that text messages between Lisa Jackson and her successor, Gina McCarthy, may have been deleted.[22] It took the agency until April 2015 to release texts and phone records but, "the agency has so far only given them two text message records from McCarthy. The agency also sent over phone billing records and texts from lower-ranking officials."[23]

Obama's EPA might be opaque to ethics investigators or conservative opponents to their ideological agenda, but they showed no discretion for leaking private information to environmental groups with whom they were colluding. The same EPA that was giving preferential treatment to environmental groups and stonewalling the release of their own emails, released the personal information of over 80,000 private farms and ranches to left-wing activists in response to a FOIA request. This information included individual names, email addresses, phone numbers and personal addresses—which raised concerns for the safety of those people. The release of information by the EPA was so egregious that senators from both sides of the aisle demanded answers. Many wondered why such information was even collected.[24]

Naturally, the media deemed these Obama administration scandals unworthy of coverage. When the Windsor scandal broke, the press paid little attention; stories were "virtually non-existent" according to analysis by the Media Research Center. Neither the Associated Press nor *The New York Times* felt it was worth mentioning that, in Barack Obama's supposedly transparent administration, his own EPA Administrator was actively trying to evade transparency laws.[25] It's a disturbing story made so much worse by the complicity of the press.

When Lisa Jackson resigned from the EPA, *USA Today* lauded her, saying the most notable aspect of her four-year stint as head of the EPA was her efforts to curb greenhouse gases. They praised her for her handling of "repeated battles with industry groups and GOP lawmakers," and explained her departure as commonplace turnover from one presidential term to the next. The email scandal was a mere blip in the story, with only enough room to print her bogus excuse for the alias, and none for the stonewalling.[26] *The New York Times* report on the resignation wasn't much different, citing only Jackson's explanation, but none of the evidence against her.[27] Left-wing "journalists" painted Jackson as a tireless advocate for the environment, the first African-American to head the EPA, and a constant target of Republicans. No one paid any mind to Mark Levin's battle against the EPA. Judge Lamberth's ruling that the EPA had lied, and his warning to the agency to stop discriminating against conservative groups in FOIA requests, got no network coverage.[28] It's enough to make a patriot wonder: what could a Democrat do that would make reporters angry enough to call him or her to account?

The Pigford Scandal

Pigford v. Glickman was a 1997 class-action lawsuit against the United States Department of Agriculture (USDA) alleging African-American were victims of racial discrimination when the USDA denied their loan applications. The case was settled in 1999, and the injured parties were awarded $50,000 each. These payouts were plagued by fraudulent claims almost from the moment they began, and they continued right through the Obama presidency. The late Andrew Breitbart worked tirelessly to expose the rampant fraud, which became endemic on Obama's watch. He would not live to see it happen, but he was finally vindicated on April 26, 2013, when *The New York Times* published an explosive front-page, above-the-fold investigative report acknowledging that Pigford payouts "had proved a magnet for fraud" and that the claims process by design encouraged people to lie to get a payout. In 2007 then Senator Obama sponsored legislation for even more claimants—despite the prevalent fraud even back then. As president, he delivered on his past efforts in a huge way, turning the Pigford case into a pig's trough for people who never farmed and were never even in contact with the USDA.[1]

How did the Pigford judgment go from a narrow class-action lawsuit to a multibillion-dollar wealth transfer scheme? After the 1999 settlement for black farmers, 81 Hispanic and 10 women farmers wanted the same deal and sued to get it, arguing that they also faced systemic discrimination. The courts disagreed, but the Obama administration, seeing a political opportunity, promised to pay these settlements without a court decision. Obama set aside "$1.33 billion to compensate not just the 91 plaintiffs but thousands of Hispanic and female farmers who had never claimed bias in court."[2] Current and former government officials who spoke with *The New York Times* said the deal was "fashioned in White House meetings despite the vehement objections—until now undisclosed—of career lawyers and agency officials who had argued that there was no credible evidence of widespread discrimination."[3]

Once the Obama administration broadened the terms of the Pigford settlement, the number of fraudulent claimants exploded to the thousands:

> But an examination by The New York Times shows that it became a runaway train, driven by racial politics, pressure from influential members of Congress and law firms that stand to gain more than $130 million in fees. In the past five years, it has grown to encompass a second group of African-Americans as well as Hispanic, female and Native American farmers. In all, more than 90,000 people have filed claims. The total cost could top $4.4 billion. [4]

The Obama administration turned the *Pigford* settlement fund into an open-access ATM, costing billions of tax dollars. And when I say anyone, I don't just mean farmers who weren't denied a loan. People who weren't farmers got payouts. According to the 2007 Agricultural Census, there were not even 40,000 African-American farmers in the entire United States. By 2010, there were over 86,000 applicants for Pigford payouts. There were only four hundred African-American farmers in the original 1997 lawsuit.[5] The system was so easy to exploit that one person received payouts from multiple claims and others were paid for claims on behalf of children. There were even claims made on behalf of the deceased.[6]

Why would Obama be so intentionally reckless with taxpayer dollars? The Pigford payouts became a successful vote-buying scheme. Even as a U.S. senator, Obama was using the *Pigford* settlement issue to curry favor with important constituencies. Obama's support of late-filers for *Pigford* earned him the endorsement of a black farmers' association with a membership of 109,000 during the 2008 presidential primaries. And black farmers weren't the only votes Obama was buying. One expert claimed, even though Native American farmers were eligible to get Pigford payouts after a new settlement with the government, there was no evidence of systemic discrimination against them. "If they had gone to trial, the government would have prevailed," the expert said. "I was so disgusted. It was simply buying the support of the Native Americans."[7]

By now, it should not surprise you that the media ignored *Pigford* fraud for years. There was ample evidence of fraud, and the Obama administration's role in enabling that fraud, that the mainstream media could have uncovered well before the post-Obama-reelection exposé. Besides *Breitbart*, there was also coverage of the fraud at the *Washington Times*, which called for the payments to halt and the fraud investigated in early 2011,[8] and *National Review*. *The New York Times* did previously cover the *Pigford* settlement in a February 2010 editorial titled "Pay Up"—only this editorial lamented that not all victimized black farmers had gotten their payouts yet. "The Pigford settlement will remain a misnomer until the nation rights this historic injustice and pays what it owes," they wrote. There was no mention of the fraudulent redistributive scheme. I wonder: would they and the rest of the mainstream media have been so blasé if a Republican administration was buying votes with unearned tax money?

The IRS Scandal

In May 2013, the "scandal-free" Obama administration was rocked by another huge scandal when America learned that the Internal Revenue Service (IRS) was targeting conservative groups seeking tax-exempt status as non-profits for unfair scrutiny from 2010 onward. Groups with "tea party" or "patriot" in their names or mission statements applying for 501(c)(4) status found their applications denied or delayed, and the applicants often found themselves abusively audited.

A preemptive apology from Lois Lerner, the Director of the IRS Exempt Organizations division, did little to prevent the controversy from blowing up into a huge scandal. Despite the partisan nature of the abuses, Lerner claimed the targeting—which she conceded was "absolutely inappropriate"—resulted from an attempt to streamline the processing of applications for organizations requesting tax-exempt status and had no partisan motives.[1] And I'm sure the fact that this happened during the 2012 presidential campaign and ensnared few left-wing groups was just a bizarre coincidence.

Damage control was now in order. Attorney General Holder ordered a criminal investigation. "We are examining the facts to see if there were criminal violations."[2] Obama also spoke out: "It's inexcusable, and Americans are right to be angry about it, and I am angry about it," he said in a statement. "I will not tolerate this kind of behavior in any agency, but especially in the IRS, given the power that it has and the reach that it has into all of our lives." He also promised that the guilty parties would face consequences.[3] Neither Holder nor Obama won an Academy Award for their portrayals of shocked bystanders demanding accountability, though it was a close call.

Obama next tried to distance himself from the scandal by claiming, "I first learned about it from the same news reports that I think most people learned about this." There's that old saw again. Obama's press secretary Jay Carney seemed to contradict this claim the next day when he said that the White House was alerted that the IRS was targeting conservative groups several weeks prior—though, according to Carney, neither he nor Obama were individually notified.[4]

As the Executive Branch scrambled for cover, several of their claims meant to downplay the scandal fell apart. Lerner blamed two low-level employees out of the IRS Cincinnati office for the targeting. This claim, which the White House supported, proved false. Employees interviewed by members of the House Oversight Committee said the directive to target conservative groups came right out of the Exempt Organizations Technical Unit in Washington, D.C. One employee even complained that she was "being micromanaged to death."[5] Twelve different IRS units took part in the targeting of conservative groups and were receiving direction out of Washington, D.C.[6]

They claimed liberal groups were also on the list for higher scrutiny. Not so. Groups with left-leaning identifiers in their names appearing on that list saw their tax-exempt status applications approved quickly. The Treasury Department inspector general who investigated the IRS targeting said his audit "did not uncover instances of groups that could be identified as liberal that were treated in the manner that these tea party cases were."[7]

Don't imagine that Obama was innocent in this, either. The *Washington Times* reported that "IRS employees were 'acutely' aware, in 2010, that President Obama wanted to crack down on conservative organizations and were egged into targeting tea party groups by press reports mocking the emerging movement."[8] Douglas Shulman, the IRS Commissioner, visited the White House a whopping 157 times—more than anyone in Obama's cabinet—while the abuses were occurring.[9] Just a coincidence?

How about the revelation that the IRS was providing confidential taxpayer information to the White House?[10] The Treasury Inspector General for Tax Administration (TIGTA) blocked a FOIA request for thousands of documents related to this exchange of confidential information.[11] The IRS denied the allegations, but refused to provide the documents, and seemed determined to prevent all efforts to make those records available to Congress.[12] It would be much easier to believe they did nothing wrong if they weren't acting like they had something to hide. Was there collusion between the White House and the IRS?

The abuses of the IRS weren't limited to improper targeting of conservative groups. Individual donors to Mitt Romney's presidential campaign also found themselves the target of IRS audits, some within weeks of donating to Romney's campaign.[13] Eric Bolling of Fox News said he was audited by the IRS after criticizing Obama.[14] When Dr. Ben Carson criticized Obama during his speech at the 2013 National Prayer Breakfast, the White House demanded an apology. When Carson refused, the IRS audited him, too.[15] A cancer patient who appeared on Fox News to discuss how Obamacare cost him his health insurance was audited shortly after his interview aired.[16] Hollywood's only conservative group, Friends of Abe, became another target; their tax exempt status was kept under review for over two years, and the IRS even demanded to see their membership list.[17] Yet Obama still had the audacity to tell Bill O'Reilly in an interview that there was "not even a smidgen of corruption." In all, the IRS audited a whopping 10 percent of Tea Party donors—a rate ten times higher than the national average.[18]

So, what became of the investigation that Holder ordered? With all the damning revelations that poured out, Obama kept his promise of accountability, right? Wrong. The FBI investigation turned out to be a complete sham. First, Holder appointed DOJ lawyer Barbara Bosserman to lead the investigation. Her primary qualification to handle this investigation was that she was an Obama donor.[19] On January 13, 2014, just days after Bosserman's role in the investigation and her conflict of interest were exposed, law enforcement officials announced that even though the investigation was still ongoing, the FBI was *not* planning to file any criminal charges related to the scandal.[20]

Perhaps they held back because the FBI wasn't doing much investigating. Cleta Mitchell, a D.C.-based political law attorney representing several conservative and Tea Party groups, said the FBI concluded there was no criminal targeting "without ever speaking to a single conservative or Tea Party organization leader or attorney to learn what actually happened." Mitchell called it a "new low for the FBI, which appears to have been completely silenced by this administration, starting with the president's appointment of the very political Eric Holder, who in turn appointed Barbara Bosserman."[21]

The investigation by the House Committee on Oversight and Government Reform, however, determined that Lois Lerner "was keenly aware of acute political pressure to crack down on conservative-leaning organizations." She "created unprecedented roadblocks for Tea Party organizations, worked surreptitiously to advance new Obama administration regulations that curtail the activities of existing 501(c)(4) organizations— all the while attempting to maintain an appearance that her efforts did not appear, in her own words, 'per se political.'" The committee found that she gave many false statements during the investigation.[22]

Another explosive revelation came, in April 2014, when Judicial Watch released emails–previously hidden from Congress and obtained by a FOIA lawsuit–showing Lerner not only shared confidential tax information with Democrat Congressman Elijah Cummings, but she also discussed pursuing criminal investigations of conservative groups with Obama's Justice Department the day before the scandal broke.[23] So, Obama's Department of Justice that was "investigating" the scandal had a conflict of interest from the moment it broke. That explains a lot.

Efforts to stonewall the investigation continued as Lois Lerner refused to testify and was found in contempt of Congress.[24] Then came a truly Nixonian cover-up. After stonewalling for a year, the Obama administration claimed it had "lost" two years of Lerner's emails in a computer crash. The excuse fooled no one. "Isn't it convenient for the Obama administration that the IRS now says it has suddenly realized it lost Lois Lerner's emails requested by Congress?" asked Rep. Darrell Issa. "Do they really expect the American people to believe that, after having withheld these emails for a year, they're just now realizing the most critical time period is missing?"[25] The committee also accused IRS Commissioner John Koskinen of making false statements under oath and obstructing the investigation. He nearly faced impeachment.[26]

Sadly, the Obama administration wasn't alone in hiding the scandal; the media did their part. As the scandal grew, the media's interest remained virtually nil. According to an analysis by the Media Research Center, ABC,

CBS, and NBC covered the scandal in May and June 2013, but soon tried to forget it. "After producing 136 stories on their morning and evening news show during the first seven weeks of the scandal, broadcast news coverage dried up, with just 14 more reports over the next 10 months, as the 'Big Three' ignored numerous damning developments in the case."[27] CBS only broke their embargo after the FBI said they didn't expect to file any charges.[28] Remember the two years of Lois Lerner's emails that were supposedly lost in a crash? Remote backup tapes containing those emails later surfaced, conveniently forgotten by the IRS. The emails proved the decision to target conservative groups came out of Washington, D.C., not Cincinnati, and the IRS was trying to cover up the scandal well before it became public.[29] Even when the FBI ended their sham investigation in fall of 2015, ABC, CBS, and NBC pretended like the scandal didn't exist.[30] "The media's blackout of the IRS scandal continued through 2016 despite a constant trickle of new, damning developments in the case. On June 15, 2016, the IRS finally released an almost complete list of organizations that the tax agency scrutinized in the Tea Party targeting scandal, but the Big Three networks (ABC, CBS, NBC) ignored this stunning development."[31]

Despite Democrats' claims to the contrary, and the media whitewashing that followed, the IRS targeting of Tea Party groups was a huge scandal. The FBI investigation was a fraud from day one, and the congressional investigation was plagued by Obama administration cover-ups and stonewalling that would make Richard Nixon blush. No one was held accountable. Sure, Lois Lerner resigned four months after the scandal erupted, but she never faced justice for her contempt of Congress, or for her crimes at the IRS. She walked away unscathed and with a six-figure pension and the Obama administration retained "not even a smidgen" of credibility.

Media Spying Scandals

Obama proved to be quite the enemy of the free and independent press during his time in the White House. We learned of several high profile abuses in May 2013—around the same time the IRS scandal broke. First, the Associated Press (AP) announced that the Justice Department took two months of AP reporters' phone records. Next came the revelation that the Department of Justice spied on Fox News reporter James Rosen, naming him a "criminal co-conspirator" in a leak investigation. Soon after that, CBS News investigative reporter Sharyl Attkisson claimed someone in the government compromised both her personal and work computers—she suspected the breach was related to what happened to James Rosen. I'll take a closer look at each abuse of power.

When the Associated Press learned the Department of Justice had secretly seized two months' worth of phone records of reporters and editors, including their home phones and cellphones, AP president Gary Pruitt called it a "massive and unprecedented intrusion" into newsgathering activities. The DOJ gave no reason federal investigators gathered the records, but an investigation into leaks of classified information overlapped with the time from which the records originated. "There can be no possible justification for such an overbroad collection of the telephone communications of The Associated Press and its reporters," Pruitt wrote in a letter to Attorney General Eric Holder. "These records potentially reveal communications with confidential sources across all of the newsgathering activities undertaken by The A.P. during a two-month period, provide a road map to A.P.'s newsgathering operations, and disclose information about A.P.'s activities and operations that the government has no conceivable right to know." Holder had to be the one to approve the subpoena, according to Justice Department regulations.[1] Even so, the White House played dumb. "We don't have any independent knowledge of that, [President Obama] found out about the news reports uh yesterday on the road." Obama spokesman Jay Carney said.[2]

After the story broke, S.E. Cupp, a conservative columnist for the *New York Daily News*, explained what was so frightening about the AP spying scandal—not just for the media, but for all Americans. "If you believe we're better off as a nation knowing the truth about our military operations in Vietnam, as outlined by the Pentagon Papers, or about Watergate and Nixon administration's break-in at the Democratic National Committee headquarters, or about the abuses at Abu Ghraib prison and the Bush administration's stated reasons for invading Iraq, then you should have serious concerns about the DOJ's efforts to disrupt the critical relationship between reporters and their sources."[3]

The AP spying scandal was still a fresh bombshell when *The Washington Post* reported that James Rosen, the chief Washington, D.C., correspondent at Fox News, was also a target of the Obama administration. The DOJ monitored his activities and collected phone records and emails while investigating leaks of classified information by State Department contractor Stephen Ji-Woo Kim about North Korea's nuclear ambitions.[4] To obtain a secret search warrant, the Justice Department went much further than they had with the Associated Press, as they named Rosen a "co-conspirator" in the investigation, invoking *The Espionage Act of 1917*. The same law used by the Nixon administration after the leak of the Pentagon Papers to go after *The New York Times* and the source of the leak, Daniel Ellsberg.[5] "We are outraged to learn today that James Rosen was named a criminal co-conspirator for simply doing his job as a reporter," said Fox News Executive Producer Michael Clemente. "In fact, it is downright chilling."[6]

It gets worse. The DOJ monitored over thirty different phone numbers connected to Rosen and Fox News including the home phone of Rosen's parents.[7] Their own documents confirmed this. Although the DOJ *claimed* there was probable cause to conclude Rosen had committed a crime, a law enforcement official said they had no plans to charge Rosen. Attorney Jesselyn Radack, director of national security and human rights with the Government Accountability Project, expressed concern that the Obama administration was only using the Espionage Act to get access to Rosen's communications. "We should take a hard look at how the Espionage Act, a favorite tool of Nixon, is being used to go after any organization who's saying things the administration doesn't like."[8] Recall, the Obama administration used the Espionage Act to target whistleblowers and journalists more than any White House in history, and it wasn't even close.

On May 15, just days before the Rosen story broke, Attorney General Holder appeared before Democrat Congressman Hank Johnson of Georgia at a Congressional hearing to answer questions about the targeting of reporters by the Justice Department. He said, "With regard to the potential prosecution of the press for the disclosure of material, that is not something I've ever been involved in, heard of, or would think would be wise policy."[9] Remember the secret warrant naming Rosen a "co-conspirator"? Guess who approved that warrant. I know you'll be stunned to learn that it was Attorney General Eric Holder.

On the Friday before Memorial Day weekend, the Justice Department confirmed that "senior officials including Attorney General Eric Holder vetted a decision to search an email account belonging to a Fox News reporter [James Rosen] whose story on North Korea prompted a leak investigation."[10] Holder and the DOJ had to explain Holder's apparent perjury, which prompted a formal investigation by the House Judiciary committee. The DOJ defended Holder's felonious statement by saying he had no intention of charging Rosen with a crime.[11] No big deal; they were just accusing him of espionage—which the United States has imprisoned and executed people for. Move along—nothing to see here.

The committee's investigation concluded that Holder in fact "gave deceptive and misleading testimony before the Committee," which is a fancy way of saying, "yes, he committed perjury." The committee also determined that the Justice Department "inappropriately interpreted the Privacy Protection Act of 1980 to obtain a search warrant for Mr. Rosen's emails."[12] In other words, Holder lied, and the DOJ twisted the law to get the search warrant. The report also said the committee took "little comfort in Mr. Holder's assurances to us now that the Department never intended to prosecute Mr. Rosen when it labeled him a criminal suspect in 2010."[13] If the Department of Justice makes bogus accusations of espionage against journalists for doing their job, what will stop them from spying on anyone they want? All they need do is accuse you of a crime, and you could be next. Think about that.

Lastly, there's the curious case of the hacking of Sharyl Attkisson's computers. Attkisson's investigative reporting on the Fast and Furious gun-walking scandal and Benghazi did not earn her any friends in the Obama administration and according to Attkisson, the Obama administration fought back. Attkisson said, on a Philadelphia-based radio station affiliated with CBS, that she believed her home and work computers were compromised since at least February 2011 and possibly further back. If true, it meant that someone was watching her computers while she was investigating Fast and Furious.[14] Though she didn't go into specifics, she said: "there could be some relationship between these things and what's happened to James [Rosen]." In response to the allegations, Obama's Department of Defense offered the non-denial-denial: "To our knowledge, the Justice Department has never compromised Ms. Attkisson's computers, or otherwise sought any information from or concerning any telephone, computer, or other media device she may own or use."[15]

A cybersecurity firm performed a forensic analysis on Attkisson's work computer and concluded that it had been "accessed by an unauthorized, external, unknown party on multiple occasions in late 2012," according to CBS News. "While no malicious code was found, forensic analysis revealed an intruder had executed commands that appeared to involve search and exfiltration of data. This party also used sophisticated methods to remove all possible indications of unauthorized activity and alter system times to cause further confusion."[16] The DOJ Inspector General also investigated Attkisson's claims. She gave the IG her home computer, but CBS News did not provide them with her work computer since it had already been examined. Their investigation was, therefore, inconclusive. The media then falsely rushed to claim that the IG report debunked her claims.[17]

Attkisson would later reveal more details about the hacking of her computer in her memoir *Stonewalled: My Fight for Truth Against the Forces of Obstruction, Intimidation, and Harassment in Obama's Washington*. One of Attkisson's sources, to whom she refers as Number One and is "connected to government three-letter agencies," examined her computer and determined that it was hacked by "a sophisticated entity that used commercial, non-attributable spyware that's proprietary to a government agency: either the CIA, FBI, the Defense Intelligence Agency, or the National Security Agency." The spyware logged keystrokes, exposing her emails and passwords. Whoever hacked her computer planted three classified documents deep within her computer's operating system, possibly intending to accuse her of a federal crime. Espionage, perhaps? Number One was "shocked" and "flabbergasted" from the analysis. "This is outrageous," he said. "Worse than anything Nixon ever did. I wouldn't have believed something like this could happen in the United States of America."[18] This is Obama we're talking about, sir. You need a better imagination.

Attkisson resigned from CBS in March 2014 over complaints that the network silenced her investigative reporting on the Obama administration.[19] It's not surprising, given their record of protecting the Obama administration. In January 2015, Attkisson sued the Obama administration for the hacking, seeking $35 million in damages.[20] That lawsuit is still ongoing as of this writing. A government motion to dismiss Attkisson's lawsuit was dismissed on March 19, 2017. In June 2017, the Department of Justice was still fighting discovery[21] and, "won't even help us find out who had access to govt IP address found in my computer,"[22] Attkisson told me on Twitter. "Why wouldn't they help with that if we all want the truth?"[23]

With Obama's scandals, neither the government nor the media really want the truth. But he didn't get a free pass from the media for his assaults on the free press. Sure, protecting Obama was the *modus operandi* of the mainstream media for over eight years, but the press defends itself before it defends any politician and Obama went too far, eliciting significant criticism, at least at first. Nevertheless, NBC News senior investigative correspondent Lisa Myers distanced Obama from the scandal by suggesting that Obama was unlikely aware about the wiretapping of Associated Press reporters because "from a political standpoint" it would anger "one of the president's most important constituencies, the press."[24] I think she meant "cheerleaders" not "constituencies," but I'm amused at the idea that NBC's journalists think so much of themselves that they believed they were one of Obama's most important support groups.

The revelation that the Obama administration had named James Rosen a criminal "co-conspirator" to obtain a warrant to search his emails went unnoticed by ABC and CBS.[25] I suppose a Fox News reporter is fair game, given the network's political leanings. CNN ignored the fact that Eric Holder approved the bogus search warrant attacking Rosen. Dana Milbank of *The Washington Post*, who had previously dismissed Obama scandals, conceded the situation was "flagrantly an assault on civil liberties" and it "uses technology to silence critics in a way Richard Nixon could only have dreamed of." He also lamented that "the administration's actions shatter the president's credibility and discourage allies who would otherwise defend the administration against bogus accusations such as those involving the Benghazi 'talking points.'" That Milbank suggested Obama had any credibility at that point demonstrates his bias, but his disillusionment was, I confess, amusing. "If the administration is spying on reporters and accusing them of criminality just for asking questions—well, who knows what else this crowd is capable of doing?"[26] Welcome to my world, Dana.

Left-wing journalist and Obama-apologist Juan Williams, to his credit, accused the Obama administration of having "criminalized journalism" for investigating Rosen. "How do you do journalism if you are treated as a criminal for asking for information?" That was obviously the point, Juan.

Media coverage of the Attkisson hacking was lacking, however—barely a story at all. The media was, however, quick to close the lid on the scandal with the inconclusive Inspector General report.[27] The Obama administration's abuse of the media was unprecedented in scope and criminally dangerous in the repercussions for freedom of the press. According to a report by the Committee to Protect Journalists, a nonprofit organization that promotes press freedom worldwide, "in the Obama administration's Washington, government officials are increasingly afraid to talk to the press."[28] The Obama administration didn't want the media to be a watchdog over them and they usually weren't. When it was their turn to face the tyrant, it must have felt very strange.

NSA Surveillance Scandals

On March 12, 2013, James Clapper, Barack Obama's Director of National Intelligence, testified before the Senate Intelligence Committee. During his testimony, Senator Ron Wyden (D-OR) asked for a yes or no answer to the question, "Does the NSA collect any type of data at all on millions or hundreds of millions of Americans?"

"No, sir," Clapper told him.

"It does not?" Wyden asked again.

"Not wittingly," Clapper said. "There are cases where they could inadvertently perhaps collect, but not wittingly."[1]

Not much was made of this exchange at the time, but three months later, Americans would learn the truth after former CIA employee Edward Snowden stole and leaked sensitive documents from the National Security Agency (NSA) to the media. The leaks were not only a devastating blow to national security but also exposed a pattern of out of control domestic spying by the Obama administration—including bulk data collection. Despite being a critic of domestic surveillance as a U.S. Senator and presidential candidate, as president, Obama embraced his inner Big Brother. Under Obama, surveillance programs that began under the Bush administration designed to intercept intelligence on enemies abroad morphed into something that should terrify all Americans. Obama's NSA collected the phone records of millions of Verizon customers through a Foreign Intelligence Surveillance Court (FISA) order for three months. What made this order unprecedented was the scope of the surveillance. Rather than a targeted order aimed at a terror suspect, this was a large-scale collection of records, without cause or a warrant.[2]

The Washington Post published a piece showing that the NSA and FBI were "extracting audio and video chats, photographs, emails, documents, and connection logs that enable analysts to track foreign targets" from the servers of nine American internet companies, including Microsoft, Yahoo, Google, Facebook, Apple, and others under a program code called PRISM.[3]

Even *The New York Times* editorial board couldn't hold back criticism. "The administration is saying that, without any individual suspicion of wrongdoing, the government is allowed to know whom Americans are calling every time they make a phone call, for how long they talk and from where," they wrote. "To casually permit this surveillance—with the American public having no idea that the executive branch is now exercising this power—fundamentally shifts power between the individual and the state, and it repudiates constitutional principles governing search, seizure and privacy."[4]

Another program, codenamed EvilOlive, collected internet metadata from millions of Americans.[5] An Obama-era rule change that empowered the NSA to conduct warrantless searches of phone calls and emails of American citizens also came to light.[6] According to *The Guardian*, "the authority, approved in 2011, appears to contrast with repeated assurances from Barack Obama and senior intelligence officials to both Congress and the American public that the privacy of U.S. citizens is protected from the NSA's dragnet surveillance programs." Yeah, that's an understatement.

As more damaging information appeared, Obama came out in defense of his decision to expand surveillance on his watch. "You can shout Big Brother or program run amok, but if you actually look at the details, I think we've struck the right balance," he said.[7] Obama's Attorney General Eric Holder even tried to spin the leaks as a positive. "You know, we can certainly argue about the way in which Snowden did what he did, but I think that he actually performed a public service by raising the debate that we engaged in and by the changes that we made."[8]

Despite assurances from the Obama administration that the program was in our national security interests, the White House had to admit that there was no evidence the bulk collection of phone data ever prevented a terrorist attack.[9] So the government violated our privacy for nothing.

In May 2015, a federal appeals court ruled that the bulk collection of Americans' phone records was illegal, finding the Patriot Act provision known as Section 215, which Obama used to support his claim the spying was legal, "cannot be legitimately interpreted to allow the bulk collection of domestic calling records."[10]

When Americans learned that the U.S. government was spying on the U.S.-allied world leaders of France, Spain, Mexico, and Germany, Obama played dumb yet again, claiming he only learned about it from the leak.[11] *How many times have we heard that one?* That excused turned out not to be true; imagine my surprise. Both the White House and State Department signed off on surveilling friendly foreign leaders, according to intelligence agency staffers who weren't amused by Obama's attempt to distance himself from the controversy.[12] According to intelligence officials, the State Department has input on any decision to spy on a foreign leader, and the White House is given any useful intelligence gleaned from it. So Obama graduated from playing dumb to *being* dumb. After this embarrassing revelation, Obama publicly claimed the NSA would stop surveilling friendly foreign leaders. Except they didn't. Big Brother Obama needed that intelligence, and he had no intention of giving it up.

In December 2015, the voters found out the NSA also spied on Israeli Prime Minister Benjamin Netanyahu during the Iran nuclear talks. The White House claimed the surveillance was for national security purposes. That was another lie. The White House was attempting to gain information to counter Netanyahu's campaign against Obama's deal with Iran. Netanyahu's conversations with members of Congress were also monitored, violating the bonds of trust between the executive and legislative branches and sparking vitriol across the political spectrum.[13] The White House knew they could be accused of spying on Congress...so they covered their tracks. From *The Wall Street Journal*:

> White House officials believed the intercepted information could be valuable to counter Mr. Netanyahu's campaign. They also recognized that asking for it was politically risky. So, wary of a paper trail stemming from a request, the White House let the NSA decide what to share and what to withhold, officials said. 'We didn't say, 'Do it,'' a senior U.S. official said. 'We didn't say, 'Don't do it.''[14]

Beautiful. What a *tidy* arrangement.

Fred Fleitz, senior vice president for policy and programs with the Center for Security Policy, said this "suggests major misconduct by the NSA and the White House of a sort not seen since Watergate." The comparisons to Nixon keep mounting! According to Fleitz, these intercepts should have never been provided to the White House in the first place because they involved a policy dispute between Congress and the president. Fleitz also said, "the White House bears significant responsibility for this scandal. By encouraging and accepting this intelligence, the White House used the NSA as an illegitimate means to undermine its legislative opponents. This represented a major abuse of presidential power since it employed the enormous capabilities of an American intelligence service against the U.S. Congress. It also probably violates the U.S. Constitution's separation-of-powers principles and the Fourth Amendment, since surveillance may have been conducted against U.S. citizens without a warrant."[15]

When the details of Obama's aggressive intelligence gathering campaign surfaced, the media covered the growing spying scandal but did its best to make sure it wasn't connected to Obama in any way.[16] Often, the discussion at roundtables and in commentaries about the NSA's abusing spying program centered on George W. Bush and the Patriot Act. Whatever your view on the Patriot Act, it's difficult to avoid the conclusion that Obama abused the law far, *far* more than Bush did. Domestic surveillance didn't start with the Obama administration, but it grew exponentially on his watch, and, once they realized it, an already skeptical American citizenry lost what little faith they had in their government.

The fallout from the NSA spying scandal also had both political and economic ramifications. American tech companies lost business worldwide, including with foreign governments, out of concern that the Obama administration was spying on them.[17] Intelligence and diplomatic relationships with European countries also suffered because of the scandal.

So, what about James Clapper? The exposure of mass data collection by the NSA proved he had given false testimony under oath. According to Citizens for Responsibility and Ethics in Washington (CREW), a left-leaning government watchdog group, "Director Clapper appears to have violated laws prohibiting false statements and obstruction of a

congressional inquiry. In 1977, in an analogous situation, DOJ prosecuted then CIA Director Richard Helms for lying to a congressional
committee about CIA operations in Chile."[18] Spoiler alert: Clapper never
faced prosecution for lying to Congress. Like many Democrats who find
themselves in trouble, survived with a simple apology. "My response was
clearly erroneous–for which I apologize," he wrote in a letter to Senator
Dianne Feinstein, then chairman of the Senate Intelligence committee.
"Mistakes will happen, and when I make one, I correct it."[19]

Mistakes? That's one hell of a mistake, Jim. Are we to believe you
simply *forgot* about the most expansive and outrageous domestic spying
program in U.S. history? That excuse would never work for everyday
people. Especially when it proved to be *impossible.*

After the Snowden leaks exposed Clapper's lies, Senator Wyden said,
"So that he would be prepared to answer, I sent the question to Director
Clapper's office a day in advance. After the hearing was over, my staff and
I gave his office a chance to amend his answer."[20] Mistake indeed.

Despite the scandal created by Clapper's false testimony, and many
calls for his resignation, Clapper didn't submit his resignation until after
the 2016 presidential election, and remained in his position as Obama's
Director of National Intelligence until Obama left office. Obama didn't
care enough about Clapper's dishonesty to demand his resignation when
it would have mattered. I don't know about you, but I don't see that as a
great way to encourage transparency.

The VA Scandal

Obama made many promises during his 2008 campaign, and, believe it or not, I agreed with a few. Reducing the backlog of benefits claims through the Veterans Health Administration was one such honorable promise. Even though the VA has struggled with backlog issues for decades, on the campaign trail, Obama attacked George W. Bush for the state of VA hospitals, accusing him of ignoring the deplorable conditions and failing to plan for the care of military personnel returning home from the wars in Afghanistan and Iraq. "America's veterans deserve a President who will fight for them not just when it's easy or convenient, but every hour of every day for the next four years," Obama said.[1] Sadly, he didn't make that promise out of genuine concern for the brave men and women who fought for our country, but rather, from a desire to exploit their suffering for political gain. What happened with the VA on Obama's watch was appalling.

When Obama took office, the backlog was in decline. Outstanding claims fell by nearly 100,000 during George W. Bush's second term. This trend did *not* continue under Obama, however. Instead, it more than doubled during his first term, from approximately 390,000 outstanding claims (with 22 percent backlogged over 180 days) to roughly 884,000 outstanding claims (with 65.8 percent backlogged for over 125 days), increasing by 116,000 outstanding claims in 2011 alone.[2] Under Obama, the number of veterans who died while waiting to receive care because of the backlog also skyrocketed.[3] As the problem spiraled out of control, Obama VA Secretary General Eric Shinseki promised to end the backlog by 2015.[4]

Obama and Shinseki ignored the problem until, in April 2014, even more disturbing details came to light. Whistleblowers surfaced claiming at least forty veterans in a Phoenix VA hospital died waiting for care after being placed on a secret list designed to hide long wait times for medical appointments. Internal VA emails obtained by CNN showed management at the Phoenix VA hospital knew of the secret list and defended it. Officials in D.C. received an abridged "official" list that gave the impression veterans were receiving care within the required 14 to 30 days. To hide the backlog, doctor's appointments weren't scheduled on the VA computer system. "They enter information into the computer and do a screen capture hard copy printout," explained Dr. Sam Foote, a retired doctor out of the Phoenix VA hospital. "They then do not save what was put into the computer so there's no record that you were ever here." That information was kept on a secret list, and the hard copy indicating when the appointment was supposed to have been scheduled was destroyed. According to Foote, "they wouldn't take you off that secret list until you had an appointment time that was less than 14 days so it would give the appearance that they were improving greatly the waiting times, when in fact they were not." The secret list contained an estimated 1,400 to 1,600 sick veterans waiting for care.[5]

Sadly, this problem wasn't isolated to the Phoenix hospital. Whistleblowers came forward alleging that at least seven other VA hospitals around the country were also manipulating waitlists.[6] Despite increasing evidence of systemic problems, Attorney General Eric Holder said there were no plans to launch an investigation.[7] The White House, like a broken record, claimed this was yet another scandal that Obama was unaware of until he saw it on television. Even if I take Obama's proclaimed ignorance at face value, I must ask, what happened to the Obama Americans saw in 2008?

But, this was more than just a broken campaign promise. Obama's transition team was warned about the problems in 2008. According to documents obtained by the *Washington Times*, "Veterans Affairs officials specifically warned the Obama-Biden transition team in late 2008 that the department should not trust the wait times its facilities were reporting."[8] The Obama administration was also warned in writing twice about the secret waiting lists, in 2010 and again in 2012, but did nothing.[9] Instead of fighting "every hour of every day" for our veterans, Obama ignored them for five long years until the problems became a matter of public outrage. After bipartisan calls for VA Secretary Eric Shinseki's ouster, Obama reluctantly accepted his resignation on May 30, 2014.[10] But, that did little to stop the scandal from getting worse.

In fact, the scandal developed another twist when the Office of Special Counsel (OSC) announced, a few weeks later, that it was investigating allegations that the VA retaliated against dozens of whistleblowers who exposed the systemic problems in the agency. Employees who tried to expose the falsified record-keeping at the VA got suspended or demoted. "The frequency with which VA employees are filing these complaints is one of the highest levels in the federal government," an OSC spokesman reported.[11] By July 2014, complaints of retaliatory actions had been filed in 28 states at 45 separate facilities, prompting an apology from a top VA official, but not any change in behavior at the VA.[12]

A year later, an internal VA document provided to *The Huffington Post* revealed the horrific extent of the scandal. Of the 847,822 veterans waiting for care in the VA system, a staggering 238,647 of them, nearly a third, died before receiving treatment.[13]

In a final, heartbreaking indignity to our brave men and women of the military, as late as 2016, nearly a third of all calls to the VA's suicide prevention hotline *went unanswered,* according to the hotline's former director, Greg Hughes.[14] To make matters worse, the main reason for the high failure rate was laziness by call screeners.

Laziness!

And nothing was done under two different Obama-appointed heads of the VA to address a problem as basic as that. Suicide is far too common among veterans, many of whom suffer from serious mental illnesses like post-traumatic stress disorder and clinical depression. A suicide prevention hotline exists to get help to people on the brink of taking their own lives *immediately.* Prevention often hinges on early intervention. But, at the VA, if you called the suicide hotline feeling hopeless and alone, you had a one in three chance to get shunted to a less-experienced counselor at a backup call center or even an *answering machine.* If that doesn't get your blood boiling, you have no blood. This is incomprehensible!

Obama didn't think the problems at the VA were important enough to address until after public outcry. The media, however, didn't seem to think it was important enough to cover even then. The Media Research

Center calculated that, despite significant investigative reporting by CNN and Fox News, "none of the networks bothered covering the story until May 6, 2014, almost two weeks after it broke." Criticism of the Obama administration was virtually nonexistent in the coverage. New Jersey governor Chris Christie's Bridgegate scandal got more coverage.[15] The scandal fell off the radar after Shinseki's resignation.[16] When the news broke that Obama had been warned about the falsified wait times, "*CBS Evening News* and Fox News' *Special Report with Bret Baier* were the only evening news programs to cover the report while *NBC Nightly News* and *ABC World News Tonight* remained silent."[17]

Obama never stopped lying to save face over this scandal. First, he falsely claimed to have been unaware of the problems with the VA. Then, towards the end of his presidency, he claimed his administration had held the guilty parties in the VA accountable: "we have, in fact, fired a whole bunch of people who are in charge of these facilities." But that's not true, according to *The Washington Post*'s fact checker Michelle Ye Hee Lee. Only one senior executive was fired (due to an unrelated ethics violation) and five non-senior employees in leadership positions lost their jobs over patient wait times.[18] To their credit, NBC broke the story about failure and corruption at the VA suicide prevention hotline and unleashed an unequivocal condemnation in the process.

Obama promised to be an advocate for our veterans and, despite repeated warnings of falsified waiting lists and deficient care, he let the problem explode out of control, betraying our nation's heroes, many of whom died waiting for their country to take care of them. Two years after the scandal broke, with Obama just months away from leaving office, patients still were not receiving timely care.[19] I can think of very few things that the Commander in Chief of the U.S. Armed Forces could do to further harm the men and women under his command. And Democrats wonder why the military despises Obama?

Oh, and one more thing. In the first few months of the Trump administration, VA Secretary David Shulkin fired over 500 employees in the department and demoted dozens more.[20] As for the suicide hotline... by June 2017, 9 out of every 10 calls was answered in eight seconds or less.[21] So don't presume to tell me that this problem couldn't be solved. No, Obama could have solved this *years* ago...if he gave a damn. I wonder...how many servicemen and women died because Obama had other priorities?

The Bergdahl Swap

To say Obama is a horrible dealmaker would be an understatement. The nuclear deal with Iran comes to mind as the chief example. A sworn enemy of the United States, the world's number one state sponsor of terrorism, got everything it wanted and the U.S. got nothing. There are others, but right now I want to focus on one terrible deal that quickly became a scandal. In 2014, Obama released five senior Taliban leaders to Qatar in exchange for Army Sgt. Bowe Bergdahl, "captured" by the Taliban in 2009. Soldiers who served with him say that Bergdahl was a deserter who voluntarily left his post. The Obama administration wanted to keep reports of Bergdahl's desertion secret and his fellow soldiers were forced to sign nondisclosure agreements. But, many spoke out anyway.

Josh Cornelison, the medic in Bergdahl's platoon, explained that the men who defied Obama and speak out made their choice when President Obama spoke at the White House with Bergdahl's parents, presenting Bergdahl as a hero. He said:

> When the president was there with Bergdahl's parents, we got this feeling that the American people needed to be told the truth. We were there, this is not hearsay, we were on the ground, the first ones to go looking for him. The American public needs to know the truth about Bergdahl before treating him like any kind of war hero, because that is completely false.[1]

Former Sgt. Matt Vierkant, a member of Bergdahl's platoon, also spoke out:

> I was pissed off then, and I am even more so now with everything going on. Bowe Bergdahl deserted during a time of war, and his fellow Americans lost their lives searching for him." Another member of the

platoon, former U.S. Army Sgt. Josh Korder, was similarly upset. "Any of us would have died for him while he was with us, and then for him to just leave us like that, it was a very big betrayal. I don't think I could have continued to go on without being able to share with you and the people the true things that happened in this situation, because if you guys aren't made aware of it, it will just go on, and he'll be a hero, and nobody will be able to know the truth.[2]

The Eclipse Group, a private intelligence agency and subcontractor of the Department of Defense, investigated Bergdahl. They learned that, while in captivity, Bergdahl converted to Islam and called himself a warrior for Islam. Their reports contained amazing detail, including eyewitness accounts.

> Conditions for Bergdahl have greatly relaxed since the time of the escape. Bergdahl has converted to Islam and now describes himself as a mujahid. Bergdahl enjoys a modicum of freedom, and engages in target practice with the local mujahedeen, firing AK47s. Bergdahl is even allowed to carry a loaded gun on occasion. Bergdahl plays soccer with his guards and bounds around the pitch like a mad man. He appears to be well and happy, and has a noticeable habit of laughing frequently and saying "Salaam" repeatedly.[3]

Retired Gen. Stanley McChrystal, who was commander of U.S. troops in Afghanistan at the time Bergdahl left his post, confirmed the Army knew Bergdahl was a deserter. "I had been in command about a month or so when he left in 2009. My initial understanding based upon the reporting I got is that he had walked off intentionally."[4]

Despite the questions surrounding Bergdahl's disappearance, the Obama administration seemed intent on presenting him as a hero, not a deserter. Bergdahl's parents had joined Obama for a media event at the White House Rose Garden to celebrate the prisoner swap. Obama's national security advisor Susan Rice claimed Bergdahl "served the United States with honor and distinction," and that "he was an American prisoner of war captured on the battlefield."[5]

Who wrote those absurdities? They remind me of the Benghazi talking points. Obama shrugged off the brewing scandal, saying, "I'm never surprised by controversies that are whipped up in Washington.

Right? That's par for the course."[6] When you are as corrupt and incompetent as Obama, perhaps.

The administration also gave every signal they would not pursue punishment for Bergdahl for his act of desertion. An anonymous senior Defense official told CNN that five years in captivity was enough for Bergdahl not to face punishment. Pentagon spokesman Rear Adm. John Kirby said, "We really don't know why he left the base and under what circumstances."[7]

However, when the Obama administration realized that the Bergdahl swap was backfiring on them, there was a concerted effort to distance Obama from it and make Defense Secretary Chuck Hagel the fall guy. Administration officials told Congress that it was Hagel who made the final call, despite the fact that Hagel had previously explained on *Meet The Press* that Obama had made the final call. "I signed off on the decision. The president made the ultimate decision. We did spend time looking at this," he told host David Gregory.[8]

Though Obama and his cabinet appeared to prefer not to punish Bergdahl, on March 25, 2015, the U.S. Army Forces Command charged him "under the Uniform Code of Military Justice with 'Desertion with Intent to Shirk Important or Hazardous Duty' and 'Misbehavior Before The Enemy by Endangering the Safety of a Command, Unit or Place.'" Under the latter charge, Bergdahl faces a possible life sentence.[9] To the surprise of many in the military, Obama elected not to pardon Bergdahl, though he granted a commuted sentence to former Army Private Bradley Manning, now called Chelsea Manning, who compromised national security by leaking thousands of classified documents.[10] Perhaps if Bergdahl was transgender, he would have had more luck. I guess we'll never know.

Bergdahl pleaded guilty to desertion in October 2017. There have also been two verdicts on the Obama administration's actions. The Government Accountability Office found that the Pentagon violated the 2014 Defense Appropriations Act by swapping the five Taliban leaders for Bergdahl. The law states that Congress must be alerted at least 30 days before any detainee may be transferred from the prison at Guantanamo Bay. The Obama administration gave no such warning.

"It is extremely troubling that the president chose to ignore this notification requirement despite the previous bipartisan opposition to this ill-conceived swap," said Senator Susan Collins (R-ME) after the release of the GAO report. "It is highly likely that these men will return to the fight against our country after their year in Qatar. That is the assessment of the administration's own intelligence experts." Collins was not swayed by the administration's argument that informing Congress could have compromised the negotiations because "dozens" in his administration had advance knowledge of the swap. "The president's decision is part of a disturbing pattern where he unilaterally decides that he does not have to comply with provisions of laws with which he disagrees," she added.[11]

An investigation by the House Armed Services Committee released more than a year later also concluded that the Obama administration broke the law and went to great lengths to keep the negotiations secret, even lying to the media and to Congress about it. Some Department of Defense officials who would typically be involved in the negotiations weren't informed. Both Republicans and Democrats in Congress were angry at the actions of the Obama administration, not just for hiding the negotiations from them but for violating U.S. policy not to negotiate with terrorists, thereby incentivizing more hostage-taking. The five Taliban leaders weren't even eligible for transfer at the time of the swap. The report speculated that the Obama administration kept the negotiations secret to help Obama achieve his 2008 election campaign promise of closing Guantanamo Bay. Democrats on the committee *concurred* that Obama violated the law, but issued their own dissenting report because they objected to language that implied the Obama administration broke the law for political reasons.[12] I suppose they deserve credit for not debating that Obama broke the law.

And what happened to the Taliban leaders exchanged for Bergdahl? The House Armed Services Committee investigation found that they were welcomed as heroes in Qatar and resumed "threatening activities." The committee added, "Despite the current restrictions of the [Memorandum Of Understanding], it is clear...that the five former detainees have participated in activities that threaten U.S. and coalition personnel and are counter to U.S. national security interests–not unlike their activities before they were detained on the battlefield."[13] According to the Counter Extremism Project, a nonpartisan and nonprofit international policy organization, Qatar likely influenced former Guantanamo detainees, including those exchanged for Bowe Bergdahl, to return to terrorist activities.[14] So, how was this trade a good deal for the United States?

Leaders in the press certainly did their part to paint the deal as a triumph and a foreign policy success, even as the facts came to light and the swap backfired on Obama. *The New York Times* was so eager to come to Obama's defense that they whipped up a hastily written editorial titled "The Politics of the Bergdahl Case." It was so poorly written that the editorial team revised it five times after it appeared on their website. They even changed the title to the more derisive "The Rush to Demonize Sgt. Bergdahl". The editorial, according to the Media Research Center, impugned "the motives, integrity and basic decency of Bergdahl's comrades in Afghanistan and sympathizers who have had the unmitigated gall to help them tell their story to the press." When politicians who originally expressed joy over Bergdahl's release began backtracking, *The New York Times* editorial board became outraged, exclaiming: "This duck-and-cover response is the result of the outrageous demonization of Sergeant Bergdahl in the absence of actual facts. Republican operatives have arranged for soldiers in his unit to tell reporters that he was a deserter who cost the lives of several soldiers searching for him."[15] The *Times* later published another hit piece against Bergdahl's unit in an attempt to discredit their claims against him. They described the men as "a misfit platoon" and blamed them for Bergdahl's desertion.[16]

Think that's absurd? Well, a writer for the *Daily Beast* tried to blame George W. Bush for Bergdahl's desertion. Nancy A. Youssef, the Senior National Security Correspondent, wrote, "The administration celebrated negotiating [Bergdahl's] release after years of failed bids by both the current and former administration."[17] Uh, no...Bergdahl abandoned his post in June 2009, when *Obama* was president.

When Bergdahl was charged with desertion, CNN news anchor Brooke Baldwin said of him, "this is someone who was held–you know, for five years by terrorists. Is that not–this is what some say–is that not punishment enough?"[18] When the big three networks reported on the desertion charges, they conveniently "forgot" that national security advisor Susan Rice had praised Bergdahl a year earlier as having served "with honor and distinction."[19] I guess they didn't want to point out that the Obama administration tried to paint a false narrative to justify his plans to purge Gitmo.

That soldiers died looking for Bergdahl didn't register with the major media outlets.[20] Even two years after the swap, *The New York Times* falsely claimed no soldiers died looking for Bergdahl.[21] When reports surfaced that at least one of the five released Taliban leaders was trying to rejoin the fight against the United States, the media covered that up too.[22]

The question isn't whether we should have tried to get Bergdahl back. The U.S. doesn't leave its men behind unfought for. The real question is: why did we swap *five* Taliban leaders intent on rejoining the fight against us, instead of, say, one or two. It looks to me like Obama thought closing the prison at Guantanamo Bay was more important than protecting American lives. The Army personnel involved in Bergdahl's case sure seem to think so.

President Stonewall

For obstruction of justice and stonewalling investigations, the Obama administration is in a league of its own. Whatever was necessary to protect Obama and his allies, he did it. Justice under Obama became highly politicized. I've already documented several examples of how the DOJ became a shield for Obama and his senior cabinet officials earlier in this book. The dismissal of the New Black Panther Party voter intimidation case, the Fast and Furious investigation, the Benghazi terror attack investigation, and the IRS targeting scandal investigation all featured stonewalling tactics aided and abetted by the Justice Department.

When the Obama administration wasn't protecting itself, it was protecting its allies. Obama's Department of Justice prevented a federal investigation into Senate Minority Leader Harry Reid after local prosecutors found evidence of illegal campaign contributions and shady financial dealings.[1] They also blocked an FBI probe of the Clinton Foundation without a stated justification.[2] Obstruction of justice was integral to the entire operation of the Obama administration.

In August 2014, forty-seven of seventy-three inspectors general wrote an open letter to Congress accusing the Obama administration of obstructing investigations by not allowing them full access to the information they need to conduct their investigations. The letter described obstruction of investigations at Environmental Protection Agency, the Department of Justice and the Peace Corps, but acknowledged "that many other IGs have faced similar obstacles to their work, whether on a claim that some other law or principle trumped the clear mandate of the IG Act or by the agency's imposition of unnecessarily burdensome administrative conditions on access." According to the Justice Department Inspector

General Michael Horowitz—an Obama appointee—all requests for access to DOJ documents had to go through Attorney General Eric Holder, giving Holder veto power over the release of documents for ongoing investigations, a clear violation of the *Inspector General Act of 1978.* "Refusing, restricting, or delaying an IG's access to documents leads to incomplete, inaccurate, or significantly delayed findings or recommendations, which in turn may prevent the agency from promptly correcting serious problems and deprive Congress of timely information regarding the agency's performance," they wrote.[3] It's worth noting here that many of these IGs were Obama appointees.

House Oversight Chairman Darrell Issa called the letter unprecedented, "there has never been a letter even with a dozen IGs complaining." Hans von Spakovsky, a senior legal fellow at the Heritage Foundation, agreed. "This unprecedented complaint by a majority of the federal government's inspectors general that the Obama administration is obstructing their ability to investigate corruption shows just how far the administration is willing to go to hide its wrongdoing."[4] Systemic obstruction by the Obama administration of government watchdogs? Richard Nixon faced impeachment not only for the DNC break-in but for obstructing the investigation thereof. And we're talking about Nixon-level abuse of power as a normal part of life under Obama. Sounds like a scandal to me—a big one...and impeachable.

But the Obama administration didn't sweat too much. In fact, they were emboldened by it. In the summer of 2015, the Obama administration imposed new restrictions on the investigative powers of inspectors general. The Office of Legal Counsel at the Justice Department issued a legal opinion stating that all inspectors general would have to get permission from their respective agency heads to obtain information necessary for their investigations. To clarify, the new rule forced IGs to ask permission of an agency head before they could conduct an investigation that potentially involved that agency head. I hope you can see the problem here. The DOJ's opinion received criticism from both sides of the aisle.[5]

A few months later, several inspectors general came forward saying there were "at least 20 investigations across the government that have been slowed, stymied or sometimes closed because of a long-simmering dispute between the Obama administration and its own watchdogs over the shrinking access of inspectors general to confidential records, according to records and interviews." These new restrictions had the result Obama intended; among the investigations hampered by the Obama administration were NSA spying, intelligence sharing before the 2013 Boston Marathon bombing, Fast and Furious, and the deadly 2012 Honduran drug raid. The Obama administration's antipathy for independent watchdogs was so egregious that, once again, Republicans *and* Democrats united in their criticism.[6] Considering how rare bipartisanship is these days, it's hard to deny that the Obama administration was up to no good if Obama's own party, which so often blindly defended him, questioned his administration's actions.

The culture of obstruction in the Obama administration was such a problem that it literally took an act of Congress to address it. The *Inspector General Empowerment Act* of 2016 was drafted in response to the aforementioned 2015 legal opinion from the Justice Department Office of Legal Counsel and passed by unanimous consent in both the House and Senate.[7] Obama signed the bill into law on December 16, 2016, a month before he left office. No doubt, he figured he didn't need to worry about watch dogs once he left the White House.

In a statement announcing the signing, Obama's press secretary, Josh Earnest, ironically called the legislation a continuation of "the commitment to transparency in government that has been a hallmark of this Administration from day one."[8] It takes a lot of gall to spin legislation written in response to the Obama administration's obstruction as a positive aspect of Obama's legacy.

Intelligence Manipulation Scandals

When Obama ran for reelection, he leaned heavily on the successful raid of Osama bin Laden's Pakistani hideout in May 2011 to position himself as strong on terrorism and to claim that al Qaeda was "on the path to defeat." But this claim was false, and the administration's efforts to manipulate intelligence reports to confirm his talking points began a pattern of deception and selective disclosure that dogged Obama's entire second term in office and, worse, slowed America's response as both al Qaeda and the Islamic State in Iraq and Syria (ISIS or ISIL) expanded, leading to countless attacks the world over.

Thanks to the raid on Osama bin Laden's compound, which resulted in his death, the U.S. uncovered a treasure trove of intelligence on al Qaeda operations across the globe. Millions of documents, the best collection of terrorist material ever collected in one place, were now in the hands of the United States government. Exploitation of these documents could have given us an edge in the fight to eradicate al Qaeda if we used it properly. We didn't. Stephen Hayes of *The Weekly Standard* reported, over three years after the raid, that a comprehensive analysis of the intelligence never took place:

> In the days immediately following the bin Laden raid, the document haul was taken to a triage center where a CIA-led interagency team of analysts and subject-matter experts began to comb through it for perishable intelligence. It was, by all accounts, a fruitful effort.
>
> The initial scrub took several weeks. It was never meant to be comprehensive. "It was more data-mining than analysis," says one intelligence official with knowledge of the project. Researchers and analysts searched the documents for key names, phone numbers, and addresses

that could be used by U.S. troops to target senior al Qaeda leaders. In subsequent congressional testimony, James Clapper, director of national intelligence, reported that there were "over 400 intelligence reports that were issued in the initial aftermath immediately after the raid."

Then the document exploitation stopped. According to sources with detailed knowledge of the handling of the documents, the CIA did little to build on the project after the initial burst of intelligence reports.[1]

What happened next was inexcusable. Obama's CIA limited access to the documents, declassifying only handpicked information that reflected the administration's public narrative that al Qaeda was "on the run." But, as Hayes noted, "As the public heard this carefully managed story about al Qaeda, analysts at CENTCOM had documents that showed something close to the opposite."

> The exploitation by the CENTCOM team, though far from comprehensive, generated "hundreds of additional reports" on al Qaeda that were distributed throughout the intelligence community, according to congressional testimony from Lieutenant General Michael Flynn, then director of the Defense Intelligence Agency. The findings were briefed to senior intelligence and military officials, including Robert Cardillo, deputy director of national intelligence, and Admiral Michael Mullen, former chairman of the Joint Chiefs of Staff. Several members of Congress were briefed as well on the findings.[2]

Derek Harvey, who supervised the team of analysts from the United States Central Command (CENTCOM) and the Defense Intelligence Agency (DIA), said the conclusions they reached contradicted what the Obama administration was telling the public. "They were saying al Qaeda was on the run. We were telling them al Qaeda was expanding and growing stronger."[3]

Next came a cover-up. "Analysts on the CENTCOM/DIA team were told they could not include information from the bin Laden documents in finished intelligence products. As word of the contents of the documents began to circulate informally in intelligence circles, one official on the team was summoned to Washington and ordered to quit analyzing the documents."[4] DIA intelligence analyst Michael Pregent said Obama's National Security Council canceled an opportunity for DIA and CENTCOM analysts to more thoroughly review the documents and gave no explanation for the change of plans. Hayes asked, "Why would the president's National Security Council intervene to block access to the bin Laden documents for analysts from the DIA and CENTCOM—analysts who are providing intelligence to those on the frontlines of America's battle with jihadists?" The answer is political:

> Four sources with knowledge of the bin Laden documents tell *TWS* that the White House was intimately involved in limiting access to them. NSC officials handpicked the first set of documents released to the public—chosen to reinforce the impression that bin Laden was weak and isolated when he was killed and that al Qaeda was in disarray. The release of those documents, six months before the 2012 presidential election, coincided with a push by the White House and the Obama campaign to position Obama as strong on terror.[5]

As Hayes noted, "The allegations that intelligence on ISIS was being manipulated at CENTCOM are not noteworthy because they're new. In this case, they're noteworthy because they're not."[6]

Covering up the intelligence also meant not acting on the threat. Three months before the presidential election, a classified Defense Intelligence Agency report warned that Al Qaeda in Iraq (which became ISIS) was poised to make a comeback due to the deteriorating situation in Syria. The White House ignored the report because, according to Lt. Gen. Michael Flynn, who was Obama's DIA Director at the time, "it didn't meet the narrative." Obama also received warnings from the CIA, State Department, the Iraqi government, and others; but ignored those warnings and *refused* to act.[7]

Let's not forget that Democrats, Barack Obama included, spent years falsely accusing George W. Bush of manipulating pre-war intelligence about Iraq's weapons of mass destruction. Many on the left *still* believe it. Yet, when it was Obama's turn at the helm of the ship of state, he and his administration did exactly that to save his reelection. Obama's scandalous deception and inaction came at a major cost, the rise of ISIS, yet his allies on the left see no problem with his actions.

In 2014, Barack Obama said, "if a jayvee team puts on Lakers uniforms, that doesn't make them Kobe Bryant."[8] ISIS had just captured Fallujah, Iraq, much to the surprise of his administration. This analogy haunted him for the rest of his presidency as ISIS, under his watch, grew in strength and number, carrying out successful terror attacks around the globe. Obama later claimed his comment "wasn't specifically referring" to ISIS—a claim *PolitiFact* rated false[9], and *The Washington Post* gave four Pinocchios.[10]

Obama's pathetic deflection meant to distract Americans from his failure to understand the threat posed by ISIS was bad, but it pales in comparison to what he did next to improve his image as commander-in-chief. In an interview on CBS's *60 Minutes*, correspondent Steve Kroft asked Obama, "How did [ISIS] end up where they are in control of so much territory? Was that a complete surprise to you?"

Rather than accept responsibility for underestimating the threat of ISIS, he blamed his Director of National Intelligence. "Well I think our head of the intelligence community, Jim Clapper, has acknowledged that I think they underestimated what had been taking place in Syria."[11]

Soon after Obama threw the intelligence community under the bus many stepped forward, eager to refute his claim. "Unless someone very senior has been shredding the president's daily briefings and telling him that the dog ate them, highly accurate predictions about ISIL have been showing up in the Oval Office since before the 2012 election," one national security staffer told the *Daily Mail*. "We were seeing specific threat assessments and many of them have panned out exactly as we were told they would."[12] Senior intelligence officials told the *Daily Beast* similar stories. "Either the president doesn't read the intelligence he's getting or he's bullshitting," said one former senior Pentagon official.[13] A military intelligence official told Fox News that the ISIS threat "was well-documented in the president's daily brief for over a year, but the White House failed to act."[14]

Obama was lying when he blamed the intelligence community for failing to catch the threat of ISIS. The media, however, didn't think this was worth mentioning. The day after Obama's interview aired, *Newsbusters* documented a complete lack of interest by the major networks. "*ABC World News Tonight with David Muir* chose to ignore the story all together while the *CBS Evening News with Scott Pelley* simply re-aired Obama's comments from 60 Minutes the night prior without acknowledging the criticisms since the interview aired."[15]

Obama's problems with ISIS and the intelligence community continued to get worse, becoming a huge scandal with serious implications. An explosive report in August 2015 by *The New York Times* revealed the that the Pentagon inspector general was "investigating allegations that military officials have skewed intelligence assessments about the United States-led campaign in Iraq against the Islamic State to provide a more optimistic account of progress."[16] Two weeks later, the *Daily Beast* revealed that this investigation was prompted by complaints from over intelligence analysts from CENTCOM that "their reports on ISIS and al Qaeda's branch in Syria were being inappropriately altered by senior officials." The purpose of the manipulation was to ensure the intelligence did not conflict with the administration's public statements that the United States was winning against the so-called jayvee team. Despite the severity of the scandal, only CBS and Fox News covered the story. It only merited a brief 18-second mention on ABC's *Good Morning America* and was skipped entirely by NBC.[17]

The news got even worse when *The Guardian* reported that Clapper was in "frequent and unusual contact" with Army Major General Steven Grove, the head of CENTCOM's intelligence wing implicated in the Pentagon investigation. "In communications, Clapper, who is far more senior than Grove, is said to tell Grove how the war looks from his vantage point, and question Grove about Central Command's assessments. Such a situation could place inherent pressure on a subordinate..." [18]

Two separate congressional investigations, by Republicans and Democrats, concluded that senior officials at CENTCOM had manipulated intelligence on the war with ISIS.[19] Why? While the Democrat-led investigation agreed that someone manipulated the intelligence on the war with ISIS, Congressman Adam Schiff, the top Democrat on the House Intelligence Committee, said there was no evidence of political pressure coming from the White House.[20] But Congressman Mike Pompeo, who was part of the Republican investigation, told the *Daily Beast*, "The most senior leaders in Central Command and the J2 [CENTCOM's Joint Intelligence Center] had a deep understanding of the political narrative the administration was putting forth. The culture was one where you were rewarded for embracing that political narrative."[21] Clapper's regular contact with Grove raised questions about whether Obama played a role in establishing that culture of self-delusion.

That delusion came at a heavy price. Obama's CIA Director John Brennan told the Senate Intelligence Committee in June 2016, "The number of ISIL fighters now exceeds what al Qaeda had at its height."[22] The rise of ISIS has resulted in terror attacks worldwide, including Europe, Australia, Canada, Africa, and the Middle East, and in the United States, killing and injuring thousands.[23] That's a huge price to pay—that we are *still* paying—for Obama protecting his political career.

Hillary Clinton's Email Scandal

During the intense battle for the Democratic nomination in 2008, a campaign ad for Barack Obama said of Hillary Clinton, "She'll say anything, and change nothing." To unite the Democratic Party, when Obama became president, he made Hillary his first Secretary of State. She came into her former rival's administration with plenty of baggage and left behind a dark cloud of scandal.

Her use of an unsecured private email server out of her Chappaqua, New York, home to skirt transparency laws launched an FBI investigation that turned her inevitable presidential victory into perhaps the most stunning upset in history. The left and the mainstream media continue to write off the scandal as insignificant, but the truth is worse than a tale of personal corruption. This new scandal, in the heat of the 2016 presidential election, cast a dark cloud over both Obama *and* Clinton, just as the Benghazi cover-up did. Threaten one and the other suffers. This was one of the best examples of the culture of scandal that plagued the entire Obama administration and, like so many others, it reached all the way to the top.

On March 2, 2015, *The New York Times* revealed that Hillary Clinton "exclusively used a personal email account to conduct government business as secretary of state, State Department officials said, and may have violated federal requirements that officials' correspondence be retained as part of the agency's record." Hillary's aides "took no actions to have her personal emails preserved on department servers at the time, as required by the Federal Records Act."[1] Hillary left the State Department in February 2013, but she didn't turn over any of her emails for almost two years. When the State Department requested those emails, she and her advisors handpicked about 30,000 pages and *deleted* another 30,000 emails she claimed were personal. She also refused to turn over the server to investigators.[2] Whatever she didn't want investigators to find was worth the risk of *looking* guilty.

Hillary's office claimed "nothing nefarious was at play" regarding the decision to use a private, unsecured server instead of—not along-side—a secure State Department email. CNN reviewed the evidence and concluded that not only was the server difficult to trace back to Clinton, but it was insecure. From their report: "Clinton's accounts were regis-tered under the names of aides, according to the review. She also used a proxy company to shield her involvement...Clinton's computer server wasn't using trusted Web certificates—something that's frowned upon by computer security experts."[3] It's more than just "frowned upon" when transmitting classified and top secret information; it's criminally negli-gent. So multiple investigations were launched.

Forced to go into damage control mode, Hillary's excuses for the private email server were as plentiful as they were absurd. "I opted, for convenience, to use my personal email account, which was allowed by the State Department, because I thought it would be easier to carry just one device for my work and for my personal emails instead of two," she said at a press conference.[4] That story fell apart two weeks later when evidence surfaced that she was using both an iPad and a Blackberry to send emails.[5] Hillary also claimed to have gone "above and beyond" taking "unprece-dented steps" to make the emails public.[6] Well, we know that's not true. But she went above and beyond when she had 13 of her mobile devices destroyed—at least two smashed with a hammer—before the FBI could examine them.[7]

Deleted emails...Destroyed mobile devices...Refusal to cooperate with an investigation...Does that sound like unprecedented transparency or a cover-up? It sure sounded like the latter to veteran journalist Bob Woodward, who helped break the story of Richard Nixon's cover-up of the Watergate break-in. He even likened Hillary Clinton to the disgraced former president. "So, you've got a massive amount of data. It, in a way, reminds me of the Nixon tapes," he said during an interview on MSNBC. "Thousands of hours of secretly recorded conversations that Nixon thought were exclusively his. Hillary Clinton initially took that position, 'I'm not turning this over, there'll be no cooperation...'"[8]

The State Department Inspector General also criticized Hillary's actions. According to the inspector general's report, Hillary didn't get approval for using a private server, and, if she'd asked, the would have said no. The IG concurred with earlier reporting that the server was insecure and expressed frustration that Hillary and her top aides refused to cooperate with his investigation. A Clinton campaign spokesman claimed Hillary refused an interview with the inspector general because "it made sense to prioritize the review being conducted by the Justice Department."[9] If I were Hillary Clinton, I'd probably prioritize an investigation by the Obama administration over an independent watchdog, too.

And boy did they come through for her. Obama predictably came to Hillary's defense. "I continue to believe she has not jeopardized America's national security," he said in a *Fox News Sunday* interview. "There's a carelessness in terms of managing emails that she has owned and she recognizes. But I also think it is important to keep this in perspective." He also suggested that even though Hillary emailed classified information it was no big deal. "What I also know is that there's classified and then there's classified. There's stuff that is really top secret top secret, and then there's stuff that is being presented to the president, the secretary of state, you may not want going out over the wire." Despite his defense of Hillary, he "guaranteed" that there would be no political influence on the investigation, and that his Justice Department would not protect Hillary.[10] But protect his heir apparent, he and the Justice Department did.

Former federal prosecutor and bestselling author Kevin C. McCarthy found that, throughout their investigation, "the Obama Justice Department would not use the grand jury or help the FBI obtain search or surveillance warrants. As a result, the FBI had no power to compel the production of evidence. Suspects had to be cajoled into cooperating. The only thing the Justice Department was willing to do was grant highly unusual immunity deals, ensuring that suspects could not be prosecuted if they disclosed incriminating evidence."[11] Why no grand jury? "Commencing a grand-jury investigation suggests that a matter is very serious and an indictment (which only the grand jury can issue) is likely. In this case, the Justice Department was determined to maintain the illusion that Clinton and her underlings hadn't committed crimes, so the grand jury was avoided."[12] Another sham investigation by Obama's Justice Department? By now, this should surprise no one.

Various emails that came to light reflected poorly on Hillary's motivations. One email released because of a FOIA lawsuit showed that Huma Abedin rejected the suggestion that Hillary should be using a secure, state.gov email account.[13] In another email, Hillary told her Deputy Chief of Staff she didn't want some of her emails "accessible" via transparency laws.[14]

Hillary Clinton was interviewed by the FBI on Saturday, July 2, 2016. The interview wasn't recorded, and she wasn't under oath.[15] Very convenient. The details of the interview weren't released until two months later, when we learned that, amongst other things, she claimed she couldn't recall any training on how to handle classified information, and that she didn't understand that the "C" before a paragraph meant "classified." She *claimed* she thought it indicated alphabetical order.[16] It's amazing, the absurd things you'll say when you're *not* under oath.

A mere three days after her interview, FBI Director James Comey gave a press conference to announce the findings of the FBI's so-called investigation. "Although we did not find clear evidence that Secretary Clinton or her colleagues intended to violate laws governing the handling of classified information, there is evidence that they were extremely careless in their handling of very sensitive, highly classified information."[17] Comey acknowledged that Hillary had sent and received classified information, contradicting Hillary's claim that she "never received nor sent any material that was marked classified" on her private email server while secretary of state. Even the left-wing fact-checking site *PolitiFact* conceded she had lied.[18]

I want to make one other point. Comey based his decision not to recommend criminal charges for Clinton on the lack of evidence that she intended to violate the law, but negligent handling of classified information is still a felony. As Ben Shapiro, the editor-in-chief of *DailyWire.com*, explained, "Comey tried to say he wouldn't recommend prosecution because she didn't have the requisite intent, but the law doesn't require intent; it requires merely 'gross negligence' under 18 U.S.C. 793. In fact, even the level of intent required to charge under statutes like 18 U.S.C. 1924 and 18 U.S.C. 798 was clearly met: the intent to place classified information in a non-approved, non-classified place."[19]

And yet, Comey recommended no charges. Anyone else would get the book thrown at them for doing what she did. Even an MSNBC legal analyst acknowledged, "People do go to jail for mishandling classified information, they have been prosecuted in the Obama administration for that."[20] He probably meant to say, "People who weren't allies of the president have been prosecuted."

Need more proof the investigation was a total sham? Although Hillary had mishandled classified information and should have faced prosecution, Barack Obama made his debut appearance on the campaign trail with Hillary in Charlotte, North Carolina, *the same day* as Comey's announcement. That's a gutsy move for a sitting president who claimed not to know what Comey was going to say. It could have been awkward had Comey announced he would recommend prosecution. Was it confidence, dumb luck, or perhaps *collusion*?

Obama knew what Comey would say—his Justice Department allies agreed on the outcome long before Comey's press conference. A week earlier, former president Bill Clinton and attorney general Loretta Lynch *just happened* to find themselves on the same tarmac at the Phoenix Sky Harbor International Airport in Arizona. They spoke for about 30 minutes; if you suspend common sense, you might buy Lynch's claim that the conversation was about grandchildren and personal matters. Both Republicans *and* Democrats were quick to criticize the meeting. In response, Lynch said she would accept whatever recommendation the FBI gave on Hillary Clinton, claiming it was to avoid the appearance of impropriety. "It's important to make it clear that that meeting with President Clinton does not have a bearing on how this matter will be reviewed and resolved," Lynch said.[21] Yeah, sure, Loretta.

In August 2017, the American Center for Law and Justice (ACLJ) released more than 400 pages of Department of Justice documents relating to the infamous meeting between Loretta Lynch and Bill Clinton—documents that the DOJ told the ACLJ did not exist just weeks before the 2016 presidential election. The ACLJ described the documents as painting "a clear picture of a DOJ in crisis mode as the news broke of Attorney General Lynch's meeting with former President Clinton. In fact, the records appear to indicate that the Attorney General's spin team immediately began preparing talking points for the Attorney General regarding the meeting."[22] Lynch was heavily involved in these discussions using a secret email alias and DOJ email account she also used to conduct other Department of Justice business.[23] Seriously, what is with Obama administration officials and secret email aliases?

From early in the investigation, Obama had Hillary's back. In February 2016, the White House blocked the release of eighteen emails between Hillary and Barack Obama found on her private server. The emails contained no classified information, but the Obama administration refused to release them to "protect the President's ability to receive unvarnished advice and counsel."[24] In other words, whatever was in those emails, Obama didn't want you to know about it. According to Former federal prosecutor Kevin C. McCarthy, the implications of this explanation were serious. "Not only is it obvious that President Obama knew Mrs. Clinton was conducting government business over her private email account, the exchanges the president engaged in with his secretary of state over this unsecured system clearly involved sensitive issues of policy."[25] Americans later learned from FBI documents related to the investigation that Obama used a pseudonym when emailing Hillary's private email.[26]

McCarthy believes this doomed any possibility of Hillary being prosecuted:

> In terms of the federal laws that criminalize mishandling of classified information, Obama not only engaged in the *same type of misconduct* Clinton did; he engaged in it *with Clinton*. It would not have been possible for the Justice Department to prosecute Clinton for her offense without its becoming painfully apparent that 1) Obama, too, had done everything necessary to commit a violation of federal law, and 2) the communications between Obama and Clinton were highly relevant evidence.[27]

And then he abused his executive power to hide his crime.

Hillary's scandal was Barack Obama's as well. Even the Hillary campaign knew this situation was bad news for the president. Leaked emails published by WikiLeaks show Hillary's campaign freaking out about emails between the Secretary of State and President Obama and showing intent to cover it up. Emails obtained by Judicial Watch via FOIA lawsuit also suggested that the State Department knew about Hillary's email problem for three years, but covered it up.[28] Want to take a guess why?

The same day the House Select Committee on Benghazi subpoenaed Hillary's emails, John Podesta emailed Cheryl Mills, an attorney for the Clinton campaign, "Think we should hold emails to and from potus? That's the heart of his exec privilege. We could get them to ask for that. They may not care, but I [sic] seems like they will."[29] A few days later Mills emailed Podesta, concerned over Obama's claim he found out about Hillary's private email server on the news: "we need to clean this up—he has emails from her—they do not say state.gov".[30] They did a poor job cleaning up their mess, but they sure tried.

Later that month, Trey Gowdy (R-SC), chairman of the House committee investigating the 2012 terror attack on the U.S. consulate in Benghazi, revealed that Hillary's private server was wiped clean in 2014 after the State Department requested she turn over her emails to comply with the Federal Records Act. Hillary was under a House committee subpoena order to provide all documents—including emails—relating to the attack.[31] According to an FBI report, an employee of Platte River Networks, a Denver-based IT company managing Hillary's email server, deleted Hillary's email archive using software designed to prevent the recovery of data.[32]

Hillary's actions, and her litany of excuses, weren't even convincing to people in her circle. Another Clinton attorney, Erica Rottenberg, questioned Hillary's use of the private email server, and Hillary's taking it upon herself "to review them and delete documents without providing anyone outside her circle a chance to weigh in."[33] When one of your own attorneys acknowledges that you acted inappropriately, you've got problems. Rottenberg's exact words, according to the leaked email, were: "It smacks of acting above the law." *You think*?

Comey's refusal to recommend charges in July 2016 made less and less sense with time. Congress asked for a new investigation, which Comey rejected. Then, on October 28, 2016, less than two weeks before Election Day, the investigation reopened after emails relevant to the case were discovered on the laptop of Anthony Weiner and Huma Abedin during a separate investigation involving Weiner's sexting an underage girl. Comey felt it was necessary to inform Congress of the new develop-ment.[34] For nearly a week, the scandal again dominated news coverage. Huma Abedin had been forwarding emails, including ones marked clas-sified, to her husband Anthony Weiner to print out. Some of us hoped that Hillary might now be held accountable, but it didn't happen that way. She was "cleared" again.[35]

To my relief, she lost an election that most people believed she was destined to win. She paid a huge price for her arrogance but, as far as I'm concerned, she got off easy. She still hasn't been held accountable for her crimes. Obama also came out of the scandal unscathed, despite his lying to the American people about what he knew, and his administration doing everything it could to protect Hillary and stonewall the investiga-tion. What's a little cover-up between former political rivals?

The scandal was so big, it didn't end with the election, or even with Obama's departure from the White House. In the summer of 2017, more damning emails came to light thanks to a Judicial Watch lawsuit alleging that the State Department stonewalled multiple FOIA requests. They showed that Hillary sent emails marked classified to employees of the Clinton Foundation (also under investigation for pay to play deals with foreign government officials) who did not have the proper security clear-ance. This was more proof that Hillary had lied when she said all relevant emails had been released. "The casual violation of laws concerning clas-sified material and noxious influence peddling show the Clinton State Department was 'corruption central' in the Obama administration," said Judicial Watch president Tom Fitton.[36]

A week later, while testifying under oath to the before the Senate Intelligence Committee, the now former FBI Director James Comey said Barack Obama's Attorney General Loretta Lynch pressured him to downplay the investigation of Hillary Clinton. "At one point, the attorney general had directed me not to call it an investigation, but instead to call it a matter, which confused me and concerned me." According to Comey, it wasn't "a hill worth dying on," and he said okay, but he became concerned because "that language tracked the way the campaign was talking about FBI's work and that's concerning."[37]

Emails released by Judicial Watch in August 2017 showed more previ-ously undisclosed emails, some including classified information, taken from Clinton's private server. Other emails showed that Clinton Foundation donors were getting special perks from the State Department while Hillary was Secretary of State. Several emails showed "the free flow of information and requests for favors between Clinton's State Department and the Clinton Foundation and major Clinton donors."[38]

Former Attorney General Michael Mukasey said this was important. "What makes it egregious is the fact—and I think it's obvious that it is a fact—that the attorney general of the United States was adjusting the way the department talked about its business so as to coincide with the way the Clinton campaign talked about that business," he said in an interview with *Newsmax*. "In other words, it made the Department of Justice essentially an arm of the Clinton campaign."[39] In another interview with Fox Business, Mukasey also said he felt Obama was guilty of obstruction of justice when he came to Hillary's defense. "President Obama's statement that he thought she shouldn't be charged because she didn't intend to violate the law is the real Clinton obstruction because that is a statement by him that 'this is the way I want that investigation to come out.'"[40] And it came out exactly as he requested.

Oh, but, it's worse than you think. In the summer of 2017 we learned that the now-former FBI Director James Comey had drafted his statement exonerating Clinton of any wrongdoing *months before* interviewing key witness, including as Clinton herself.[41] The FBI confirmed this several months later. [42] It would be useless to claim the investigation wasn't rigged by the Obama administration to prevent Clinton from being held accountable.

Hillary and her allies have consistently downplayed all the damning revelations during and after the investigations. Despite the undeniable corruption, Hillary called the scandal "the biggest nothingburger ever."[43] Do you suppose her staff focus-grouped that expression? No matter how you slice it, this scandal had everything: mishandling classified information, deliberately sharing classified information, obstruction of justice, lies, a cover-up, collusion, conflicts of interest, a sham investigation, and more lies. Or, as the Obama administration calls it, standard operating procedure. Obama himself was ensnared by the scandal. This was a *some-thing*burger with everything on it, for crying out loud.

And the media did its best to sweep it under the rug—not just for Hillary's sake, but Obama's as well. While the media covered the original *New York Times* bombshell in March 2015, coverage tapered off dramatically within a few weeks.[44] What little coverage there was of the scandal was often dismissive. Journalist Ashleigh Banfield of CNN declared it wasn't "even a scandal" during a discussion about the sordid affair. "It's really a controversy," Banfield claimed. "But 'scandal' is the Republicans' word for it. So far, no one has determined there's any scandal there."[45]

The media did its best to make sure the public didn't think so. Coverage of Hillary's (and, by extension, Obama's) scandal was buried under a mountain of anti-Trump press coverage. Coverage of Hillary was less negative, and she enjoyed far less scrutiny than her opponent.[46] Incriminating emails exposed by Wikileaks were barely mentioned, and never in detail. They even ignored an email showing that Hillary's campaign received presidential debate questions in advance.[47] The Wikileaks revelation that Obama knew about the private email account, contradicting his original claim he heard about it "on the news" was ignored by ABC and downplayed by NBC. CBS gave it a scant mention.[48] The Associated Press buried the story that Obama had used a pseudonym to communicate with Hillary via her private email account.[49] The DOJ documents released by the ACLJ in August 2017 also showed clear evidence of collusion...between the media and the Department of Justice to bury the story of Attorney General Lynch's meeting with Bill Clinton.

> A Washington Post reporter, speaking of the Clinton Lynch meeting story, said, "I'm hoping I can put it to rest." The same Washington Post reporter, interacting with the DOJ spin team, implemented specific DOJ requests to change his story to make the Attorney General appear in a more favorable light. A New York Times reporter apologetically told the Obama DOJ that he was being "pressed into service" to have to cover the story. As the story was breaking, DOJ press officials stated, "I also talked to the ABC producer, who noted that they aren't interested, even if Fox runs with it."[50]

And what about the bombshell report that former FBI Director James Comey had decided to exonerate Hillary Clinton long before the investigation was complete? The three major networks completely ignored the story in favor of fluff pieces. [51]

With all that help from the media, it's no wonder Hillary was confused why she wasn't "50 points ahead" of Trump. She may have lost the election anyway, but, she still should be grateful for Barack Obama. Had it not been for him and his corrupt administration, she'd probably be in prison.

The OPM Hacking Scandal

Obama promised in his first presidential campaign to make cybersecurity a top priority. "We can—and must—strengthen our cyber-defenses in the 21st century," he said in the summer of 2008. "We know that cyber-espionage and common crime is already on the rise. And yet while countries like China have been quick to recognize this change, for the last eight years we have been dragging our feet."[1] If cyber-security was a "top priority" for Obama, why did the largest breach of government data in American history occur on his watch when it could have been prevented with a modicum of competence and nonpartisan judgment?

On June 4, 2015, the Office of Personnel Management (OPM) announced that the records of four million government employees were compromised by Chinese hackers.[2] It soon became clear that many more than the originally stated number were at risk and that the administration had tried to keep the full extent of the data breach under wraps. *The Wall Street Journal* reported, "The Obama administration, for more than a week, avoided disclosing the severity of an intrusion into federal computers by defining it as two breaches but divulging just one." The administration only disclosed the breach of personnel files, but sensitive security-clearance forms were also taken. Those forms "contain information that foreign intelligence agencies could use to target espionage operations." The hackers also compromised Social Security numbers, forcing the administration to revise the number of people exposed upward to a whopping 18 million.[3] Next, investigators realized the hackers had access to government servers for more than a year before being detected.[4] The long duration of exposure increased the number of former and current government employees at risk to as high as 32 million.[5]

115

As the situation got worse, so did the lies. The Obama administration claimed OPM discovered the breach while undertaking "an aggressive effort to update its cyber-security posture." But, that wasn't true. *The Wall Street Journal* noted that the breach was discovered during a sales demonstration by a cyber-security company. The company, Virginia-based CyTech Services, was running diagnostics on the OPM network to demonstrate how their cyber-security platform worked, when they stumbled upon the malware.

OPM answered CyTech's valuable contribution to national security by stiffing CyTech on an $818,000 bill for cyber-security services performed and publicly denying CyTech's role in uncovering the data breach. They implied that CyTech CEO Ben Cotton "angled for undeserved praise in the media," damaging the reputation of the company.[6] No good deed goes unpunished.

Government watchdogs often call a disaster or mistake in government management "preventable" and, upon reviewing the evidence, walk away thinking "maybe, but only in hindsight." In this case, however, the hack really was preventable, and not just looking backward. U.S. intelligence agencies expressed concerns over OPM's cyber-security as early as 2010. They were so concerned about it, they refused to share classified personnel records with OPM out of fear that "it could expose the personal information of covert operatives to leakers and hackers." Did that stop the merging of records? Nope. Michael Adams, a veteran of U.S. Special Operations Command told *The Daily Beast* "The U.S. government either doesn't understand or is obfuscating the national-security implications of this cyber-attack. These people either need serious help or need to come clean now."[7]

So, how did this happen? Paul Conway, the former Chief of Staff of OPM during the Bush administration thinks it all comes down to Obama's appointment of Katherine Archuleta as OPM director. "The political appointment of Katherine Archuleta to OPM director was a devastating example of the poor personnel judgment exercised by President Obama," he said. "It highlighted his willingness to elevate ideological purity over competency [sic] when selecting appointees whose job is to protect America."[8] She was unqualified for the position.

How unqualified? Imagine a community organizer deciding to run for president of the United States after only two years in the U.S. Senate. It was like that, with similar unfortunate results. Except Archuleta's appointment, and the epic failure that followed, falls entirely on Obama and not on millions of voters. As *National Review*'s Jim Geraghty noted, before Obama appointed Archuleta to head OPM, she "had no background in the kind of work the agency does." She was, however, national political director for Obama's reelection campaign and had experience in community organizing—hey, just like Obama!

She had other credentials, but, as Geraghty explained, "Nothing in this record suggests any expertise in the vitally important human resources and record-keeping functions OPM is supposed to serve." Prior to the hack, Archuleta focused on increasing the diversity of government employees and overseeing changes in government employee health insurance caused by the implementation of Obamacare.[9] Despite her lack of qualifications and her inability to secure the data on OPM's servers, Obama still had confidence that she was "the right person for that job."[10]

Archuleta testified to Congress that she made upgrading OPM's cyber-security a top priority, but OPM Inspector General Patrick McFarland repeatedly warned Archuleta that OPM's network was vulnerable to attack and she *ignored* those warnings. Archuleta ultimately resigned her position due to the scandal. Her resignation was welcome news on both sides of the aisle.[11]

In a final twist, as the hack was being investigated, government analysts realized that KeyPoint, the contractor they relied upon to process background checks, was the likely source of the hack.[12] The hackers gained access to OPM files by accessing KeyPoint's system through corrupted user data and snatching security credentials for the government mainframe. Guess what the Obama administration did once they realized the source of the breach? They hired that company for government record-keeping *again*.[13]

When the media reported on the scandal, coverage was absent of criticism of the Obama administration, or Obama's broken promise on cyber-security. "The broadcast news networks protected the president and his administration on cyber security issues by refusing to criticize the administration in 90.2 percent of cyber stories (139 of 154)," analysis from the Media Research Center showed. "Those stories included reports of serious data breaches at OPM and the IRS, the theft of emails from the Joint Chiefs of Staff and top administration officials, possible hacks of major airlines and Wall Street, hackers taking over cars on America's highways as well as cyber-bullying."[14]

Obama appointed a political crony to a position she was unqualified for, and that decision compromised tens of millions of government employees' personal records. That's a pretty big scandal. If only the media cared to acknowledge it. *The Washington Post's* editorial board, to their credit, eviscerated Obama over the hacking, accusing him of "inexcusable negligence" on cybersecurity.[15]

In retrospect, when Obama said cyber-security would be a top priority on the campaign trail, he was more interested in taking a swipe at the Bush administration than solving the problem. The U.S. government's cyber-security was so bad that Obama's Secretary of State, John Kerry, said in an interview that it was "very likely" Chinese and Russian hackers were reading his emails—and he wrote emails under the assumption they were reading them. If that's taking cyber-security seriously, I'd hate to know what *indifference* to cyber-security looked like in the Obama administration. Oh, right...Hillary Clinton's private email server. If great minds think alike, the corollary might be that weak minds make the same mistakes.

EPA Environmental Scandals

The Environmental Protection Agency (EPA) was a hotbed of corruption, as I discussed earlier, but given the agency's extremist political agenda, you might expect that it would, at least, protect the environment. You'd be wrong. In truth, the agency caused or exacerbated several major environmental disasters in the name of prevention. I'll look at two such cases.

In August 2015, the Animas River in Colorado turned orange. The EPA *claimed* approximately one million gallons of wastewater from the abandoned Gold King Mine that should have been pumped out and filtered spilled into the river following the breach of a dam. That figure was revised upward to three million gallons. One local resident described the river as looking like it had "turned to carrot juice." Rivers in Colorado, New Mexico, Utah, the Navajo Nation, and Southern Ute Reservation were contaminated by the spill, posing significant risks to fish, plant life, and local drinking water. It was a devastating environmental disaster. And it was caused by the Environmental Protection Agency.

An EPA cleanup crew caused the spill; they deliberately breached the dam but didn't check the water pressure before doing so.[1] To make matters worse, after contaminating the river, the EPA waited over a day before alerting residents downriver in Arizona and New Mexico about the toxic water headed their way and only announced the correct volume of wastewater spillage several days later.[2] They were also still unsure about the threats it posed to humans and animal life.[3] Residents complained when the EPA initially *downplayed* the short-term impacts, believing those false reports to be deliberate deception.[4] An Interior Department report on the accident also said the EPA did not have the proper skills to handle this type of cleanup project, and that the accident was avoidable with proper training and safety procedures.[5]

And where was Obama during this disaster? Nowhere. Well, maybe he was golfing, but since Obama's poll numbers took a beating after his inept response to the BP oil spill, the White House wasn't interested in getting caught up in *another* environmental disaster scandal, so they let the EPA twist in the wind. After the BP oil spill, Obama said he wanted to find out "whose ass to kick." This time, there was no tough talk from Obama, or demands for accountability, because now it was his own administration at fault.

With no one to blame but themselves, the EPA seemed intent on minimizing the impact of the spill to the public. A week after the accident, EPA Administrator Gina McCarthy claimed the water was safe again and that the river was "restoring itself."[6] More than a year after the incident, a GAO investigation and an internal EPA probe still languished, unfinished and no one at the EPA was punished.[7] Obama's DOJ even refused to prosecute the EPA employee who caused the spill.[8] That no one paid a price is appalling; it's amazing how attitudes shift when your own people are the guilty parties.

The Obama administration also refused to pay the price of civil claims against the EPA, which had taken responsibility for the damage and said it would make thing right. Just before Obama left office, "the Environmental Protection Agency refused to pay 73 claims totaling $1.2 billion filed by tribes, farmers, river-rafters and local governments from the August 2015 wastewater spill, citing sovereign immunity under the Federal Tort Claims Act (FTCA)." They also argued that the blowout would have occurred anyway had they not caused it even though internal documents flushed out by the Associated Press indicate that the agency knew their plan carried a significant risk of catastrophic collapse.[9] This infuriated Republican Colorado Congressman Scott R. Tipton. "For the EPA now to say it's not a big deal shows that it's an agency that's looking out for itself and not looking out for the people that it impacts," he said.[10]

I'm sure Colorado Republicans were even angrier when the EPA inspector general officially cleared the agency of any wrongdoing in this disaster.[11] Their excuse was laughable; the IG found that there were no rules for the cleanup of mines prone to blowout. To which I would say...so?

Negligence does not depend on the existence of rules. Environmentalists often preach the 'precautionary principle' when attempting to convince Americans to back aggressive regulations, even in situations where the risk is poorly understood. Here, the EPA knew the risk of blowout was high and proceeded with a rushed dam-break plan without taking basic precautions. Any reasonable person would call that negligence.

Obama's EPA did little to redeem itself with its handling of the Flint Water Crisis. In 2014, the city of Flint, Michigan, changed their water source from treated Detroit River water to improperly treated water from the Flint River. The corrosive water caused lead from old pipes to leach into the water supply, exposing thousands to drinking water with high lead levels and causing severe health problems. In the fall of 2015, the state told Flint residents to stop drinking the water and switched back to the original water source, but it was too late. Damage to the pipes caused continued leaching of lead into the drinking water, and it remained unsafe.[12] Michigan state officials may have caused the problem, but the EPA made it much worse.

In January 2016, Obama declared a federal emergency in Flint, allowing FEMA to coordinate disaster relief.[13] A few days after the declaration, Obama addressed the crisis in Flint during a visit to the United Auto Workers General Motors training center in Detroit. "I know that if I was a parent up there, I would be beside myself that my kids' health could be at risk," he said. In the same speech, he resorted to his favorite pastime: blaming Republicans for the problem. He called the crisis, "a reminder of why you can't short change basic services that we provide to our people and that we together provide as a government to make sure that public health and safety is preserved."[14] Never let a good crisis go to waste; he'll pin the problem on his political rivals even though every member of the Flint City Council was a Democrat.[15]

Administration officials knew about the problem long before they got involved. It took a whopping seven months for the EPA to issue a Safe Drinking Water Act (SDWA) Emergency Order to intervene on behalf of the residents of Flint on January 21, 2016. The EPA knew of high lead concentrations in the water back in February 2015, but Michigan state officials claimed they had it under control so, understandably, they didn't take it further. When the EPA learned in June that state officials couldn't handle the disaster on their own, they still did nothing. An internal memo from EPA official Miguel Del Toral confirmed "the presence of high lead results in the drinking water, which is to be expected in a public water system that is not providing corrosion control treatment." According to the memo, one home had lead levels of 13,200 parts per billion. Federal intervention triggers at 15 parts per billion, by law.[16]

In response to this, the EPA chose not to intervene and, instead, issued a press release calling the data "initial results," doing nothing to intervene on behalf of the residents of Flint.[17] Obama once said, "If he had a son, he would have looked like Trayvon [Martin]." Well, if he had a son in Flint, he wouldn't have lead poisoning because the Obama administration would have intervened at once instead of sitting on their hands for several months and keeping the contamination on the down-low even after they knew people were getting sick from lead exposure. They only took action when the crisis became a national story. Internal emails unveiled during congressional hearings showed reluctance to send more aid to Flint. In one shocking email, an EPA official said they weren't sure "Flint is the community we want to go out on a limb for."[18]

Alongside the congressional investigation, the EPA Inspector General also investigated the water crisis. The IG report included a scathing indictment of the EPA's response confirming that the EPA regional office knew of the high lead levels in the water and that "state and local authorities were not acting quickly to protect human health." The report also faulted the EPA for not intervening when they first realized the problem, allowing it to get worse. "In the absence of EPA intervention in Flint, the state continued to delay taking action to require corrosion control or provide alternative drinking water supplies," the report stated.[19] Flint's water was still not safe to drink when Obama left office.[20] While responsibility for creating the crisis belongs to state and local officials, the scandalous inaction of Obama's EPA made a bad situation much worse.

The media covered the Gold King Mine disaster extensively, but committed leftists sometimes placed the blame on the mines.[21] Although the EPA's negligence caused the spill, an environmental reporter on MSNBC described the EPA as innocent bystanders and seemed to blame locals for the spill.[22] One environmental activist on MSNBC even compared the EPA's job to defusing a bomb in a crowded marketplace, depicting the agency's missteps as understandable and difficult to avoid.[23] The media also didn't want to call them out for their inaction in Flint. CNN didn't mention the EPA once during a segment on Flint water crisis. Apparently their knowledge of the high lead levels and their subsequent inaction wasn't newsworthy.[24] If only Obama had a son in Flint, things would have played out differently.

The Iran Ransom Scandal

The next Obama scandal broke in January 2016, just months after Obama had completed negotiations for his signature foreign policy "achievement," a nuclear non-proliferation pact with the theocratic and anti-American regime in Iran, a pact with zero chance of stopping Iran from developing nuclear weapons.[1] Iran showed their appreciation by capturing and humiliating a boat of U.S. Navy sailors who they claimed had traveled into Iranian waters, and Secretary of State John Kerry responded with *gratitude* to Iran "for their cooperation" after they freed the soldiers.[2] One day prior, he exchanged seven Iranian citizens in U.S. custody as suspected terrorists for four Americans captured as bartering tools by Iran.[3] But on January 17, 2016, Obama gave the world's number one state sponsor of terrorism another gift. Alongside a nuclear agreement that lifted sanctions, unfreezing as much as $150 billion in Iranian assets, the Obama administration gave Iran $1.7 billion. They claimed they owed that money to Iran as part of a settlement from a failed 1979 arms deal.[4]

While Iranian Mullahs were busy laughing at us and rallying their countrymen in chants of "death to America," Obama made it his mission to leave a legacy of "peace" with the country. What could go wrong with that? What would the world's top state sponsor of terrorism do with all that money? Secretary of State John Kerry conceded that Iran would fund terrorism with money they got from sanctions relief. "I think that some of it will end up in the hands of the [Islamic Revolutionary Guard Corps] IRGC or other entities, some of which are labeled terrorists. You know, to some degree, I'm not going to sit here and tell you that every component of that can be prevented."[5]

While many people weren't happy with the settlement announcement, the real controversy exploded on August 3 when *The Wall Street Journal* revealed that the White House secretly paid $400 million in cash to Iran, timed to coincide with the release of the four American prisoners held in Tehran. The money was delivered on wooden pallets in an unmarked plane which departed the U.S. in the dead of night, raising suspicion that the cash was a ransom payment.[6] A cash payment? An unmarked plane? It sounds like something out of a James Bond flick—something the *Russians* would do. Not even Congress knew of the payment.[7]

Obama denied that the payment was a ransom. "We do not pay ransom. We didn't here, and we won't in the future," he said. "And the notion that we would somehow start now, in this high-profile way, and announce it to the world, even as we're looking in the faces of other hostage families whose loved ones are being held hostage, and saying to them we don't pay ransom, defies logic." The payment, Obama claimed, had been part of the $1.7 billion settlement announced in January. The Obama administration claimed the negotiations for the prisoner swap were separate from the settlement negotiations and the nuclear deal.[8] But, not everyone in the Obama administration thought the $400 million payment was good policy. Justice Department officials objected to it but were overruled by the State Department.[9] Secretary of State John Kerry echoed Obama's claim that the ransom wasn't a ransom, "The United States of America does not pay ransom and does not negotiate ransoms with any country. We never have and we're not doing that now. It is not our policy."[10]

It may not be policy, but it *was* a ransom. *The Wall Street Journal* reported on August 18, 2016, that the transfer of money was contingent upon the release of the prisoners.

> New details of the $400 million U.S. payment to Iran earlier this year depict a tightly scripted exchange specifically timed to the release of several American prisoners held in Iran, based on accounts from U.S. officials and others briefed on the operation.
>
> U.S. officials wouldn't let Iranians take control of the money until a Swiss Air Force plane carrying three freed Americans departed from Tehran on Jan. 17, the officials said. Once that happened, an Iranian

cargo plane was allowed to bring the cash back from a Geneva airport that day, according to the accounts.[11]

State Department spokesman John Kirby confirmed this during a press briefing the same day. A journalist asked, "In basic English, you're saying you wouldn't give them $400 million in cash until the prisoners were released, correct?" Kirby replied, "That's correct." This explanation contradicted Obama's and Kerry's statements two weeks prior, proving that both of them lied.[12] A senior Iranian military official, Brigadier General Mohammad Reza Naqdi, also called the payment a ransom. "This money was returned for the freedom of the U.S. spies, and it was not related to the nuclear negotiations."[13] One of the American hostages, Pastor Saeed Abedini, also reported that the hostages couldn't leave until another plane—presumably the plane carrying the $400 million ransom—had arrived. According to Abedini, the prisoners were waiting many hours at the airport before he asked the police why they weren't being let go. The police, Abedini recalled, said, "We are waiting for another plane so if that plane doesn't come, we never let [you] go."[14]

Despite the controversy, the Obama administration insisted the money was Iran's all along. "This $400 million is actually money that the Iranians had paid into a U.S. account in 1979 as part of a transaction to procure military equipment," Obama spokesman Josh Earnest said.[15] While appearing on MSNBC, John Kirby also claimed the money was Iran's from the start. "First of all, this was Iran's money, OK? It was money that they were going to get back, anyway."[16] Only, the $400 million in Iran's frozen military sales (FMS) account in the U.S. Treasury was earmarked by the Clinton administration for victims of Iranian terrorism. Those payments were never deducted from the FMS account and the victims of Iranian terrorism were paid damages from U.S. taxpayers, not Iran. Iran forfeited that money when they began attacking Americans.[17]

When asked why the payment was made in cash, Obama explained, "We had to give them cash precisely because we are so strict in maintaining sanctions and we do not have a banking relationship with Iran that we couldn't send them a check and we could not wire the money." But that explanation fell apart months later when the Treasury Department acknowledged that the United States had made two separate wire transfers to Iran. The first wire transfer payment, for approximately $848,000, was made in July 2015, the same month they announced the nuclear deal. The second payment of $9 million arrived in April 2016. A senior Obama administration official claimed this didn't contradict Obama's earlier claim but didn't explain why. Republicans suggested the administration used case to make payments difficult to trace.[18] "It seems the Obama administration will bend over backwards to accommodate the world's biggest state sponsor of terrorism," said Financial Services Committee Chairman Jeb Hensarling (R-TX), in a statement.[19] Oh, they did more than bend over backward; they also broke the law.

Former federal prosecutor Kevin C. McCarthy explained that it didn't matter what form of payment Iran received because Iran is still on the government's list of state sponsors of terrorism and anti-terrorism sanctions still in place make any form of payment to them illegal.

> Obama had our financial system issue U.S. assets that were then converted to foreign currencies for delivery to Iran. Both steps flouted the regulations, which prohibit the clearing of currency of any kind if Iran is even minimally involved in the deal; here, Iran is the beneficiary of the deal. The regs further prohibit supplying things of value to Iran, regardless of whether it is done "directly or indirectly." Expressly included in the "indirect" category are transfers of assets to another country with knowledge that the other country will then forward the assets, in some form, to Iran. That's exactly what happened here, with Obama pressing the Swiss and Dutch into service as intermediaries.[20]

"By his own account," McCarthy added, "President Obama engaged in the complex cash transfer to end-run sanctions that prohibit the U.S. from having 'a banking relationship with Iran.' The point of the sanctions is not to prevent banking with Iran; it is to prevent Iran from getting value from or through our financial system—the banking prohibition is a corollary."[21] By paying with cash, the U.S. allowed Iran to use that money for terrorism with fewer hurdles—and Obama violated the law to make it happen.

It should come as no surprise that the Obama administration did everything it could to block a congressional investigation. Attorney general Loretta Lynch refused to answer questions from Congress about the payments. "Who knew that simple questions regarding Attorney General Lynch's approval of billions of dollars in payments to Iran could be so controversial that she would refuse to answer them?" Congressman Mike Pompeo (R-KS) said. "This has become the Obama administration's coping mechanism for anything related to the Islamic Republic of Iran—hide information, obfuscate details, and deny answers to Congress and the American people."

What was the Obama administration trying to hide? If the payments were on the level, there would be no reason to obstruct an investigation. Details of the deal weren't classified, but the Obama administration hid key documents at a secure site to make access difficult.[22] *The Washington Free Beacon* argued that the Obama administration decided ignoring Congress was their best strategy because the details of the negotiations were so damning.[23]

Since I've established that the payment was a ransom, one might assume the media would take an interest in the scandal. But, no. Analysis from the Media Research Center shows that the media almost entirely ignored the story. Rather than give the ransom scandal the attention it deserved, they covered the story that three Olympic swimmers had fabricated an alleged robbery in Rio de Janeiro. That story received ten times more coverage from ABC, CBS, and NBC than the ransom scandal. The Olympic swimmer story "garnered a whopping 37 minutes and 31 seconds. In comparison, the cash payout to Iran, which looked suspiciously like ransom, only amounted to a scant 3 minutes and 46 seconds."[24]

The New York Times editorial board called the ransom scandal fake, and spun the story as a positive for Obama, arguing that the timing of the payment and the release of the prisoners was "pragmatic diplomacy not capitulation."[25] A *Washington Post* editorial similarly praised Obama, calling the $400 million payment "American diplomacy at its finest," and saying it "represented continued adherence to a masterful feat of American diplomacy and to the peaceful resolution of disputes under international law."[26] The left-wing fact checking site *PolitiFact* also covered for Obama, rating the claim that the $400 million payment was a ransom as "Mostly False" despite the concession that it was a "quid pro quo."[27] Google the definition of ransom and get back to me, *PolitiFact*.

While *The New York Times* gave the story about the $400 million payment being tied to the release of the prisoners a spot on the front page and above the fold, *The Washington Post* buried the story, even though one of the ransomed prisoners was one of their own reporters![28] The reporter, Jason Rezaian, later sued the Iranian government in federal court, "claiming he was taken hostage and psychologically tortured during his 18 months in prison in an effort by Tehran to influence negotiations for a nuclear agreement with Iran," the *Post* reported. According to the suit, Rezaian believes he was targeted "to gain advantage in a prisoner exchange and to 'extort' concessions from the U.S. government in the multinational talks over lifting sanctions if Iran agreed to limits on its nuclear program."[29]

> Iranian officials repeatedly told Rezaian and his wife, Yeganeh Salehi, who also was detained for more than two months, that Rezaian had "value" as a bargaining chip for a prisoner swap, the suit says. The filing also links key moments in the nuclear negotiations to Rezaian's treatment in the judicial system, from arrest to conviction to sentencing, and ultimately his release on the day the deal was implemented.
>
> "For nearly eighteen months, Iran held and terrorized Jason for the purpose of gaining negotiating leverage and ultimately exchanging him with the United States for something of value to Iran," the suit states.[30]

That really, *really* sounds like a ransom, doesn't it? Of course it does. Yet, Rezaian's own paper felt it had to push the Obama administration's version of the events and bury damaging stories. That isn't just yellow journalism; that's indecent and cruel.

Rezaian alleges that Javad Karim Ghodousi, a member of Iran's parliament, said Iran "didn't give up anything and got everything [in the negotiations]. We gave [up] Jason Rezaian—who/whose usefulness had been exhausted and would have only manifested a loss from then on—and in return we got four concessions. They included the release of seven Iranians from U.S. prisons and the release of $1.7 billion in frozen Iranian assets [.]" The lawsuit also states: "Although the U.S. Government has disputed that any money was paid in exchange for the release of the Iranian-American prisoners...it is the Iranian Government's intent that is relevant to the legal question of whether or not Jason was taken hostage."[31]

Marc Thiessen at the American Enterprise Institute argues, "Rezaian is arguing that even if the U.S. insists that the payment was not a ransom, it is irrelevant because Iran took him hostage with the intent to extort a ransom payment. So long as Iran saw it as a ransom, how the U.S.

describes it is legally irrelevant." He added, "It seems increasingly clear that the only ones who don't believe a ransom was paid are officials of the Obama administration."[32] Since the mainstream media is now an arm of the Democratic Party, their stated belief that the payment was not a ransom doesn't invalidate that argument.

The Trump Surveillance Scandal

At long last, on January 20, 2017, the era of Barack Obama came to an end. With the most corrupt chief executive in U.S. history out of government, the endless parade of scandals surrounding his administration was over. Except it wasn't. Even from beyond the confines of the White House, Obama's long, dark shadow still hangs over the nation's capital.

On March 4, 2017, President Donald J. Trump tweeted, "Terrible! Just found out that Obama had my 'wires tapped' in Trump Tower just before the victory. Nothing found. This is McCarthyism!" and "How low has President Obama gone to tap my phones during the very sacred election process. This is Nixon/Watergate. Bad (or sick) guy!"[1] Trump offered no proof, but it set off a firestorm of reactions, denials, counter accusations, and often slanderous claims against Trump, all of which amounted to the charge that his tweet was a lie.

After Trump's accusation, Obama's spokesman, Kevin Lewis, issued a statement on Obama's behalf. "A cardinal rule of the Obama administration was that no White House official ever interfered with any independent investigation led by the Department of Justice. As part of that practice, neither President Obama nor any White House official ever ordered surveillance on any U.S. citizen. Any suggestion otherwise is simply false."[2] Like many other statements made by former Obama staffers, Lewis' claim stopped short of denying that the administration had Trump's wires tapped. Obama's former speechwriter, Jon Favreau, warned journalists not to report that there had been no wiretap at all. "I'd be careful about reporting that Obama said there was no wiretapping," Favreau tweeted. "Statement just said that neither he nor the WH ordered it." Obama's former advisor David Axelrod also refused to say there hadn't been a wiretap, arguing that if there had been a wiretap, a court would have had a valid reason for approving it.[3]

No denial was possible because the Department of Justice did tap Trump's office phones. *The New York Times* even reported that these wiretapped recordings existed. On Trump's Inauguration Day, a front-page story appeared, titled, "Wiretapped Data Used In Inquiry of Trump Aides." In the wake of Trump's tweets, *The New York Times* changed the headline of the online version of the story to the more innocuous "Intercepted Russian Communications Part of Inquiry Into Trump Associates."[4] Wiretapped conversations between Trump's national security adviser Michael Flynn and the Russian ambassador leaked, ultimately leading to Flynn's resignation.[5] It's worth noting that the FBI found *no evidence* of wrongdoing or illicit ties to the Russian government in their review of Flynn's communications with the Russian ambassador.[6] It was his dishonesty about speaking with Russian officials that ended his political career.

The controversy surrounding Flynn made one thing clear: Trump's offices were under surveillance just as he claimed. Former federal prosecutor Andrew McCarthy said Obama officials knew that, under the Foreign Intelligence Surveillance Act (FISA) process, the FISA court 'orders' surveillance and the Justice Department represents the government in court. The question wasn't who showed up in court or approved the tap but who sought the tap in the first place? Why did they spy on a Republican presidential candidate?

Originally, the White House and Department of Justice pursued a criminal investigation of Trump's associates, and perhaps Trump himself, over concerns of his alleged Russian connections in the spring of 2016. When initial inquiries found nothing nefarious, the Obama Justice Department converted it into a national-security investigation under the FISA, rather than shut down the investigation. This allowed the Obama administration to conduct sweeping electronic surveillance.[7]

But the FISA court turned down the Obama administration's first request—a significant detail as 99.7 percent of FISA warrant requests are approved[8]—so they tried again in October with a more narrowly focused surveillance request, which gained approval.[9] The surveillance was likely legal, but McCarthy suggested:

Whether done inside or outside the FISA process, it would be a scandal of Watergate dimension if a presidential administration sought to conduct, or did conduct, national-security surveillance against the presidential candidate of the opposition party. [Without substantial evidence the candidate] was actually acting as an agent of a foreign power, such activity would amount to a pretextual use of national-security power for political purposes. That is the kind of abuse that led to Richard Nixon's resignation in lieu of impeachment.[10]

Those classified recordings of Flynn's conversations were leaked by someone in Washington intending to undermine President Trump; that amounts to using security laws as a cudgel for political gain.

Two weeks after Trump's accusatory tweets, House Intelligence Chairman Devin Nunes claimed, while there was no evidence that Trump was directly or personally wiretapped, foreign intelligence monitoring may have picked up Trump and his associates "incidentally." Democrats cried foul over this statement, which appeared to bolster Trump's original allegations, and Nunes was eventually forced to recuse himself from the investigation into Russian interference with the 2016 election.[11]

As you can imagine, Obama's cheerleaders answered Nunes' revelation with more denials. Former national security advisor Susan Rice told Judy Woodruff of *PBS Newshour*, "I know nothing about this. I was surprised to see reports from Chairman Nunes on that account today." Two weeks later, *Bloomberg* columnist Eli Lake published a bombshell report proving that Susan Rice not only knew about it, she "requested the identities of U.S. persons in raw intelligence reports on dozens of occasions that connect to the Donald Trump transition and campaign." The intelligence reports were summaries of conversations monitored "primarily between foreign officials discussing the Trump transition, but also in some cases direct contact between members of the Trump team and monitored foreign officials."[12]

The pattern of Rice's requests was discovered in a National Security Council review of the government's policy on "unmasking" the identities of individuals in the U.S. who are not targets of electronic eavesdropping, but whose communications are collected incidentally. Normally those names are redacted from summaries of monitored conversations and appear in reports as something like "U.S. Person One."

The National Security Council's senior director for intelligence, Ezra Cohen-Watnick, was conducting the review, according to two U.S. officials who spoke with Bloomberg View on the condition of anonymity because they were not authorized to discuss it publicly. In February Cohen-Watnick discovered Rice's multiple requests to unmask U.S. persons in intelligence reports that related to Trump transition activities.[13]

Former U.S. Attorney Joseph diGenova told *The Daily Caller* News Foundation that Rice also wanted detailed spreadsheets on these calls:

> What was produced by the intelligence community at the request of Ms. Rice were detailed spreadsheets of intercepted phone calls with unmasked Trump associates in perfectly legal conversations with individuals. [...] In short, the only apparent illegal activity was the unmasking of the people in the calls.[14]

Multiple sources confirmed Rice's request for spreadsheets to Fox News. The unmasked names of Trump's associates and family members "were then sent to all those at the National Security Council, some at the Defense Department, then Director of National Intelligence James Clapper and then-CIA Director John Brennan–essentially, the officials at the top, including former Rice deputy Ben Rhodes."[15]

Under pressure, Rice admitted that she ordered the unmasking of Trump officials on the intelligence reports—proving that her prior claim that she knew nothing about incidental monitoring of Trump associates was a lie. She denied there were any political motives behind it, and no one with half a brain bought it. With the truth out, Rice's new excuse was that it was part of her job of protecting the American people and securing the country.[16] How does one go from saying "I know nothing about this" to "We only do it to protect the American people and to do our jobs"? The only explanation is that Rice tried cover up either the political motives behind the unmasking or Barack Obama's involvement. If she had any credibility left to lose when this scandal broke it evaporated.

Andrew McCarthy rejected the premise of her final excuse writing at *National Review*:

> There would have been no *intelligence* need for Susan Rice to ask for identities to be unmasked. [...] The national-security adviser is not

an investigator. She is a White House staffer. The president's staff is a *consumer* of intelligence, not a generator or collector of it. [...] If Susan Rice was unmasking Americans, it was not to fulfill an intelligence need based on American interests; it was to fulfill a political desire based on Democratic-party interests.[17]

In light of Susan Rice's role in the unmasking, the *New York Post* accused the Obama administration of trying to sabotage Trump.

It's no surprise that U.S. spooks intercept foreign officials' calls. But intelligence community reports don't disclose the names of U.S. citizens on the other end. To get that info, a high official must (but rarely does) push to "unmask" the Americans' names.

Bloomberg's Eli Lake now reports that Rice started doing just that last year.

That was perfectly legal. But we also know that the Obama administration later changed the classification of the "unmasked" transcripts, and other similar material, in order to spread the information as widely as possible within the government.

The motive for that was (supposedly) to prevent Team Trump from burying it all once it took over. But the result was that it made it relatively safe for someone (or someones) to leak the info to the press.

Which made it likely somebody would leak. So Team Obama's "spread the info" initiative certainly broke the spirit of the laws.[18]

Susan Rice's role in the scandal prompted the House Intelligence Committee to issue several subpoenas for information on the unmasking.[19] In August 2017, that investigation implicated Ben Rhodes as a person of interest, suggesting he may have played a role in unmasking requests coming from the White House.[20] Another person of interest, former U.N. Ambassador Samantha Power, may have unmasked hundreds of names in intelligence reports during the last year of Obama's presidency.[21] Judicial Watch also filed a FOIA lawsuit against the Department of Justice and the National Security Agency for information.[22] We can only guess what other damaging information they had because all documents related to the unmasking were taken to the Obama Library and sealed for five years.

Judicial Watch president Tom Fitton was none too pleased:

Prosecutors, Congress, and the public will want to know when the National Security Council shipped off the records about potential intelligence abuses by Susan Rice and others in the Obama White House to the memory hole of the Obama Presidential Library.[23]

A House Intelligence Committee source told the *Washington Times* in the summer of 2017 that the transfer "appeared to reflect an effort by former administration officials to obscure evidence on whether Ms. Rice and other top officials in the Obama White House illegally tried to identify which Trump campaign and transition aides had been caught up in the U.S. intelligence intercepts of Russian interference in the presidential race."[24]

It gets worse. CNN reported in April 2017 that the FBI used a thirty-five-page anti-Trump dossier full of allegations against Donald Trump to win FISA court approval to monitor Trump campaign officials as part of the investigation into Russian meddling of the 2016 election.[25] The dossier was produced by Fusion GPS, a Democrat opposition research firm, which hired former British spy Christopher Steele to investigate any connections between Donald Trump and Russia.[26] The FBI even agreed to fund Steele's efforts—but ultimately did not after his connections to the dossier and Fusion GPS became public.[27] This information did not amuse Senate Judiciary Committee Chairman Chuck Grassley. "The idea that the FBI and associates of the Clinton campaign would pay Mr. Steele to investigate the Republican nominee for president in the run-up to the election raises further questions about the FBI's independence from politics, as well as the Obama administration's use of law enforcement and intelligence agencies for political ends," Grassley wrote in a letter to then FBI director James Comey.[28] Comey would later describe the dossier as being full of "salacious and unverified" material in testimony before the Senate Select Committee on Intelligence.[29]

In October 2017, *The Washington Post* broke the story that between April and October 2016, the Hillary Clinton campaign *and* the DNC financed the dossier through the Democratic Party's law firm, Perkins Coie—though they'd previously denied any knowledge of it.[30] According to Byron York of the *Washington Examiner,* this new revelation raised serious questions. "What did the FBI do with the dossier material? Did judges make surveillance decisions in the Trump-Russia investigation based in whole or in part on the dossier? To what degree is the "salacious and unverified" dossier the source of what we think we know about allegations of collusion between Russia and the Trump campaign?"[31] All good questions. As of this writing, they have yet to be answered, but, considering we're talking about the Obama administration, the answers are likely to be as troubling as the fact that we even have to ask the questions. We do know, thanks to the ongoing investigation, that Steele was in *repeated* contact with an associate deputy attorney general in the Obama Justice Department[32]—a very significant development that further fuels speculation that the Justice Department under Obama was actively and improperly trying to thwart Donald Trump.

Just as Obama's accumulation of scandals didn't end with his presidency, the media's covering up of his scandals didn't end then either. Over at CNN, Don Lemon said he'd ignore the bombshell of Susan Rice's ordering the unmasking, and called it a "fake scandal ginned up by right-wing media and Trump." Chris Cuomo claimed the bombshell was not true and a fake scandal. Jim Sciutto, CNN's Chief National Security Correspondent, tried to excuse Rice's earlier lie that she'd been unaware of the unmasking of Trump officials. "From her perspective, she didn't know what specific unmasking Devin Nunes and others are talking about."[33] CBS also defended Rice while NBC and ABC ignored the bombshell report.[34]

There were also the usual accusations of sexism and racism. MSNBC anchor Chris Matthews called Rice's critics sexist, as did David Corn, the D.C. bureau chief at *Mother Jones* and political analyst for MSNBC. According to Corn, Republicans were "defaming" Rice, "maybe because she's a black woman."[35] Some things never change.

As for the "salacious and unverified" dossier, the media did its part to downplay the fact that the Hillary's campaign and the DNC helped fund it—if they covered that bombshell development at all. According to analysis from the Media Research Center, the story was covered on NBC for a mere four minutes, CBS for two and a half minutes, and ABC a trifle thirty seconds. The White House correspondent at NBC even tried to suggest that how the dossier created wasn't important compared to what its contents were.[36] Somehow, nothing damaging about Obama or his administration is ever considered important enough to the mainstream media.

NSA/FISA Scandal

The NSA, under Obama, targeted American citizens for illegal and unwarranted seizure of phone records and emails, as I've already documented, but they weren't content to settle for one scandal. In the final days of Obama's presidency, investigative reporter Sara Carter, national security correspondent at *Circa*, unearthed new evidence that the NSA "routinely violated American privacy protections while scouring through overseas intercepts and failed to disclose the extent of the problems until the final days before Donald Trump was elected president."[1]

> More than 5 percent, or one out of every 20 searches seeking upstream Internet data on Americans inside the NSA's so-called Section 702 database violated the safeguards Obama and his intelligence chiefs vowed to follow in 2011, according to one classified internal report reviewed by Circa.
>
> The Obama administration self-disclosed the problems at a closed-door hearing Oct. 26 before the Foreign Intelligence Surveillance Court that set off alarm. Trump was elected less than two weeks later.
>
> The normally supportive court censured administration officials, saying the failure to disclose the extent of the violations earlier amounted to an "institutional lack of candor" and that the improper searches constituted a "very serious Fourth Amendment issue," according to a recently unsealed court document dated April 26, 2017.[2]

Thanks to Obama administration policy that loosened privacy rules, there was a three-fold increase in NSA data searches on Americans and "a rise in the unmasking of U.S. person's identities in intelligence reports." Administration officials, including National Security Adviser Susan Rice, said the NSA searches were not legal and monitored to avoid abuses. Not so, according to National Security Agency's inspector general. "Since 2011, NSA's minimization procedures have prohibited use of U.S.-person identifiers to query the results of upstream internet collections under Section 702," according to an unsealed court ruling, reported by *Circa*. "The Oct. 26, 2016 notice informed the court that NSA analysts had been conducting such queries in violation of that prohibition, with much greater frequency than had been previously disclosed to the Court." [3]

The American Civil Liberties Union (ACLU) called these new revelations of Obama administration violations of civil liberties "some of the most serious to ever be documented." [4] Another report by Sara Carter published the same day at *Circa* showed that, according to newly declassified government documents, the FBI "illegally shared raw intelligence about Americans with unauthorized third parties and violated other constitutional privacy protections." [5] This despite assurances by the agency that officials properly handled such sensitive data to avoid abuses and leaks. As Andrew McCarthy noted in *National Review,* Obama created an environment favorable to leaks and abuses on a massive scale.

> Other reporting indicates that there was a significant uptick in unmasking incidents in the latter years of the Obama administration. More officials were given unmasking authority. At the same time, President Obama loosened restrictions to allow wider access to raw intelligence collection and wider dissemination of intelligence reports.
>
> This geometrically increased the likelihood that classified information would be leaked—as did the Obama administration's encouragement to Congress to demand disclosure of intelligence related to the Trump campaign (the purported Trump-Russia connection). And of course, there has been a stunning amount of leaking of classified information to the media. [6]

University of Tennessee law professor and prominent blogger Glenn Reynolds claimed the scandal raised serious questions about the intelligence community. "It now seems apparent that we overestimated the patriotism and professionalism of the people in these agencies, who allowed them to be politically weaponized by the Obama administration." [7]

These massive constitutional abuses by the Obama administration make for a massive scandal. Except the media couldn't be bothered by it. None of the big three news networks covered the story.[8] The Obama administration routinely violated civil liberties of Americans on a huge scale, but that wasn't worth telling the American people? I wonder how the people would react if they knew the truth? Is it any wonder the media is now among the least trusted of our civic institutions?

Uranium One Scandal

In 2010, the Committee on Foreign Investment in the United States, a panel of Obama appointees and cabinet members, unanimously approved a deal that allowed Rosatom, a Russian-owned nuclear energy company, to buy the Toronto-based uranium mining company Uranium One. This acquisition gave Russia control over twenty percent of America's uranium supply. Back then, Obama was in denial about the threat Russia posed to the United States, but Republicans on the House Foreign Relations Committee expressed opposition to the deal, citing national security concerns.[1] So why would an administration that would later claim to view Russia as our greatest threat and accuse high-level Russian officials of meddling in the 2016 presidential election, make this deal?

The New York Times examined the Uranium One deal more than a year and a half before the 2016 presidential election, including research from Peter Schweizer, the author of *Clinton Cash*. After much scrutiny they revealed:

> As the Russians gradually assumed control of Uranium One in three separate transactions from 2009 to 2013, Canadian records show, a flow of cash made its way to the Clinton Foundation. Uranium One's chairman used his family foundation to make four donations totaling $2.35 million. Those contributions were not publicly disclosed by the Clintons, despite an agreement Mrs. Clinton had struck with the Obama White House to publicly identify all donors. Other people with ties to the company made donations as well.
>
> And shortly after the Russians announced their intention to acquire a majority stake in Uranium One, Mr. Clinton received $500,000 for

a Moscow speech from a Russian investment bank with links to the Kremlin that was promoting Uranium One stock.[2]

Despite the damning evidence they uncovered during their investigation, *The New York Times* stopped short of saying the deal gained approval thanks in part to those donations.

> Whether the donations played any role in the approval of the uranium deal is unknown. But the episode underscores the special ethical challenges presented by the Clinton Foundation, headed by a former president who relied heavily on foreign cash to accumulate $250 million in assets even as his wife helped steer American foreign policy as secretary of state, presiding over decisions with the potential to benefit the foundation's donors.[3]

The circumstances behind the Uranium One deal were thrust back into the limelight after an October 2017 bombshell report from *The Hill*. They found "the FBI had gathered substantial evidence that Russian nuclear industry officials were engaged in bribery, kickbacks, extortion and money laundering designed to grow Vladimir Putin's atomic energy business inside the United States, according to government documents and interviews."[4]

> They also obtained an eyewitness account—backed by documents—indicating Russian nuclear officials had routed millions of dollars to the U.S. designed to benefit former President Bill Clinton's charitable foundation during the time Secretary of State Hillary Clinton served on a government body that provided a favorable decision to Moscow, sources told *The Hill*.
>
> The racketeering scheme was conducted "with the consent of higher level officials" in Russia who "shared the proceeds" from the kickbacks, one agent declared in an affidavit years later.[5]

So, the Obama administration knew of a bribery plot *before* they approved the deal and went ahead with it? Given the money in play for the Clintons, one can't help but conclude that the fortunes of high-ranking Democrats mattered more to Obama than national security.

Congress began investigations[6] and soon after the Russian bribery scheme came to light, a former FBI informant and whistleblower who worked at Uranium One from 2009 to 2014 claimed he "was intimidated by Obama administration lawyers into dropping a civil suit against the government." The informant's lawyer, Victoria Toensing, claimed Obama Justice Department lawyers told him to stay quiet because "his reputation and liberty [was] in jeopardy" if he did not.[7]

The Trump administration released the informant from his gag order, which will allow him to testify before Congress about his undercover work at Uranium One.[8] According to Toensing, her client has "specific information about contributions and bribes to various entities and people in the United States."[9] In November 2017, Attorney General Jeff Sessions "directed senior federal prosecutors to evaluate 'certain issues' requested by congressional Republicans, involving the sale of Uranium One and alleged unlawful dealings related to the Clinton Foundation, leaving the door open for an appointment of another special counsel."[10]

Another massive scandal involving Barack Obama *and* Hillary Clinton? How many does it take to get the attention of the mainstream press? Well, it hasn't happened yet. All three network evening news shows combined spent precisely three minutes and one second covering this story...in the two years since the story first broke.[11] Dan Gainor, the Vice President for Business and Culture at the Media Research Center, accused the broadcast networks of suppressing the scandal. "We finally have a compelling Russia story and the news media report on it like they did Harvey Weinstein for decades—cowering under their desks."[12]

Will Obama and the Clintons be held accountable? That question won't be answered for some time, but this scandal isn't going anywhere anytime soon. Thankfully, Obama is no longer in power to press any reset buttons or threaten any whistleblowers.

Project Cassandra Scandal

As you can see, Obama's presidency was rife with scandal, so much so that just before this book went to press, another undeniably huge scandal broke when, after an extensive investigation, *Politico* dropped a bombshell report just a week before Christmas 2017. According to the report, in order to protect Obama's nuclear deal with Iran, his administration "derailed an ambitious law enforcement campaign targeting drug trafficking by the Iranian-backed terrorist group Hezbollah, even as it was funneling cocaine into the United States."[1]

The eight-year campaign, called Project Cassandra, began under the Bush administration and tracked an international drug trafficking and money laundering network, which agents traced all the way "to the innermost circle of Hezbollah and its state sponsors in Iran."[2] But the Obama administration rolled out tons of red tape to stop the project in its tracks:

> But as Project Cassandra reached higher into the hierarchy of the conspiracy, Obama administration officials threw an increasingly insurmountable series of roadblocks in its way, according to interviews with dozens of participants who in many cases spoke for the first time about events shrouded in secrecy, and a review of government documents and court records. When Project Cassandra leaders sought approval for some significant investigations, prosecutions, arrests and financial sanctions, officials at the Justice and Treasury departments delayed, hindered or rejected their requests.
>
> The Justice Department declined requests by Project Cassandra and other authorities to file criminal charges against major players such as Hezbollah's high-profile envoy to Iran, a Lebanese bank that allegedly laundered billions in alleged drug profits, and a central player in a

U.S.-based cell of the Iranian paramilitary Quds force. And the State Department rejected requests to lure high-value targets to countries where they could be arrested.[3]

David Asher, a veteran U.S. illicit finance expert at the Pentagon involved with Project Cassandra, said the actions of the administration to thwart the campaign were a systemic policy decision. "They serially ripped apart this entire effort that was very well supported and resourced [sic], and it was done from the top down."[4]

Katherine Bauer, a U.S. Treasury Department official under Obama, informed the House Committee on Foreign Affairs that Hezbollah investigations were "tamped down for fear of rocking the boat with Iran and jeopardizing the nuclear deal." And the results are infuriating. According to Bauer's testimony, "some Hezbollah operatives were not pursued via arrests, indictments, or Treasury designations that would have blocked their access to U.S. financial markets."[5]

The Obama Justice Department even refused to investigate and prosecute Abdallah Safieddine, Hezbollah's longtime Iran envoy, who Project Cassandra agents described as "the linchpin of Hezbollah's criminal network." One such case involved a Hezbollah assault weapons deal out of Philadelphia. The DEA and FBI built up a strong case against Safieddine but were rebuffed without explanation.[6] This decision spared Hezbollah's entire illegal financial network in the United States from scrutiny.

From the *Politico* report:

> The administration also rejected repeated efforts by Project Cassandra members to charge Hezbollah's military wing as an ongoing criminal enterprise under a federal Mafia-style racketeering statute, task force members say. And they allege that administration officials declined to designate Hezbollah a "significant transnational criminal organization" and blocked other strategic initiatives that would have given the task force additional legal tools, money, and manpower to fight it.[7]

Many Israeli politicians were furious at the report. Yair Lapid, chairman of the centrist Yesh Atid party said, if the report is true, Obama should return his Nobel Peace Prize. "Israel warned repeatedly that there can be no connection between the nuclear deal and anti-terror activity, certainly against Hezbollah....We also warned of this specifically, because of the proven link between Hezbollah and Iran."[8] Tzachi Hanegbi, Israel's Minister for Regional Cooperation, said the report wasn't surprising, given Obama's efforts to legitimize Iran. "Up until the Obama Administration, every American President fought terrorism uncompromisingly." Michael Oren, the former Israeli ambassador to the United States, said the report "wouldn't surprise any Israeli involved in the attempts to prevent a bad nuclear deal with Iran." Israeli Communications Minister Ayoob Kara accused the Obama administration of allowing Hezbollah to grow stronger.[9]

Former Obama administration officials denied that political reasons played a role in how the administration handled Hezbollah and downplayed the story as ridiculous and the sources used as "low-level" people. But, the evidence presented by *Politico*'s bombshell report fits an all too disturbing pattern of the Obama administration being soft on terror in the name of a misguided policy. Josh Meyer, who wrote the *Politico* report, defended his sources in an interview with Fox News, insisting they were neither flawed nor ideologues. "These were the people, one was a Pentagon person, one was a DEA person. But I also talked to many, many dozens of other people to get sort of ground truth and see what their allegations were held up to the light of day. So this is not a story in 14,000 words where I was just taking spin from some people."[10]

Because this scandal broke just before this book went to press, there's no telling what else we'll learn going forward. But, make no mistake, this is a scandal of epic proportions. Jonathan S. Tobin in the *New York Post* asked the right question: "What if a president used his power to interfere with a federal investigation involving foreign powers committing serious crimes in the United States as well as elsewhere?" His answer: "Such a thing would be considered a terrible scandal and, no doubt, lead to a federal probe by a special counsel who would be expected to get to the bottom of such a mess."[11]

With such a major story, the media jumped all over it, right? Nope. As you likely expected if you've read the rest of this book, the media was still covering for Obama long after he left office. According to analysis by the Media Research Center, neither ABC, CBS, nor NBC covered the scandal in the days following the bombshell *Politico* report.[12] The Obama administration sabotaged a drug trafficking investigation of a terrorist organization to preserve a deeply flawed nuclear deal with the world's number one state sponsor of terrorism, and the media yawned.

This scandal, and several others that broke after Obama left office, will be investigated. The media may try to ignore them all, but perhaps someone will face consequences. We can only hope.

Conclusion

In his defense of the British soldiers in the Boston Massacre trials on December 4, 1770, John Adams said, "Facts are stubborn things; and whatever may be our wishes, our inclinations, or the dictates of our passion, they cannot alter the state of facts and evidence."[1] Barack Obama's supporters had—and still have—an undeniable passion that has convinced them to ignore a mountain of evidence right in front of their faces. Obama spoke so eloquently in his first presidential campaign about his Utopian image of America—an America fundamentally transformed into something beautiful and noble in the eyes of the political left. His soaring rhetoric established his good intentions to the people who shared his leftist ideology; for this, he was deemed virtually infallible. No level of corruption, no scandal, no pattern of dishonesty would diminish their belief that Obama was their savior—an unsullied, selfless political leader.

Partisan loyalty might cause them to miss the inconvenient truth of Obama's corruption, but it doesn't change the facts. It's up to us to stand for those facts and keep our cultural influencers from rewriting history to fit their misguided, rose-colored view of the man. Understand, this will not be an easy task. They've held this unshakable faith in Obama since he first appeared on the national stage and they won't give it up without a fight.

Even before Obama took office, the gatekeepers of popular culture (Hollywood, the media, and academia) wanted the world to see him as one of the most successful world leaders in history. His supporters believed anything but praise for their chosen icon was blasphemous, racist, or ignorant. I am reminded of an incident during Obama's first presidential campaign. Speaking before a crowd of 17,000 at a rally of adoring supporters in Dallas, Texas, Obama, who was suffering from a cold, had to interrupt his speech. "I'm going to blow my nose here for a second," he told the crowd. As he performed the task, the crowd, according to reports, went wild. CNN correspondent Jeanne Moos called this swooning of Obama's supporters "practically religious." Rather than finding it creepy, she described this reverence for Obama almost poetically. "He's bathed in light. They hand him flowers. Hands reach out to touch him—cue the angels."² I'd hate to see how Obama's supporters would react if they followed him into the bathroom. Such euphoria might be too much for them to handle.

Their emotional investment in his presidency made a serious and honest discussion about his record impossible. The assumption of Obama's greatness took many forms. The undeserved accolades (such as the Nobel Peace Prize, the JFK Profile in Courage award, heck, even the presidency itself) came first. Then, his opponents faced a barrier so impenetrable that it permitted no form of criticism to pass, not even *satire*. *Saturday Night Live* political writer Jim Downey once claimed it was impossible to joke about Obama because he had no definitive comic flaw. He also described *SNL* as "an arm of the Hollywood Democratic establishment...We just stopped doing anything which could even be misinterpreted as a criticism of Obama."³ God save the wretched soul of the man who questioned Obama's good intentions or the efficacy of his worldview; the knee-jerk cries of racism and bigotry drowned out debate time after time.

Believe me, I've been there. You should read leftists' reactions to my previous book, *The Worst President in History: The Legacy of Barack Obama*. They didn't want to read that book and they probably won't read this one either. As before, they'll write it off as racist to justify why no one should read it. When actor Billy Baldwin—you may have heard of him, he has a famous brother named Alec—learned about my last book on Twitter, he called me a hack and said he'd rather burn it or use the pages to wipe his ass than read it.⁴ I told him I would gladly send him a copy, but he still hasn't taken me up on the offer—which still stands. I'm more than happy to send him a copy of this book too. Maybe he'll read it. Okay, probably not, but, at least there's the potential opportunity of causing him some terribly uncomfortable paper cuts...either way, the truth will hurt.

The lack of honesty on the cultural left has not abated since Obama left office. In fact, it's worse than ever. I understand their optimistic and hopeful outlook as he arrived in the Oval Office, but the fantasy has to end sometime. Rather than face the last eight years with an honest desire to seek the truth, the press has abdicated its vital role as watchdog in favor of ideological warfare, the education system has chosen indoctrination over an education based in reason, and Hollywood has abandoned entertainment for heavy-handed propaganda wherever its films enter the political arena.

All three branches of the cultural elite agree on one pernicious and dangerous untruth: Obama's administration was "scandal-free." This is so absurd that it's difficult to write this sentence without using an expletive, or to literally laugh out loud. If you've read this far, you know there were scandals aplenty in the Obama administration, some directly connected to Obama, some involving the White House, and others various agencies within the administration. Pretending they didn't happen or weren't a big deal will only empower future chief executives to all new heights of corruption. But, that doesn't stop Obama's allies from trying to sanitize his record, future consequences be damned.

It shouldn't be so easy to cover up the existence of this many scandals in the age of the internet and social media, but the average American doesn't have time to follow every story from beginning to end, read every source, and check every factual claim. Those who make the "scandal-free" claim know it's nonsense, but their strategy is time-tested. They know if they repeat a lie often enough, many people will believe it. I hate to tell you this, but it's working. There are many people who believe Obama's tenure was devoid of scandal. When one side has a virtual monopoly on the legacy media, the halls of academia, the creative heartbeat of the culture, and even the vast majority of the internet (Google and its various subsidiary internet companies own about 40 percent of the traffic on the web *worldwide*[5] and they're just one of dozens of powerhouse dot coms run by leftists), as the years pass, the truth will vanish.

Now, there is a new president, and a new and ingenious tactic has emerged among Obama's allies. After eight years of ostrich syndrome during Obama's presidency, they deploy an endless scandalization of anything and everything under President Trump. The idea is to create a popular consciousness that associates Obama with relative media peace and Trump with chaos, anger, and scandal. Take a look around your Facebook walls and Twitter feeds—it's working. We should be skeptical of our leaders, and Trump is no exception, but if Barack Obama received the same treatment from the media as Donald Trump, his presidency would have lasted less than a year.

In May 2017, Matthew A. Cherry, a former wide receiver in the NFL turned writer/director opined on Twitter: "I miss the days when the biggest presidential scandal was that time Obama wore a tan suit." As of this writing, it was retweeted nearly sixty-eight thousand times and liked by almost two hundred and twelve thousand.[6] Similar sentiments abound on Facebook, usually expressed in snarky memes with no factual backing. I'm certain many Americans believe Obama's scandals were a series of nothingburgers ginned up by "racist" Republicans and Fox News based on the fact that their social media and news feeds are filled with that claim because it generates clicks, likes, and follows among the most active social media users: the young.

And that's the problem. The left isn't just denying that the scandals documented in this book played out as I have claimed. They deny that there exists any evidence that merits an investigation and they claim anyone who wants an inquiry is a racist or a fool. Obama had a free pass from the media (both legacy and social) and it served as a license to abuse his power. People on both sides of the aisle must be willing to view all corruption equally, instead of letting political allegiances dictate how we perceive corruption. When we let partisanship skew our perception, it only hurts our ability to hold our elected leaders accountable for legitimate crimes. As *New York Post* columnist Karol Markowitz noted, "Obama supporters are so invested in preserving the fiction that his presidency was 'scandal-free' and cool under fire that their lack of introspection only serves to weaken their attacks on Trump." Markowitz added, "Obamaites tell people to hush up about things that will make their side look bad and to focus all attacks in one direction. It's dishonest and counterproductive. Trump supporters see these attacks as strictly partisan and that makes them more defensive and protective over 'their' candidate. It's a cycle that we should work to break."[7]

As I mentioned earlier in this book, *The Washington Post*'s fact checker Glenn Kessler excused Obama's scandal-plagued presidency by professing, *unapologetically*, that scandals are in the eye of the beholder. "Whether something is a scandal or not—or whether an administration is 'scandal-free'—is more a matter of opinion, bound to be fiercely disputed by partisans in either camp."[8] This is *not* acceptable. I reject the notion that corruption is subjective. We live in a nation founded on the *rule of law* and standing for the principle that all men are equal under that law. When we see evidence that a politician has broken the law, it should not be a matter of subjective opinion.

Both the political left and right are guilty of tolerating corruption from members of their respective tribes, but the left's monopoly on the media, popular culture, and academia make it easier for their partisan perspective to become "fact" in the eyes of the masses, particularly the young and impressionable. We should call out *any* politician on either side of the aisle because abuse of power is not limited to one party. If there is no standard that we can all agree on, then only the media and academia can break the impasse...and we know where their loyalties are.

Obama's supporters will point to the lack of indictments and criminal convictions of administration officials as proof that his administration was ethical and bounded by the law, but what it actually proves is just how devoid of accountability his administration was. As conservative talk radio host and author Hugh Hewitt put it:

> Republicans routinely demanded special prosecutors in the era of President Barack Obama and Attorneys General Eric Holder and Loretta Lynch. There were calls for one to investigate Hillary Clinton's private email server, the Internal Revenue Service's alleged abuse of power regarding "tea party"-named groups, and the "gun walking" scandal known as Fast and Furious. But there were no special prosecutors appointed during the Obama years. The Democrats knew better than to set a seasoned prosecutor with subpoena power loose when political intrigue is afoot.[9]

Obama's Justice Department was a politicized and corrupt agency intent on protecting Obama and his allies, attacking his enemies, and stonewalling congressional investigations into administration scandals. As scandals in his administration accumulated, Republican-led investigations were dismissed as partisan witch hunts. The Obama administration's stonewalling and obstruction of justice were almost a Pavlovian response to each scandal, as was the left's denial that any corruption existed. When partisan loyalties trump our desire for accountability, government gains power and tyranny soon follows.

As Americans, we believe the power of government over the people comes from the consent of the governed. The Constitution protects us from government abuse in part by guaranteeing our right to free speech and a free press. When we, the governed, ignore or excuse the kind of corruption the Founding Fathers feared most, we give the government our consent to abuse their authority. When the free press turns into a partisan press, it becomes impossible for the people to understand the workings of their own government or to check its power and excesses. The Founding Fathers guaranteed the rights of the people and the press to speak out against the government without fear of persecution. This compulsion to canonize Obama not only as a successful president but as a scandal-free president—in spite of the evidence to the contrary—defies everything our forebears taught us. If the press had done its job, this book would not have been necessary.

The fact is, Obama spent the entirety of his presidency under a dark cloud of scandal and that dark cloud has continued to grow *after* he left office. As of this writing, new questions are being asked about the Obama administration's approval of Russia's acquisition of Uranium One.

Denial of Obama's dishonorable record has taken some absurd turns. In August 2017, Illinois established Obama's birthday as a state holiday.[10] Imagine if California had made Richard Nixon's birthday a state holiday after he resigned from the presidency. And before you protest that Obama didn't leave office in disgrace, is it not clear after reading this book that Obama's presidency was far more scandalous? Nixon's birthday being celebrated as a state holiday would be *less* insulting.

Too many liberal lies about history have become accepted as truths because of the left's virtual monopoly on our culture. The same people that claim fascism was right-wing, that Franklin D. Roosevelt ended the Great Depression, or that racist Southern Democrats switched over to the Republican Party *en masse* following passage of the Civil Rights Act of 1964, are now trying to elevate Barack Obama to the level of Martin

Luther King, Jr. or John F. Kennedy. Today's lies will become historical "fact" if we don't correct the record. I've documented dozens of separate scandals, most of which were at least as important and corrupt as Watergate, in this book. That is by no means a complete list of the Obama administration's filthy ledger, but it's more than enough to put to rest all claims that Obama was scandal-free. I sincerely hope enough people read this book that the truth about Obama's presidency won't get swept under the rug in favor of a more politically correct fairy tale. The cost of this deception is just too great. If we fail to tell the truth today, it will be our own fault when we wake up one day and find ourselves ruled by despots. Thomas Jefferson once said, "If a nation expects to be ignorant and free, in a state of civilisation, it expects what never was and never will be."[11] How right he was.

Acknowledgements

Taking on the lies and misinformation of Obama's supporters, the media, and academia is no easy task. Writing this book would not have been possible without the assistance and support of several people and organizations whose contributions to this project, direct and indirect, deserve some credit. David S. Bernstein, of Bombardier Books, for seeing the potential of this book, and making it happen. Mark Noonan, my co-author on my previous books. Our writing paths have now diverged, but it took two books written together for me to feel ready to tackle a project like this on my own. Matthew Souders, for helping me polish the manuscript. Nick Cole, for all the advice and insight.

I'd also like to thank everyone who has supported me and my writing over the years, even friends and family who may not agree with me.

The mountains of research collected for this book included many sources, two of which greatly contributed to making my job much easier: the Media Research Center, for their invaluable analyses of media coverage, and Judicial Watch, for their tireless efforts to get the answers the media didn't want to find during the Obama years.

Writing this book involved many solitary hours of researching and writing away from my family, in order complete the manuscript on time. So, many thanks to Beth, Isaac, and Zuzu for tolerating my absence many nights and weekends. I sincerely hope this book is worthy of that sacrifice.

Endnotes

Introduction Notes

1 "Transcripts President Barack Obama Holds Press Conference at APEC," *CNN*, November 20, 2016 transcripts.cnn.com/TRANSCRIPTS/1611/20/cnr.05.html. Accessed 10 May 2017.

2 Steve Kroft, "Barack Obama: Eight Years in the White House," *CBS News*, January 15, 2017 cbsnews.com/news/60-minutes-barack-obama-eight-years-in-the-white-house/. Accessed 10 May 2017.

3 Ian Schwartz, "Valerie Jarrett: Obama Hasn't Had A Scandal, Done Something To Embarrass Himself," *Real Clear Politics*, January 2, 2017 realclearpolitics.com/video/2017/01/02/valerie_jarrett_obama_hasnt_had_a_scandal_done_something_to_embarrass_himself.html. Accessed 10 May 2017.

4 "McDonough: Obama 'historically free of scandal,'" *CNN*, January 15, 2017 cnn.com/videos/politics/2017/01/15/sotu-mcdonough-scandal.cnn. Accessed 10 May 2017.

5 Jeffrey Meyer, "*Time*'s Rana Foroohar Laughably Claims Obama White House Largely Scandal Free," *Newsbusters*, May 14, 2013 newsbusters.org/blogs/nb/jeffrey-meyer/2013/05/14/times-rana-foroohar-laughably-claims-obama-white-house-largely. Accessed 10 May 2017.

6 Steve Inskeep and Cokie Roberts, "Republicans Focus on Democrats' Political Misdeeds," *NPR*, May 14, 2013, npr.org/2013/05/13/183538481/politics-in-the-news. Accessed 10 May 2017.

7 David Brooks, "I Miss Barack Obama," *The New York Times*, February 9, 2016 nytimes.com/2016/02/09/opinion/i-miss-barack-obama.html. Accessed 10 May 2017.

8 Paul Waldman, "Republicans are still pining for a real Obama administration scandal," *The Week*, May 24, 2016 theweek.com/articles/626000/republicans-are-still-pining-real-obama-administration-scandal. Accessed 10 May 2017.

9 "While Clinton, Trump Brawl, Obama Rises: Our View," *USA Today*, September 6, 2016 usatoday.com/story/opinion/2016/09/06/president-obama-approval-ratings-polls-editorials-and-debates/89770472/. Accessed 10 May 2017.

10 Joe Klein, "Amazing Grace," *TIME*, December 8, 2016 time.com/4594954/amazing-grace/. Accessed 10 May 2017.

11 Jessica Chasmar, "Tom Brokaw: Obama has been 'scandal-free,'" *Washington Times*, January 11, 2017 washingtontimes.com/news/2017/jan/11/tom-brokaw-obama-has-been-scandal-free/. Accessed 10 May 2017.

12 Mike Raust, "Joy Behar: Worst Things Obama Did Were Smoking, Putting Feet On Desk. VIDEO," *The Daily Caller*, March 6, 2017 dailycaller.com/2017/03/06/joy-behar-worst-things-obama-did-were-smoking-putting-feet-on-desk-video/. Accessed 10 May 2017.

13 Glenn Kessler, "Has the Obama White House been 'historically free of scandal'?" *Washington Post*, January 19, 2017 washingtonpost.com/news/fact-checker/wp/2017/01/19/has-the-obama-white-house-been-historically-free-of-scandal/. Accessed 10 May 2017.

14 Michael Calderone, "JournoList: Inside the echo chamber," *Politico*, March 17, 2009 politico.com/story/2009/03/journolist-inside-the-echo-chamber-020086. Accessed 17 July 2017.

15 Jonathan Strong, "Documents show media plotting to kill stories about Rev. Jeremiah Wright," *The Daily Caller*, July 20, 2010 dailycaller.com/2010/07/20/documents-show-media-plotting-to-kill-stories-about-rev-jeremiah-wright/. Accessed 17 July 2017.

16 Ibid.

17 Tucker Carlson, "Letter from Editor-in-Chief Tucker Carlson on The Daily Caller's Journolist coverage," *The Daily Caller*, July 22, 2010 dailycaller.com/2010/07/22/letter-from-editor-in-chief-tucker-carlson-on-the-daily-callers-journolist-coverage/. Accessed 17 July 2017.

18 *TIME* Staff, "10 Historians on What Will Be Said About President Obama's Legacy," *TIME*, January 20, 2017 time.com/4632190/historians-obamas-legacy/. Accessed 10 May 2017.

19 "C-SPAN Releases Third Historians Survey of Presidential Leadership," *C-SPAN*, February 17, 2017 static.c-span.org/assets/documents/presidentSurvey/C-SPAN%20Historians%20Survey%20of%20President%20Leadership%20Feb%2017%20 2017%20press%20release%20PDF.pdf. Accessed 10 May 2017.

20 Anthony Salvanto, "CBS battleground poll: Partisans divide on news of FBI, emails," *CBS News*, October 30, 2016 cbsnews.com/news/cbs-battleground-poll-partisans-divide-on-news-of-fbi-emails/. Accessed 17 July 2017.

The BlagoGate Scandal Notes

1 "Feds: Governor tried to 'auction' Obama's seat," *NBC News*, December 9, 2008 nbcnews.com/id/28139155/ns/politics/t/feds-governor-tried-auction-obamas-seat/. Accessed 19 March 2017.

2 Jeff Coen, Rick Pearson, John Chase, and David Kidwell, "Illinois Gov. Rod Blagojevich arrested on federal charges," *Chicago Tribune*, December 10, 2008 articles. chicagotribune.com/2008-12-10/news/chi-blagojevich-1210_1_political-corruption-crime-spree-blagojevich-attorney-sheldon-sorosky-blagojevich-case. Accessed 20 March 2017.

3 Monica Davey and Jack Healy, "Illinois Governor Charged in Scheme to Sell Obama's Seat," *The New York Times*, December 9, 2008. nytimes.com/2008/12/09/us/politics/10Illinois.html. Accessed 19 March 2017.

4 "Obama Is 'Appalled,' Insists He Had No Contact With Blagojevich Over Senate Seat," *Fox News*, December 11, 2008 foxnews.com/politics/2008/12/11/obama-appalled-in-sists-contact-blagojevich-senate-seat.html/. Accessed 19 March 2017.

5 "United States Of America v. Rod R. Blagojevich and John Harris," *Chicago Tribune*, n.d. chicagotribune.com/chi-blagojevich-criminal-complaint-story.html. Accessed 19 March 2017.

6 Ibid.

7 John King, "Source: Obama wants Valerie Jarrett to replace him in Senate," *CNN*, November 9, 2008 politicalticker.blogs.cnn.com/2008/11/09/source-obama-wants-valerie-jarrett-to-replace-him-in-senate/. Accessed 19 March 2017.

8 "Transition Staff Contacts with the Governor's Office," *Newsmax*, December 23, 2008 newsmax.com/Headline/Transition-Staff-Contacts/2008/12/23/id/327290/. Accessed 19 March 2017.

9 Kevin Hechtokopf, "Obama Team Completes Review Of Contacts With Gov.," *CBS News*, December 15, 2008 cbsnews.com/news/obama-team-completes-review-of-contacts-with-gov/. Accessed 19 March 2017.

10 "Blagojevich Scandal is Obama's Scandal," *Judicial Watch*, December 12, 2008 judicial-watch.org/press-room/weekly-updates/51-blagojevich-scandal-obama-s-scandal/. Accessed 19 March 2017.

11 "Judicial Watch Obtains Documents Re: Blagojevich Contacts with Obama and Transition Team," Judicial Watch, January 5, 2009 judicialwatch.org/press-room/press-releases/judicial-watch-obtains-documents-re-blagojevich-con-tacts-obama-and-transition-team/. Accessed 19 March 2017.

12 Charles Johnson, "Obama Did Discuss Senate Seat with Blagojevich — Update: KHQA Pulls Their Articles," *Little Green Footballs*, December 10, 2008 littlegreenfootballs.com/article/32137_Obama_Did_Discuss_Senate_Seat_with_Blagojevich_-_Update-_KHQA_Pulls_Their_Articles. Accessed 19 March 2017.

13 Allahpundit, "Obama: I never talked to Blagojevich about the Senate seat; Axelrod: Yes, he did; Update: Axelrod misspoke, says Obama camp," *Hot Air*, December 9, 2008 hotair.com/archives/2008/12/09/obama-i-never-talked-to-blagojevich-about-the-senate-seat-axelrod-yes-he-did/. Accessed 19 March 2017.

14 Ben Smith, "Aide: Ax 'misspoke,'" *Politico*, December 9, 2008 politico.com/blogs/ben-smith/2008/12/aide-ax-misspoke-014687. Accessed 19 March 2017.

15 Mark Guarino "Blagojevich trial delay could hamper Rahm Emanuel's run for Chicago mayor," *The Christian Science Monitor*, October 23, 2010 csmonitor.com/USA/Politics/2010/1023/Blagojevich-trial-delay-could-hamper-Rahm-Emanuel-s-run-for-Chicago-mayor. Accessed 17 March 2017.

16 Andy Barr, "Blago aide: Obama knew," *Politico*, June 25, 2010 politico.com/story/2010/06/blago-aide-obama-knew-039020. Accessed 19 March 2017.

17 "Obama, Emanuel At Center Of Blagojevich Trial," Judicial Watch, June 29, 2010 judicialwatch.org/blog/2010/06/obama-emanuel-center-blagojevich-trial/. Accessed 19 March 2017.

18 "Blago's Un-Redacted Motion to Compel President Obama to Testify," *ABC News*, April 23, 2010 blogs.abcnews.com/politicalpunch/2010/04/blagos-unredacted-mo-tion-to-compel-president-obama-to-testify.html. Accessed 19 March 2017.

19   Michael Scherer, "Faced With The Blagojevich Scandal, Did Barack Obama Tell The Whole Truth?" *TIME*, June 30, 2010 swampland.time.com/2010/06/30/faced-with-the-blagojevich-scandal-did-barack-obama-tell-the-whole-truth/. Accessed 19 March 2017.

20   Kyle Drennen, "CBS: GOP Attempts to Tie Obama to Blagojevich 'A Tough Sell'," *Newsbusters*, December 11, 2008 newsbusters.org/blogs/nb/kyle-drennen/2008/12/10/cbs-gop-attempts-tie-obama-blagojevich-tough-sell. Accessed 19 March 2017.

21   Ibid.

22   Noel Sheppard, "Jim Lehrer Defends Blagojevich: 'What's the Big Deal Here?'" *Newsbusters*, December 12, 2008 newsbusters.org/blogs/nb/noel-sheppard/2008/12/13/jim-lehrer-defends-blagojevich-whats-big-deal-here. Accessed 19 March 2017.

23   Ibid.

The Audacity of Opacity Notes

1   "Freedom of Information Act: Memorandum For The Heads Of Executive Departments And Agencies," Obama White House Archives, January 21, 2009 obamawhitehouse.archives.gov/the-press-office/freedom-information-act. Accessed 28 May 2017.

2   Matt Margolis and Mark Noonan. *The Worst President in History: The Legacy of Barack Obama*. Victory Books, 2016.

3   Bill Dedman, "Obama blocks list of visitors to White House," *NBC News*, June 16, 2009 nbcnews.com/id/31373407/ns/politics-white_house/t/obama-blocks-list-visitors-white-house/. Accessed 28 May 2017.

4   Chris Frates, "W.H. meets lobbyists off campus," *Politico*, February 24, 2011 politico.com/story/2011/02/wh-meets-lobbyists-off-campus-050081. Accessed 28 May 2017.

5   Tom Fitton, "JW Beats Obama in Court on WH Visitor Logs," Judicial Watch, August 19, 2011 judicialwatch.org/press-room/weekly-updates/33-jw-beats-obama-court-wh-visitor-logs/. Accessed 28 May 2017.

6   James Risen, "If Donald Trump Targets Journalists, Thank Obama," *The New York Times*, December 30, 2016 nytimes.com/2016/12/30/opinion/sunday/if-donald-trump-targets-journalists-thank-obama.html. Accessed 28 May 2017.

7   Luke Johnson, "Obama Promises, Including Whistleblower Protections, Disappear From Website," *Huffington Post*, July 26, 2013 huffingtonpost.com/2013/07/26/obama-whistleblower-website_n_3658815.html. Accessed 28 May 2017.

8   Angie Drobnic Holan, "Obama said he'd televise health reform negotiations on C-SPAN," *Politifact*, July 10, 2009 politifact.com/truth-o-meter/promises/obameter/promise/517/health-care-reform-public-sessions-C-SPAN/. Accessed 28 May 2017.

9   Kevin Glass, "Who Gave Us Obamacare," *National Review*, August 13, 2012 national-review.com/nrd/articles/312377/who-gave-us-obamacare. Accessed 29 May 2017.

10   Alan Silverleib, "House passes health care bill on 219-212 vote," *CNN*, March 22, 2010 cnn.com/2010/POLITICS/03/21/health.care.main/index.html. Accessed 29 July 2017.

11   Hadas Gold, "Media protest White House photo ban," *Politico*, November 21, 2013 politico.com/blogs/media/2013/11/media-protest-white-house-photo-ban-178077. Accessed 28 May 2017.

12 Jeffrey Scott Shapiro, "Worse than Nixon? Obama White House accused of hiding public information," *Washington Times*, June 30, 2014 washingtontimes.com/news/2014/jun/30/white-house-censors-and-slows-release-of-informati/. Accessed 28 May 2017.

13 Ted Bridis, "Obama's final year: US spent $36 million in records lawsuits," Associated Press, March 14, 2017 apnews.com/0b27c4d4b23b436d805328694e58c605/Obama%27s-final-year:-US-spent-%2436-million-in-records-lawsuits. Accessed 28 May 2017.

14 Jason Leopold, "It Took a FOIA Lawsuit to Uncover How the Obama Administration Killed FOIA Reform," *Vice News*, March 9, 2016 news.vice.com/article/it-took-a-foia-lawsuit-to-uncover-how-the-obama-administration-killed-foia-reform. Accessed 29 May 2017.

15 The Editorial Board, "What Happened to Transparency?" *The New York Times*, January 7, 2014. nytimes.com/2014/01/08/opinion/what-happened-to-transparency.html. Accessed 28 May 2017.

16 "Bloomberg: Obama Cabinet Flunks Disclosure Test With 19 in 20 Ignoring Law," *Newsmax*, September 29, 2012 newsmax.com/Newsfront/Obama-Cabinet-disclosure-test/2012/09/29/id/458086/. Accessed 30 May 2017.

17 Leonard Downie Jr, "The Obama Administration and the Press," *Committee to Protect Journalists*, October 10, 2013 cpj.org/reports/2013/10/obama-and-the-press-us-leaks-surveillance-post-911.php. Accessed 30 May 2017.

18 Josh Hicks, "Sunshine Week: Transparency issues persist with Obama administration," *The Washington Post*, March 17, 2014 washingtonpost.com/news/federal-eye/wp/2014/03/17/sunshine-week-transparency-issues-persist-with-obama-administration/. Accessed 30 May 2017.

19 "World Press Freedom Index 2009," Reporters Without Borders, n.d. rsf.org/en/world-press-freedom-index-2009. Accessed 29 May 2017.

20 "The United States ranks 41st in Reporters Without Borders 2016 World Press Freedom Index," Reporters Without Borders, April 20, 2016. rsf.org/en/news/united-states-ranks-41st-reporters-without-borders-2016-world-press-freedom-index. Accessed 29 May 2017.

21 Hadas Gold, "Risen: Obama administration is greatest enemy of press freedom," *Politico*, February 17, 2015 politico.com/blogs/media/2015/02/risen-obama-administration-is-greatest-enemy-of-press-freedom-202707. Accessed 30 May 2017.

22 Jack Mirkinson, "NY Times' Jill Abramson: 'This Is The Most Secretive White House...I Have Ever Dealt With,'" *Huffington Post*, January 23, 2014 huffingtonpost.com/2014/01/23/jill-abramson-white-house-secret-ny-times_n_4653014.html. Accessed 30 May 2017.

23 Margaret Sullivan, "Obama promised transparency. But his administration is one of the most secretive," *The Washington Post*, May 24, 2016 washingtonpost.com/lifestyle/style/obama-promised-transparency-but-his-administration-is-one-of-the-most-secretive/2016/05/24/5a46caba-21c1-11e6-9e7f-57890b612299_story.html. Accessed 28 May 2017.

24 Martha Joynt Kumar, "Obama Meets the Press—on His Terms," *Real Clear Politics*, August 29, 2015 realclearpolitics.com/articles/2015/08/29/obama_meets_the_press_on_his_terms_127907.html. Accessed 28 May 2017.

25 Cheryl K. Chumley, "Obama slammed for YouTube talks with GloZell, a woman who ate cereal from tub," *Washington Times,* January 23, 2015 washingtontimes. com/news/2015/jan/23/obama-slammed-for-youtube-talks-with-glozell-a-wom/. Accessed 28 May 2017.

26 Josh Earnest, "Give Obama Credit for Government Transparency," *The New York Times,* August 31, 2016 nytimes.com/2016/08/31/opinion/give-obama-credit-for-government -transparency.html. Accessed 30 May 2017.

27 Paul Fletcher, "Less Than Transparent: Journalists Fault Obama," *The New York Times,* September 16, 2016 nytimes.com/2016/09/17/opinion/less-than-transparent-jour-nalists-fault-obama.html. Accessed 30 May 2017.

The New Black Panther Scandal Notes

1 Wikipedia Contributors, "New Black Panther Party voter intimidation case," *Wikipedia, The Free Encyclopedia,* May 9, 2017 en.wikipedia.org/wiki/New_Black_ Panther_Party_voter_intimidation_case. Accessed 6 June 2017.

2 Charlie Savage, "Racial Motive Alleged in a Justice Dept. Decision," *The New York Times,* July 7, 2010 nytimes.com/2010/07/07/us/07rights.html. Accessed 6 June 2017.

3 Jerry Seper, "EXCLUSIVE: No. 3 at Justice OK'd Panther reversal," *The Washington Times,* July 30, 2009 washingtontimes.com/news/2009/jul/30/no-3-at-justice-okd-panther-reversal/. Accessed 5 June 2017.

4 Wikipedia Contributors, "Henry Louis Gates arrest controversy," *Wikipedia, The Free Encyclopedia,* February 24, 2017 en.wikipedia.org/wiki/Henry_Louis_Gates_arrest_ controversy. Accessed 6 June 2017.

5 Jerry Seper, "'Non-responsive' Justice Dept. pressed again on Panthers case," *The Washington Times,* August 8, 2009 washingtontimes.com/news/2009/aug/08/the-us-commission-on-civil-rights-on-friday-demand/. Accessed 6 June 2017.

6 Jerry Seper, "'U.S. panel chides Holder in Panther probe," *The Washington Times,* October 1, 2009 washingtontimes.com/news/2009/oct/01/justice-department-chid-ed-in-panther-probe/. Accessed 6 June 2017.

7 Jerry Seper, "Justice Department restrains lawyers in Panther probe," *The Washington Times,* December 16, 2009 washingtontimes.com/news/2009/dec/16/ justice-restrains-lawyers-in-panther-inquiry/. Accessed 6 June 2017.

8 Jerry Seper, "Justice Dept. moves Panthers pursuer to S.C.," *The Washington Times,* December 29, 2009 washingtontimes.com/news/2009/dec/29/justice-transfers-pan-thers-pursuer-out-of-dc-offic/. Accessed 6 June 2017.

9 J. Christian Adams, "Inside the Black Panther case," *The Washington Times,* June 25, 2010 washingtontimes.com/news/2010/jun/25/inside-the-black-panther-case-anger-ignorance-and-/. Accessed 6 June 2017.

10 Ibid.

11 Ibid.

12 "Anti-white bias at the Justice Department?" *Los Angeles Times,* July 8, 2010 articles. latimes.com/2010/jul/08/opinion/la-ed-panthers-20100708. Accessed 5 June 2017.

13 Hans von Spakovsky, "Justice Must Address Lawlessness Uncovered by Christopher Coates," *The Daily Signal,* September 27, 2010 dailysignal.com/2010/09/27/justice -must-address-lawlessness-uncovered-by-christopher-coates/. Accessed 5 June 2017.

14   Jerry Markon and Krissah Thompson, "Bias led to 'gutting' of New Black Panthers case, Justice official says," *The Washington Post*, September 25, 2010 washingtonpost.com /wp-dyn/content/article/2010/09/24/AR2010092403873.html. Accessed 5 June 2017.

15   Jerry Seper, "EXCLUSIVE: No. 3 at Justice OK'd Panther reversal," *The Washington Times*, July 30, 2009 washingtontimes.com/news/2009/jul/30/no-3-at-justice-okd-panther-reversal/. Accessed 5 June 2017.

16   "Justice's Black Panther Lies," Judicial Watch, August 3, 2012 judicialwatch.org/pressroom/weekly-updates/justices-black-panther-lies/. Accessed 5 June 2017.

17   J. Christian Adams, "EDITORIAL: Panther politics," *The Washington Times*, January 19, 2010 washingtontimes.com/news/2010/jan/19/panther-politics/. Accessed 6 June 2017.

18   Jennifer Rubin, "New Black Panther Party case: The facts are in," *The Washington Post*, January 27, 2011 voices.washingtonpost.com/right-turn/2011/01/the_us_commission_on_civil.html. Accessed 6 June 2017.

19   Krissah Thompson, "Report clears Justice Department in Black Panther case," *The Washington Post*, March 29, 2011 washingtonpost.com/politics/report-clears-doj-in-black-panther-case/2011/03/29/AFY6bTzB_story.html?utm_term=.c6a2ad8859b6. Accessed 6 June 2017.

20   Andrew Alexander, "Why the silence from The Post on Black Panther Party story?" *The Washington Post*, July 18, 2010 washingtonpost.com/wp-dyn/content/article/2010/07/16/AR2010071604081.html. Accessed 5 June 2017.

21   Noel Sheppard, "Bob Schieffer: I Didn't Ask Holder About Black Panther Case Because 'I Just Didn't Know About It . . . I Was On Vacation That Week'," *Newsbusters*, July 18, 2010 newsbusters.org/blogs/nb/noel-sheppard/2010/07/18/bob-schieffer-i-didnt-ask-holder-about-black-panther-case-because. Accessed 5 June 2017.

22   Brad Wilmouth, "Olbermann Absurdly Claims to Debunk FNC's Black Panther Reporting, NBP 'Impotent Idiots Who Say Racist Things' Like Limbaugh," *Newsbusters*, July 16, 2010 newsbusters.org/blogs/nb/brad-wilmouth/2010/07/16/olbermann-absurdly-claims-debunk-fncs-black-panther-reporting-nbp. Accessed 5 June 2017.

23   Hans von Spakovsky, "New Black Panther Report Confirms: Politics Over Law at Obama Justice Department," *The Washington Post*, January 28, 2011 dailysignal.com//2011/01/28/new-black-panther-report-confirms-politics-over-law-at-obama-justice-department. Accessed 5 June 2017.

The Walpin Firing Scandal Notes

1   The Cajun Boy, "Will Obama's Firing of an Inspector General Evolve Into a Major Scandal?", *Gawker*, June 16, 2009 gawker.com/5292275/will-obamas-firing-of-an-inspector-general-evolve-into-a-major-scandal. Accessed 2 May 2017.

2   Kenneth P. Vogel, "W.H.: Sotomayor what right wants," *Politico*, June 2, 2009 politico.com/story/2009/06/wh-sotomayor-what-right-wants-023272. Accessed 2 May 2017.

3   Benjamin Sarlin, "Obama's First Scandal," *Daily Beast*, June 18, 2009 thedailybeast.com/articles/2009/06/18/obamas-first-scandal. Accessed 2 May 2017.

4   "What is AmeriCorps?" Corporation for National & Community Service, n.d. nationalservice.gov/programs/americorps/join-americorps/what-americorps. Accessed 2 May 2017.

5 Associated Press, "Feds end dispute with Sacramento's celebrity mayor," *The Mercury News*, April 9, 2009 mercurynews.com/2009/04/09/feds-end-dispute-with-sacramentos-celebrity-mayor/. Accessed 2 May 2017.

6 The Cajun Boy, "Will Obama's Firing of an Inspector General Evolve Into a Major Scandal?", *Gawker*, June 16, 2009 gawker.com/5292275/will-obamas-firing-of-an-inspector-general-evolve-into-a-major-scandal. Accessed 2 May 2017.

7 Congress.gov, *S.2324 - Inspector General Reform Act of 2008*, n.d. congress.gov/bill/110th-congress/senate-bill/2324/cosponsors?q=%7B%22search%22%3A%5B%22inspector+general+reform+act+2008%22%5D%7D&r=5. Accessed 2 May 2017.

8 Associated Press, "FBI investigates Sacramento mayor's nonprofit," *The San Diego Union-Tribune*, June 17, 2009 sandiegouniontribune.com/sdut-ca-sacramento-mayor-061709-2009jun17-story.html. Accessed 2 May 2017.

9 "Fired Inspector General Gerald Walpin Responds to White House," *Fox News*, June 18, 2009 foxnews.com/story/2009/06/18/fired-inspector-general-gerald-walpin-responds-to-white-house.html. Accessed 2 May 2017.

10 Ed Morrissey, "Obama WH scrambled for story to smear Walpin," *Hot Air*, November 23, 2009 hotair.com/archives/2009/11/23/obama-wh-scrambled-for-story-to-smear-walpin/. Accessed 2 May 2017.

11 "The Firing of the Inspector General for The Corporation for National and Community Service," House Committee on Oversight and Government Reform, November 20, 2009 oversight.house.gov/wp-content/uploads/2012/01/11-20-09-The-Firing-of-the-Inspector-General-for-The-Corporation-for-National-and-Community-Service.pdf. Accessed 2 May 2017.

12 "Update and Supplement to The Initial Report: The Firing of The Inspector General for the Corporation for National and Community Service," House Committee on Oversight and Government Reform, March 2, 2010 oversight.house.gov/report/update-and-supplement-to-the-initial-report-the-firing-of-the-inspector-general-for-the-corporation-for-national-and-community-service/. Accessed 2 May 2017.

13 Brad Wilmouth, "Media Ignore Further Questions Over Obama-Fired Inspector Gen Walpin," *Newsbusters*, June 29, 2009 newsbusters.org/blogs/nb/brad-wilmouth/2009/06/29/media-ignore-further-questions-over-obama-fired-inspector-gen. Accessed 2 May 2017.

14 Brad Wilmouth, "Brokaw Touts Corrupt Obama Friend/Mayor Kevin Johnson, Skips Misuse of AmeriCorps Funds," *Newsbusters*, December 25, 2009 newsbusters.org/blogs/nb/brad-wilmouth/2009/12/25/brokaw-touts-corrupt-obama-friendmayor-kevin-johnson-skips-misuse. Accessed 2 May 2017.

The Sestak Job Offer Scandal Notes

1 Stephan Dinan, "Obama admin. sent taxpayer money to campaign to oust Netanyahu," *The Washington Times*, July 12, 2016 washingtontimes.com/news/2016/jul/12/obama-admin-sent-taxpayer-money-oust-netanyahu/. Accessed 8 April 2017.

2 Raymond Hernandez and Jeff Zeleny, "Paterson Says He Will Run, Rejecting Call From Obama," *The New York Times*, September 19, 2009 nytimes.com/2009/09/20/nyregion/20paterson.html. Accessed 6 April 2017.

3   Edward McClelland, "Can Dems hold Obama's old Senate seat?" *Salon*, January 30, 2010 salon.com/2010/01/30/illinois_senate_race/. Accessed 6 April 2017.

4   Wikipedia Contributors, "Arlen Specter," *Wikipedia, The Free Encyclopedia*, March 27, 2017 en.wikipedia.org/wiki/Arlen_Specter. Accessed 6 April 2017.

5   Carl Hulse, "Specter Switches Parties," *The New York Times*, April 28, 2009 thecaucus. blogs.nytimes.com/2009/04/28/specter-will-run-as-a-democrat-in-2010/. Accessed 6 April 2017.

6   Jeffrey Lord, "White House Accused of Federal Crime in Specter, Bennet Races," *The American Spectator*, February 22, 2010 spectator.org/40058_white-house-accused-federal-crime-specter-bennet-races/. Accessed 6 April 2017.

7   Fred Lucas, "White House Spokesman Gibbs Has Never Confirmed or Denied Sestak's Claim That He Was Offered Administration Job Not to Run Against Specter," *CNS News*, March 24, 2010 cnsnews.com/news/article/white-house-spokesman-gibbs-has-never-confirmed-or-denied-sestak-s-claim-he-was-offered. Accessed 6 April 2017.

8   Brian Montopoli, "GOP Lawmaker Darrell Issa Poised to Call for Special Prosecutor to Investigate White House," *CBS News*, March 20, 2010 cbsnews.com/news/gop-lawmaker-darrell-issa-poised-to-call-for-special-prosecutor-to-investigate-white-house/. Accessed 6 April 2017.

9   Jake Sherman and John Bresnahan, "DoJ nixes Sestak special counsel," *Politico*, May 24, 2010 politico.com/story/2010/05/doj-nixes-sestak-special-counsel-037713. Accessed 6 April 2017.

10 Mike Riggs, "Justice Department declines to appoint independent counsel for Sestak case," *The Daily Caller*, May 25, 2010 dailycaller.com/2010/05/25/justice-department-declines-to-appoint-independent-counsel-for-sestak-case/. Accessed 6 April 2017.

11 David Corn, "The First Obama Scandal?" *Mother Jones*, May 27, 2010 motherjones. com/politics/2010/05/obama-sestak-jobsgate. Accessed 6 April 2017.

12 Steven Thomma, "White House: Appointment offer to Sestak was proper," *McClatchy*, May 28, 2010 mcclatchydc.com/news/politics-government/article24584038.html. Accessed 6 April 2017.

13 Ibid.

14 Brian Montopoli, "GOP Calls for FBI Investigation in Sestak Case," *CBS News*, May 28, 2010 cbsnews.com/news/gop-calls-for-fbi-investigation-in-sestak-case/. Accessed 6 April 2017.

15 Tim Graham, "Media Reality Check: Team Obama's Grubby Federal Job-Dangling Is Not News to ABC, CBS, and NBC," *Newsbusters*, June 10, 2010 mrc.org/media-reality-check/team-obamas-grubby-federal-job-dangling-not-news. Accessed 6 April 2017.

16 Ibid.

17 "Judicial Watch Statement on Sestak Scandal," Judicial Watch, May 27, 2010 judicialwatch.org/press-room/press-releases/judicial-watch-statement-sestak-scandal/. Accessed 6 April 2017.

The Obamacare Fraud Notes

1   Stephen Dinan, "EXCLUSIVE: Cantor: Obama's not met with GOP leaders since May," *The Washington Times*, October 1, 2009 washingtontimes.com/news/2009/oct/1/cantor-obama-muted-gop-voices-on-health-care/. Accessed 6 July 2017.

2   Chip Reid, "Obama Reneges on Health Care Transparency," *CBS News*, January 6, 2010 cbsnews.com/news/obama-reneges-on-health-care-transparency/. Accessed 5 July 2017.

3   "Abuse of Power," *The Wall Street Journal*, March 3, 2010 wsj.com/articles/SB10001424052748704625004575089362731862750. Accessed 5 July 2017.

4   Steven Ertelt, "In Deal With Stupak, White House Announces Executive Order on Abortion," *Life News*, September 4, 2012 lifenews.com/2012/09/04/stupak-admits-obama-violated-his-executive-order-on-obamacare-abortion/. Accessed 6 July 2017

5   Ashley McGuire, "Why some Catholics think Obama is master of deception," *CNN*, December 30, 2013 cnn.com/2013/12/30/opinion/catholics-obamacare-opinion/index.html. Accessed 6 July 2017.

6   "Public Approval of Health Care Law," *Real Clear Politics*, n.d. realclearpolitics.com/epolls/other/obama_and_democrats_health_care_plan-1130.html. Accessed 6 July 2017.

7   Avik Roy, "White House To Delay Obamacare's Employer Mandate Until 2015; Far-Reaching Implications For The Private Health Insurance Market," *Forbes*, July 2, 2013 forbes.com/sites/theapothecary/2013/07/02/white-house-to-delay-obamacares-employer-mandate-until-2015-far-reaching-implications-for-the-private-health-insurance-market/#e56f98f375d0. Accessed 5 July 2017.

8   Stephan Dinan, "Obamacare has been amended or delayed 19 times: study," *The Washington Times*, September 11, 2013 washingtontimes.com/news/2013/sep/11/study-obamacare-has-been-amended-delayed-19-times/. Accessed 5 July 2017.

9   Grace Marie Turner, "70 Changes That Make Obamacare A Very Different Law Than Congress Passed," *Forbes*, January 26, 2016 forbes.com/sites/gracemarieturner/2016/01/26/obamacare-70-changes-make-it-a-very-different-law-than-congress-passed/#3dd234526c4d. Accessed 5 July 2017.

10 Elise Viebeck, "New O-Care delay to help midterm Dems," *The Hill*, March 3, 2014 thehill.com/policy/healthcare/199784-new-obamacare-delay-to-help-midterm-dems. Accessed 5 July 2017.

11 Devin Dwyer, "Memo Reveals Only 6 People Signed Up for Obamacare on First Day," *ABC News*, October 31, 2013 abcnews.go.com/blogs/politics/2013/10/memo-reveals-only-6-people-signed-up-for-obamacare-on-first-day/. Accessed 5 July 2017.

12 "Less Than Half of One Percent of HealthCare.gov Visitors Complete Obamacare Enrollment," *Breitbart*, October 16, 2013 breitbart.com/Big-Government/2013/10/16/one-half-one-percent-obamacare-enrollment. Accessed 5 July 2017.

13 Joe Johns and Z. Byron Wolf, "First on CNN: Obama administration warned about health care website," *CNN*, October 30, 2013 cnn.com/2013/10/29/politics/obamacare-warning/. Accessed 5 July 2017.

14 Sharyl Attkisson, "High security risk found after HealthCare.gov launch," *CBS News*, December 20, 2013 cbsnews.com/news/high-security-risks-found-after-healthcaregov-launch/. Accessed 5 July 2017.

15 Richard Pollack, "Feds reviewed only one bid for Obamacare website design," *Washington Examiner*, October 14, 2013 washingtonexaminer.com/feds-reviewed-only-one-bid-for-obamacare-website-design/article/2537194. Accessed 7 July 2017.

16 Jennifer G. Hickey, "Obamacare Website Company Had Ties to Obama Fundraising, Michelle Obama," *Newsmax*, October 27, 2013 newsmax.com/Newsfront/cgi-federal-scrutiny-obama-fundraising/2013/10/27/id/533310/. Accessed 13 July 2017.

17 "Victory Lap: Obama Says Health Care Law Is 'Here to Stay,'" *NBC News*, April 1, 2014 nbcnews.com/storyline/obamacare-deadline/victory-lap-obama-says-health-care-law-here-stay-n69091. Accessed 5 July 2017.

18 Sarah Kliff, "Who counts as an Obamacare enrollee? The Obama administration settles on a definition.," *The Washington Post*, November 11, 2013 washingtonpost.com/news/wonk/wp/2013/11/11/who-counts-as-an-obamacare-enrollee-the-obama-administration-settles-on-a-definition/. Accessed 5 July 2017.

19 Guy Benson, "Confirmed: Many of Obamacare's 'Eight Million Enrollments' are Duplicates," *Townhall*, May 7, 2017 townhall.com/tipsheet/guybenson/2014/05/07/confirmed-many-of-obamacares-8-million-enrollees-are-duplicates-n1834786. Accessed 5 July 2017.

20 Avik Roy, "RAND Comes Clean: Obamacare's Exchanges Enrolled Only 1.4 Million Previously Uninsured Individuals," *Forbes*, April 9, 2014 forbes.com/sites/theapothecary/2014/04/09/rand-comes-clean-obamacares-exchanges-enrolled-only-1-4-million-previously-uninsured-individuals/#72e12c9d3b86. Accessed 5 July 2017.

21 Avik Roy, "New McKinsey Survey: 74% Of Obamacare Sign-Ups Were Previously Insured," *Forbes*, May 10, 2014 forbes.com/sites/theapothecary/2014/05/10/new-mckinsey-survey-74-of-obamacare-sign-ups-were-previously-insured/#288a17297a92. Accessed 5 July 2017.

22 Angie Drobnic Holan, "Lie of the Year: 'If you like your health care plan, you can keep it,'" *PolitiFact*, December 12, 2013 politifact.com/truth-o-meter/article/2013/dec/12/lie-year-if-you-like-your-health-care-plan-keep-it/. Accessed 6 July 2017.

23 Colleen McCain Nelson, Peter Nicholas and Carol E. Lee, "Aides Debated Obama Health-Care Coverage Promise," *The Wall Street Journal*, November 2, 2013 wsj.com/articles/no-headline-available-1383336294. Accessed 6 July 2017.

24 Avik Roy, "Obama Officials In 2010: 93 Million Americans Will Be Unable To Keep Their Health Plans Under Obamacare," *Forbes*, October 31, 2013 forbes.com/sites/theapothecary/2013/10/31/obama-officials-in-2010-93-million-americans-will-be-unable-to-keep-their-health-plans-under-obamacare/. Accessed 6 July 2017.

25 Jeffrey Anderson, "CBO Misses Its Obamacare Projection by 24 Million People," *The Weekly Standard*, March 28, 2016 weeklystandard.com/cbo-misses-its-obamacare-projection-by-24-million-people/article/2001732. Accessed 6 July 2017.

26 Alexis Levinson, "Poll: If voters had known they'd lose insurance, Romney would have won," *The Daily Caller*, November 22, 2013 dailycaller.com/2013/11/22/poll-if-voters-had-known-theyd-lose-insurance-romney-would-have-won/. Accessed 6 July 2017.

27 Ali Meyer, "19th Obamacare Co-Op Folds, Leaving Only 4 Operating in 2018," *The Washington Free Beacon*, June 27, 2017 freebeacon.com/issues/19th-obamacare-co-op-folds-leaving-4-operating-2018/. Accessed 6 July 2017.

28 Nick Clements, "Obamacare Premiums Increase 25%: Is The 'Death Spiral' Here?" *Forbes*, October 25, 2016 forbes.com/sites/nickclements/2016/10/25/obamacare-premiums-increase-25-is-the-death-spiral-here/. Accessed 6 July 2017.

29 Robert Wilde, "Brent Bozell: ABC, CBS, NBC Nightly News Engage in Obamacare 'Cover-Up,'" *Breitbart*, March 29, 2014 breitbart.com/big-journalism/2014/03/29/cover-up-over-83-nights-abc-cbs-and-nbc-nightly-news-spent-combined-31-minutes-on-obamacare/. Accessed 6 July 2017.

30 Becket Adams, "Major media mostly giving Gruber 'stupidity' videos the silent treatment," *Washington Examiner*, November 18, 2014 washingtonexaminer.com/major-media-mostly-giving-gruber-stupidity-videos-the-silent-treatment/article/2556330. Accessed 6 July 2017.

The BP Oil Spill Response and Cover-Up Notes

1 John Broder, "Oil Spill Reports Fault Obama Administration," *The New York Times*, October 6, 2010 nytimes.com/2010/10/07/science/earth/07spill.html. Accessed 10 June 2017.

2 David Freddoso, "Later today: Damning report on oil spill response," *Washington Examiner*, June 30, 2010 washingtonexaminer.com/later-today-damning-report-on-oil-spill-response/article/1892. Accessed 10 June 2017.

3 John Broder, "Oil Spill Reports Fault Obama Administration," *The New York Times*, October 6, 2010 nytimes.com/2010/10/07/science/earth/07spill.html. Accessed 10 June 2017.

4 Ben Geman, "Spill panel hits administration on oil flow data," *The Hill*, October 6, 2010 thehill.com/policy/energy-environment/122971-spill-panel-hits-white-house-on-oil-flow-data-says-worst-case-figures-may-have-been-blocked. Accessed 10 June 2017.

5 Kate Sheppard, "The Feds' Oil-Spill Number Games," *Mother Jones*, September 17, 2010 motherjones.com/politics/2010/09/watchdogs-file-suit-govt-spill-info. Accessed 10 June 2017.

6 Kate Sheppard, "Report: White House Pressured Scientists to Underestimate BP Spill Size," *Mother Jones*, January 23, 2012 motherjones.com/politics/2012/01/report-white-house-pressured-scientists-underestimate-bp-spill-size/. Accessed 10 June 2017.

7 Dan Berman, "IG: W.H. skewed drill-ban report," *Politico*, November 9, 2010 politico.com/story/2010/11/ig-wh-skewed-drill-ban-report-044921. Accessed 10 June 2017.

8 Lawrence Solomon, "Avertible catastrophe," *Financial Post*, June 25, 2010 business.financialpost.com/fp-comment/lawrence-solomon-avertible-catastrophe. Accessed 10 June 2017.

9 Alan Silverleib, "The Gulf spill: America's worst environmental disaster?," *Financial Post*, August 10, 2010 cnn.com/2010/US/08/05/gulf.worst.disaster/index.html. Accessed 10 June 2017.

10 Ken Shepherd, "WaPo Buries, NYT Print Edition Ignores Govt. Investigation Finding Obama White House Edited BP Oil Spill Report," *Newsbusters*, November 11, 2010 newsbusters.org/blogs/nb/ken-shepherd/2010/11/11/wapo-buries-nyt-print-edition-ignores-govt-investigation-finding. Accessed 10 June 2017.

11 Rachel Burnett, "MSNBC's Joe Scarborough Defended Obama Over Oil Spill, Slams GOP's Barton," *Newsbusters*, June 24, 2010 newsbusters.org/blogs/nb/rachel-burnett/2010/06/24/msnbcs-joe-scarborough-defended-obama-over-oil-spill-slams-gops. Accessed 10 June 2017.

12 Rachel Burnett, "Matthews: Canning McChrystal Helps Obama's Oil Spill Image," *Newsbusters*, June 23, 2010 bash.newsbusters.org/blogs/nb/rachel-burnett/2010/06/23/matthews-canning-mcchrystal-helps-obamas-oil-spill-image. Accessed 10 June 2017.

13 Brent Baker, "Brian Williams Treats Obama as Oracle of Wisdom, Wonders: 'How Are You Thinking About Your Job These Days?'," *Newsbusters*, August 29, 2010 newsbusters.org/blogs/nb/brent-baker/2010/08/29/brian-williams-treats-obama-oracle-wisdom-wonders-how-are-you. Accessed 10 June 2017.

14 Brent Baker, "NBC's Williams Blames Obama's Plummeting Approval on Getting Dragged Into Gulf Oil Leak," *Newsbusters*, June 23, 2010 newsbusters.org/blogs/nb/brent-baker/2010/06/23/nbcs-williams-blames-obamas-plummeting-approval-getting-dragged-gulf. Accessed 10 June 2017.

The Slush Fund Scandal Notes

1 Neil Munro, "With landmark lawsuit, Barack Obama pushed banks to give subprime loans to Chicago's African-Americans," *The Daily Caller*, September 3, 2012 dailycaller.com/2012/09/03/with-landmark-lawsuit-barack-obama-pushed-banks-to-give-subprime-loans-to-chicagos-african-americans/. Accessed 8 June 2017.

2 "Obama's Remarks on the Economy," *The New York Times*, April 14, 2009 nytimes.com/2009/04/14/us/politics/14obama-text.html. Accessed 8 June 2017.

3 "Financial Fraud Enforcement Task Force (FFETF)," United States Department of the Treasury, n.d. fincen.gov/financial-fraud-enforcement-task-force-ffetf. Accessed 8 June 2017.

4 George F. Will, "The Justice Department's bank settlement slush fund," *The Washington Post*, August 31, 2016 washingtonpost.com/opinions/the-justice-departments-bank-settlement-slush-fund/2016/08/31/a3b4da7a-6eec-11e6-8365-b19e428a975e_story.html. Accessed 8 June 2017.

5 Byron York, "Justice Department Steers Money to Favored Groups," *Washington Examiner*, August 5, 2010 washingtonexaminer.com/justice-department-steers-money-to-favored-groups/article/11539. Accessed 8 June 2017.

6 Ed Morrissey, "Change: DoJ No Longer Sharing Lawsuit Payouts With Activist Groups," *Hot Air*, June 7, 2017 hotair.com/archives/2017/06/07/change-doj-no-longer-sharing-lawsuit-payouts-activist-groups/. Accessed 8 June 2017.

7 Ibid.

8 Melissa Jacobs, "GOP wants to eliminate shadowy DOJ slush fund bankrolling leftist groups," *Fox News*, March 1, 2017 foxnews.com/politics/2017/03/01/gop-wants-to-eliminate-shadowy-doj-slush-fund-bankrolling-leftist-groups.html. 8 June 2017.

9 Theodore H. Frank, "Oversight of the Justice Department's Mortgage Lending Settlements," House Judiciary Committee, February 12, 2015 judiciary.house.gov/wp-content/uploads/2016/02/frank-testimony-House-justice-2015-February-12.pdf. Accessed 8 June 2017.

10　Sean Higgins, "Obama's big bank 'slush fund," *Washington Examiner*, January 18, 2016 washingtonexaminer.com/obamas-big-bank-slush-fund/article/2580431. Accessed 8 June 2017.

11　Ibid.

12　Ian Tuttle, "Good Riddance to the Obama DOJ's Scandalous Settlement 'Slush Fund' Policy," *National Review*, June 7, 2017 nationalreview.com/corner/448376/trump-jus-tice-department-settlement-slush-fund. Accessed 8 June 2017.

13　Anna Giaritelli, "OMB: Obama would veto GOP's anti-slush fund bill," *Washington Examiner*, September 6, 2016 washingtonexaminer.com/omb-obama-would-veto-gops-anti-slush-fund-bill/article/2601123. Accessed 8 June 2017.

14　"DOJ ends Holder-era 'slush fund' payouts to outside groups," *Fox News*, June 7, 2017 foxnews.com/politics/2017/06/07/doj-ends-holder-era-slush-fund-payouts-to-out-side-groups.html. Accessed 8 June 2017.

15　Ibid.

16　Aly Nielsen, "Hey, Journalists: Obama Policy Diverted Settlement Cash to Soros-Funded Groups," *Newsbusters*, June 19, 2017 newsbusters.org/blogs/business /aly-nielsen/2017/06/19/obama-policy-diverted-settlement-cash-soros-fund-ed-groups. Accessed 29 July 2017.

17　Tatiana Schlossberg and Hiroko Tabuchi, "Settlements for Company Sins Can No Longer Aid Other Projects, Sessions Says," *The New York Times*, June 9, 2017 nytimes. com/2017/06/09/us/politics/settlements-sessions-attorney-general.html. Accessed 10 June 2017.

Fast and Furious Notes

1　Ken Ellingwood, Richard A. Serrano and Tracy Wilkinson, "Mexico Still Waiting for Answers on Fast and Furious Gun Program," *Los Angeles Times*, September 19, 2011, articles.latimes.com/2011/sep/19/world/la-fg-mexico-fast-furious-20110920. Accessed 2 July 2017.

2　Katie Pavlich, "Barack Obama's Bloodiest Scandal," *Townhall*, April 16, 2012 townhall. com/columnists/katiepavlich/2012/04/16/opening-the-flood-gates-on-fast-and-furi-ous-n1108425. Accessed 2 July 2017.

3　Pavlich, Katie. *Fast And Furious: Barack Obama's Bloodiest Scandal and Its Shameless Cover-Up*. Washington DC: Regnery, 2012.

4　Jake Tapper, "President Obama Falsely Claims Fast and Furious Program 'Begun Under the Previous Administration," *ABC News*, September 21, 2012 abcnews. go.com/blogs/politics/2012/09/president-obama-falsely-claims-fast-and-furi-ous-program-begun-under-the-previous-administration/. Accessed 2 July 2017.

5　Pavlich, Katie. *Fast And Furious: Barack Obama's Bloodiest Scandal and Its Shameless Cover-Up*. Washington DC: Regnery, 2012.

6　Ibid.

7　Sharyl Attkisson, "Documents: ATF used "Fast and Furious" to make the case for gun regulations," *CBS News*, December 7, 2011 cbsnews.com/news/documents-atf-used-fast-and-furious-to-make-the-case-for-gun-regulations/. Accessed 2 July 2017.

8 "Grassley on Operation Fast and Furious, Six Years Later," Chuck Grassley: United States Senator for Iowa, June 7, 2017 grassley.senate.gov/news/news-releases/grassley-operation-fast-and-furious-six-years-later. Accessed 2 July 2017.

9 Sharyl Attkisson, "8 Times Obama Says He Was Way Out of the Loop," Sharyl Attkisson, March 9, 2015 sharylattkisson.com/8-times-obama-says-he-was-way-out-of-the-loop/. Accessed 2 July 2017.

10 Sharyl Attkisson, "ATF Fast and Furious: New documents show Attorney General Eric Holder was briefed in July 2010," *CBS News*, October 2, 2011 cbsnews.com/news/atf-fast-and-furious-new-documents-show-attorney-general-eric-holder-was-briefed-in-july-2010/. Accessed 2 July 2017.

11 Charlie Savage, "Report by House Democrats Absolves Administration in Gun Trafficking Case," *The New York Times*, January 31, 2012 nytimes.com/2012/01/31/us/politics/operation-fast-and-furious-report-by-democrats-clears-obama-administration.html. Accessed 2 July 2017.

12 Katie Pavlich, "Democrats Fully Engaged in Fast and Furious Coverup," *Townhall*, January 31, 2012 townhall.com/tipsheet/katiepavlich/2012/01/31/democrats-fully-engaged-in-fast-and-furious-coverup-n662684. Accessed 2 July 2017.

13 "Judicial Watch Statement on Release of Enormous Trove of DOJ Fast and Furious Documents," Judicial Watch, November 20, 2014 judicialwatch.org/press-room/press-releases/judicial-watch-statement-release-enormous-trove-doj-fast-furious-documents/. Accessed 2 July 2017.

14 "CBS Reporter Claims White House Officials Screamed And Cursed At Her," *Huffington Post*, October 5, 2011 huffingtonpost.com/2011/10/05/cbs-white-house-screamed_n_995794.html?ncid=edlinkusaolp00000003. Accessed 2 July 2017.

15 Matthew Boyle, "Grassley: Holder refusing to provide 11 witnesses for Fast and Furious interviews," *The Daily Caller*, November 10, 2011 dailycaller.com/2011/11/10/grassley-holder-refusing-to-provide-11-witnesses-for-fast-and-furious-interviews/comment-page-1/. Accessed 2 July 2017.

16 "Holder: No cover-up in 'Fast and Furious,' no effort to hide details of the operation," *Fox News*, February 2, 2012 foxnews.com/politics/2012/02/02/holder-says-no-one-punished-yet-during-testimony-on-controversial-fast-and.html. Accessed 2 July 2017.

17 Grace Wyler, "Obama Asserts Executive Privilege Over The Department Of Justice's Gun Running Scandal," *Business Insider*, June 20, 2012 businessinsider.com/justice-department-obama-executive-privilege-fast-and-furious-contempt-eric-holder-2012-6. Accessed 2 July 2017.

18 William Douglas and Erika Bolstad, "House holds Holder in contempt over Fast and Furious; Democrats charge racism," *McClatchy*, June 28, 2012 mcclatchydc.com/news/politics-government/congress/article24732121.html. Accessed 2 July 2017.

19 Pavlich, Katie. *Fast And Furious: Barack Obama's Bloodiest Scandal and Its Shameless Cover-Up*. Washington DC: Regnery, 2012.

20 "Inspector General: DOJ misled Congress about Fast and Furious," *Washington Examiner*, September 19, 2012 washingtonexaminer.com/inspector-general-doj-misled-congress-about-fast-and-furious/article/2508476. Accessed 2 July 2017.

21 "A Review of ATF's Operation Fast and Furious and Related Matters," U.S. Department of Justice Office of the Inspector General, September 2012 oig.justice.gov/reports/2012/s1209.pdf. Accessed 2 July 2017.

22 Pavlich, Katie. *Fast And Furious: Barack Obama's Bloodiest Scandal and Its Shameless Cover-Up*. Washington DC: Regnery, 2012.

23 David A. Graham, "A White House Concession on Fast and Furious," *The Atlantic*, April 8, 2016 theatlantic.com/politics/archive/2016/04/fast-and-furious-gunwalking-white-house/477612/. Accessed 2 July 2017.

24 Joint Staff, "Fast and Furious: Obstruction of Congress by the Department of Justice," *House Committee on Oversight and Government Reform*, June 7, 2017 oversight.house.gov/wp-content/uploads/2017/06/FINAL_REPORT_2017.pdf. Accessed 2 July 2017.

25 Ibid.

26 "Committee Releases Fast & Furious Report: Obstruction Of Congress By The Department Of Justice," House Committee on Oversight and Government Reform, June 7, 2017 oversight.house.gov/report/committee-releases-fast-furious-report-obstruction-congress-department-justice/. Accessed 2 July 2017.

27 "Committee Releases Fast & Furious Report: Obstruction Of Congress By The Department Of Justice," House Committee on Oversight and Government Reform, June 7, 2017 oversight.house.gov/report/committee-releases-fast-furious-report-obstruction-congress-department-justice/. Accessed 2 July 2017.

28 Dan Gainor, "Media Coverage of 'Fast and Furious' Scandal Rare and Spurious," *Newsbusters*, June 14, 2012 newsbusters.org/blogs/culture/dan-gainor/2012/06/14/media-coverage-fast-and-furious-scandal-rare-and-spurious. Accessed 2 July 2017.

29 "Attkisson: CBS Brass Killed My Investigative Reporting," *The Washington Free Beacon*, April 11, 2014 freebeacon.com/issues/attkisson-cbs-brass-killed-my-investigative-reporting/. Accessed 2 July 2017.

30 Pavlich, Katie. *Fast And Furious: Barack Obama's Bloodiest Scandal and Its Shameless Cover-Up*. Washington DC: Regnery, 2012.

31 Kyle Drennen, "MSNBC Panel: Fast & Furious Scandal Bad for GOP, Good for Obama," *Newsbusters*, June 20, 2012 newsbusters.org/blogs/nb/kyle-drennen/2012/06/20/msnbc-panel-fast-furious-scandal-bad-gop-good-obama. Accessed 2 July 2017.

32 Ray Wasler, "Operation Fast and Furious Has Harmed U.S.-Mexican Relations," *Daily Signal*, July 27, 2011 dailysignal.com/2011/07/27/operation-fast-and-furious-has-harmed-u-s-mexican-relations/. Accessed 2 July 2017.

The Solyndra Scandal Notes

1 Mark Tapscott, "Solyndra bankruptcy exposes Obama's green jobs," *Washington Examiner*, August 31, 2011 washingtonexaminer.com/solyndra-bankruptcy-exposes-obamas-green-jobs/article/811666. Accessed 26 June 2017.

2 Ibid.

3 Ronnie Green and Matthew Mosk, "Obama administration agreed to Solyndra loan days after insiders foresaw firm's failure," Center for Public Integrity, September 14, 2011 publicintegrity.org/2011/09/14/6465/obama-administration-agreed-solyndra-loan-days-after-insiders-foresaw-firms-failure. Accessed 26 June 2017.

4 Ibid.

5 Joe Stephens and Carol D. Leonnig, "Solyndra e-mails show Obama fundraiser discussed effort to win White House help," *The Washington Post*, November 9, 2011 washingtonpost.com/politics/solyndra-e-mails-show-obama-fundraiser-discussed-lobbying-white-house/2011/11/09/gIQAqPsq5M_story.html. Accessed 26 June 2017.

6 Peter Schweizer, "How Obama's Alternative-Energy Programs Became Green Graft," *Newsweek*, November 12, 2011 newsweek.com/how-obamas-alternative-energy-programs-became-green-graft-66373. Accessed 26 June 2017.

7 Amanda Carey, "Solyndra officials made numerous trips to the White House, logs show," *The Daily Caller*, September 8, 2011 dailycaller.com/2011/09/08/solyndra-officials-made-numerous-trips-to-the-white-house-logs-show/. Accessed 26 June 2017.

8 Matthew Mosk and Brian Ross, "Solyndra: Blame It On Bush, Say Obama Officials," *ABC News*, September 14, 2011 abcnews.go.com/Blotter/solyndra-blame-bush-obama-officials/story?id=14513389. Accessed 26 June 2017.

9 Carol D. Leonnig and Juliet Eilperin, "Amid Solyndra crisis, head of federal loan program resigns," *The Washington Post*, October 6, 2011 washingtonpost.com/national/health-science/jonathan-silver-head-of-doe-loan-guarantee-program-to-step-down/2011/10/06/gIQAzQmlQL_story.html. Accessed 26 June 2017.

10 Carol D. Leonnig and Joe Stephens, "Solyndra: Energy Dept. pushed firm to keep layoffs quiet until after Election Day," *The Washington Post*, November 15, 2011 washingtonpost.com/politics/solyndra-department-of-energy-pushed-hard-for-company-not-to-announce-layoffs-until-after-2010-mid-term-elections/2011/11/15/gIQA-2AriON_story.html. Accessed 26 June 2017.

11 Carol D. Leonnig, "Top leaders of Solyndra solar panel company repeatedly misled federal officials, investigation finds," *The Washington Post*, August 26, 2015 washingtonpost.com/news/federal-eye/wp/2015/08/26/top-leaders-of-solyndra-solar-panel-company-repeatedly-misled-federal-officials-investigation-finds/?utm_term=.512a2a09386e. Accessed 26 June 2017.

12 Scott Whitlock, "CBS Exposes 'the New Solyndras'; Will ABC and NBC Cover?" *Media Research Center*, January 13, 2012 archive2.mrc.org/bias-alerts/cbs-exposes-new-solyndras-will-abc-and-nbc-cover. Accessed 26 June 2017.

13 Michael Bastasch, "As many as 50 Obama-backed green energy companies bankrupt or troubled," *The Daily Caller*, October 30, 2012 dailycaller.com/2012/10/30/as-many-as-fifty-obama-backed-green-energy-companies-bankrupt-or-troubled/. Accessed 26 June 2017.

14 Joel Gehrke, "Emails show Obama admin used DOE loan money to help Harry Reid's 2010 campaign," *Washington Examiner*, October 31, 2012 washingtonexaminer.com/emails-show-obama-admin-used-doe-loan-money-to-help-harry-reids-2010-campaign/article/2512249. Accessed 26 June 2017.

15 Joe Stephens and Carol D. Leonnig, "Solyndra e-mails show Obama fundraiser discussed effort to win White House help," *The Washington Post*, November 9, 2011 washingtonpost.com/politics/solyndra-e-mails-show-obama-fundraiser-discussed-lobbying-white-house/2011/11/09/gIQAqPsq5M_story.html. Accessed 26 June 2017.

16 Rich Lowry, "Obama's Enron," *National Review*, September 2, 2011 nationalreview.com/article/276119/obamas-enron-rich-lowry. Accessed 26 June 2017.

17 Geoffrey Dickens, "The Seven Most Undercovered Obama Scandals," *Newsbusters*, January 16, 2017 newsbusters.org/blogs/nb/geoffrey-dickens/2017/01/16/seven-most-undercovered-obama-scandals. Accessed 26 June 2017.

18 Ken Shepherd, "Nets Ignore Latest Solyndra News: Obama Administration Requested Postponing Layoffs Until After 2010 Midterm Election," *Newsbusters*, November 16, 2011 newsbusters.org/blogs/nb/ken-shepherd/2011/11/16/nets-ignore-latest-solyndra-news-obama-administration-requested. Accessed 26 June 2017.

The GSA Scandal Notes

1 Lisa Rein, "GSA chief resigns amid reports of excessive spending," *The Washington Post*, April 2, 2012 washingtonpost.com/politics/gsa-chief-resigns-amid-reports-of-excessive-spending/2012/04/02/gIQABLNNrS_story.html. Accessed 1 July 2017.

2 MJ Lee, "Spook video adds to GSA woes," *Politico*, April 6, 2012 politico.com/story/2012/04/spoof-video-adds-to-gsa-woes-074901. Accessed 1 July 2017.

3 Lisa Rein, "GSA chief resigns amid reports of excessive spending," *The Washington Post*, April 2, 2012 washingtonpost.com/politics/gsa-chief-resigns-amid-reports-of-excessive-spending/2012/04/02/gIQABLNNrS_story.html. Accessed 1 July 2017.

4 Gerry Shields, "Tub of trouble for GSA honcho over Vegas ba$h," *New York Post*, April 17, 2012 nypost.com/2012/04/17/tub-of-trouble-for-gsa-honcho-over-vegas-bah/. Accessed 1 July 2017.

5 John Hayward, "GSA commissioner Neely is still getting paid," *Human Events*, April 17, 2012 humanevents.com/2012/04/17/gsa-commissioner-neely-is-still-getting-paid/. Accessed 1 July 2017.

6 Timothy R. Smith, "Jeffrey Neely, who organized lavish GSA conference, leaves agency," *The Washington Post*, May 24, 2012 washingtonpost.com/politics/jeffrey-neely-who-organized-lavish-gsa-conference-leaves-agency/2012/05/24/gJQAgU5WoU_story.html. Accessed 1 July 2017.

7 Josh Gerstein, "Ex-GSA official pleads guilty," *Politico*, March 31, 2015 politico.com/blogs/under-the-radar/2015/03/ex-gsa-official-pleads-guilty-204800. Accessed 1 July 2017.

8 "Obama administration points to rise in GSA costs under Bush amid conference controversy," *Fox News*, April 7, 2012 foxnews.com/politics/2012/04/07/white-house-pushing-blame-on-bush-white-house-for-gsa-debacle.html. Accessed 1 July 2017.

9 Jake Sherman, "Obama 'apoplectic' about GSA scandal," *Politico*, April 22, 2012 politico.com/blogs/politico-now/2012/04/obama-apoplectic-about-gsa-scandal-121258. Accessed 1 July 2017.

10 Anita Kumar, "Report: 8 years of Obama vacations cost $85 million," *McClatchy*, December 28, 2016 mcclatchydc.com/news/politics-government/white-house/article123335079.html. Accessed 1 July 2017.

11 "Rep. Mica: White House knew about GSA scandal, withheld information," *CNN*, April 17, 2012 cnnpressroom.blogs.cnn.com/2012/04/17/rep-mica-white-house-knew-about-gsa-scandal-withheld-information/. Accessed 1 July 2017.

12 Tom Cohen, "Who's on first? Hearing shows GSA's dysfunction," *CNN*, April 17, 2012 cnn.com/2012/04/17/politics/gsa-hearing/index.html. Accessed 1 July 2017.

13 Darius Dixon, "Mica: W.H. knew about GSA waste," *Politico*, April 17, 2012 politico. com/story/2012/04/mica-wh-knew-about-gsa-waste-075238. Accessed 1 July 2017.

14 Stephen Dinan, "Obama operatives stripped Judicial Watch of 'media' status, over- charged for FOIA requests," *Washington Times*, September 29, 2016 washingtontimes. com/news/2016/sep/29/obama-operatives-stripped-judical-watch-of-media-s/. Accessed 1 July 2017.

15 Jim McElhatton, "Top GSA official tried to hide report on Vegas bash," *Washington Times*, June 5, 2012 washingtontimes.com/news/2012/jun/5/top-gsa-official-tried-to- hide-report-on-vegas-bas/. Accessed 1 July 2017.

16 Doug McKelway, "Documents show dozens of questionable GSA conferences, millions in bonuses," *Fox News*, July 31, 2012 foxnews.com/politics/2012/07/31/ documents-show-dozens-questionable-gsa-conferences-millions-in-bonuses.html. Accessed 1 July 2017.

17 Scott Whitlock, "What Happens in Vegas, Stays in Vegas: NBC's Today Skips Govt. Waste in Obama's GSA," *Newsbusters*, April 6, 2017 newsbusters.org/blogs/nb/ scott-whitlock/2012/04/06/what-happens-vegas-stays-vegas-nbcs-today-skips-govt- waste-obamas. Accessed 1 July 2017.

18 Scott Whitlock, "A Week and a Half Late, NBC's Today Finally Discovers Govt. 'Spending Spree' in Vegas," *Newsbusters*, April 16, 2017 newsbusters.org/blogs/nb/ scott-whitlock/2012/04/16/week-and-half-late-nbcs-today-finally-discovers-govt- spending. Accessed 1 July 2017.

19 Melanie Sloan, "GSA Scandal Exposes Waste – Of Congress' Time," Citizens for Responsibility and Ethics in Washington, April 24, 2012 citizensforethics.org/gener- al-services-administration-scandal-exposes-waste-of-congress-time-gsa/. Accessed 1 July 2017.

20 Brian Montopoli, "GSA scandal: Is Congress engaged in hearing overkill?" *CBS News*, April 18, 2012 cbsnews.com/news/gsa-scandal-is-congress-engaged-in-hearing- overkill/. Accessed 1 July 2017.

The Benghazi Attack and Cover-Up Notes

1 Rodney Hawkins, "Biden: We are better off, 'bin Laden is dead and General Motors is alive,'" *CBS News*, September 3, 2012 cbsnews.com/news/biden-we-are-better-off- bin-laden-is-dead-and-general-motors-is-alive. Accessed 29 June 2017.

2 Joshua Yasmeh, "Libya Was Hillary's War. Here's The Proof.," *Daily Wire*, February 16, 2016 dailywire.com/news/3398/libya-was-hillarys-war-heres-proof-joshua-yasmeh. Accessed 29 June 2017.

3 "What They Said, Before and After the Attack in Libya," *The New York Times*, Septem- ber 12, 2012 nytimes.com/interactive/2012/09/12/us/politics/libya-statements.html. Accessed 29 June 2017.

4 Ian Tuttle, "Hillary Clinton's Benghazi Defense: It Depends on What the Meaning of 'Lied' Is," *National Review*, November 5, 2015 nationalreview.com/article/426636/ hillary-clintons-benghazi-defense-it-depends-what-meaning-lied-ian-tuttle. Accessed 29 June 2017.

5 "Secretary of State Hillary Clinton's remarks at transfer of remains ceremony for Americans killed in Libya (Transcript)," *The Washington Post*, September 14, 2012

washingtonpost.com/politics/decision2012/secretary-of-state-hillary-clintons-remarks-at-transfer-of-remains-ceremony-for-americans-killed-in-libya-tran-script/2012/09/14/54fc64c0-fea2-11e1-8adc-499661afe377_story.html. Accessed 29 June 2017.

6   "Evolution of administration statements on Libya attack," *Fox News*, September 20, 2012 foxnews.com/politics/2012/09/20/evolution-administration-statements-on-lib-ya-attack.html. Accessed 29 June 2017.

7   "Evolution of administration statements on Libya attack," *Fox News*, September 20, 2012 foxnews.com/politics/2012/09/20/evolution-administration-statements-on-lib-ya-attack.html. Accessed 29 June 2017.

8   Madeleine Morgenstern, "U.N. Ambassador Susan Rice: 'Spontaneous' Libya Attack Was Prompted by 'Hateful & Offensive Video,'" *The Blaze*, September 16, 2012 theblaze.com/news/2012/09/16/u-n-ambassador-susan-rice-spontaneous-libya-attack-was-prompted-by-hateful-offensive-video/. Accessed 29 June 2017.

9   David Rutz, "Hannity Plays Montage of Obama Administration Members Falsely Blaming Video for Benghazi Attack," *The Washington Free Beacon,* October 23, 2015 freebeacon.com/national-security/hannity-plays-montage-of-obama-administra-tion-members-falsely-blaming-video-for-benghazi-attack/. Accessed 29 June 2017.

10   Tom Bevan, "What the President Said About Benghazi," *Real Clear Politics*, November 30, 2012 realclearpolitics.com/articles/2012/11/30/what_the_president_said_about_benghazi_116299.html. Accessed 29 June 2017.

11   Arshad Mohammed and Tabassum Zakaria, "Clinton forcefully defends handling of Benghazi attack," Reuters, January 23, 2013 reuters.com/article/us-usa-libya-clin-ton-idUSBRE90M0SM20130123. Accessed 29 June 2017.

12   Susan Cornwell and Tabassum Zakaria , "In Benghazi testimony, Petraeus says al Qaeda role known early," Reuters, November 16, 2012 reuters.com/article/us-usa-benghazi-idUSBRE8AF03L20121116. Accessed 29 June 2017.

13   "Judicial Watch: Benghazi Documents Point to White House on Misleading Talking Points," Judicial Watch, April 29, 2014 judicialwatch.org/press-room/press-releases/judicial-watch-benghazi-documents-point-white-house-misleading-talking-points/. Accessed 29 June 2017.

14   Ibid.

15   Ibid.

16   Ibid.

17   "Judicial Watch: Defense, State Department Documents Reveal Obama Admin-istration Knew that al Qaeda Terrorists Had Planned Benghazi Attack 10 Days in Advance," Judicial Watch, May 18, 2015 judicialwatch.org/press-room/press-releases/judicial-watch-defense-state-department-documents-reveal-obama-administration-knew-that-al-qaeda-terrorists-had-planned-benghazi-attack-10-days-in-advance/. Accessed 29 June 2017.

18   "Judicial Watch: Newly Released Documents Confirm White House Officials Set Hillary Clinton's Benghazi Response," Judicial Watch, June 25, 2015 judicialwatch.org/press-room/press-releases/judicial-watch-newly-released-documents-confirm-white-house-officials-set-hillary-clintons-benghazi-response/. Accessed 29 June 2017.

19   Stephen Hayes, "Hillary Told Chelsea Truth About Benghazi, But Not American People," *The Weekly Standard*, October 22, 2015 weeklystandard.com/hillary-told

-chelsea-truth-about-benghazi-but-not-american-people/article/1051078. Accessed 29 June 2017.

20 Marina Koren, "We Now Know Who's to Blame for Benghazi," *National Journal*, January 15, 2014 nationaljournal.com/congress/we-now-know-who-s-to-blame-for-benghazi-20140115. Accessed 29 June 2017.

21 Jake Tapper, "Documents Back up Claims of Requests Requests for Greater Security in Benghazi," *ABC News*, October 19, 2012 abcnews.go.com/blogs/politics/2012/10/documents-back-up-claims-of-requests-for-greater-security-in-benghazi/. Accessed 29 June 2017.

22 Arshad Mohammed and Tabassum Zakaria, "Clinton Forcefully Defends Handling of Benghazi Attack," Reuters, January 23, 2013 reuters.com/article/2013/01/23/us-usa-libya-clinton-idUSBRE90M0SM20130123. Accessed 29 June 2017.

23 John Parkinson, "White House Failed to Protect Benghazi Mission, House Report Concludes," *ABC News*, February 11, 2014 abcnews.go.com/Politics/white-house-failed-protect-benghazi-mission-house-report/story?id=22460489. Accessed 29 June 2017.

24 Kerry Picket, "Benghazi Survivors Remain Gagged by Federal Law," *Breitbart*, February 20, 2013 breitbart.com/Big-Peace/2013/02/20/Benghazi-Survivors-Remained-Gagged-By-Federal-Law. Accessed 29 June 2017.

25 Lauren French, "Gowdy: Clinton wiped her server clean," *Politico*, March 27, 2015. politico.com/story/2015/03/gowdy-clinton-wiped-her-server-clean-116472. Accessed 29 June 2017.

26 "More Than 10,000 Days of Delays: Obama Admin's Delays of Benghazi Documents Equivalent to Over 27 Years," The Select Committee on Benghazi, May 18, 2016 benghazi.house.gov/news/press-releases/over-10000-days-of-delays-obama-administration-s-delays-on-benghazi-documents. Accessed 29 June 2017.

27 Marina Koren, "We Now Know Who's to Blame for Benghazi," *National Journal*, January 15, 2014 nationaljournal.com/congress/we-now-know-who-s-to-blame-for-benghazi-20140115. Accessed 29 June 2017.

28 Dan Gainor, "Liberal media spin Benghazi scandal to protect Team Obama," *Fox News*, May 9, 2013 foxnews.com/opinion/2013/05/09/liberal-media-spin-benghazi-scandal-to-protect-team-obama.html. Accessed 29 June 2017.

29 L. Brent Bozell III, "Why is ABC News ignoring emails related Obama's Libya scandal?" *Fox News*, October 26, 2012 foxnews.com/opinion/2012/10/26/why-is-abc-news-shielding-obama-over-benghazi-attack.html. Accessed 29 June 2017.

30 Cheryl K. Chumley, "Sharyl Attkinsson: CBS hid Benghazi clip to protect Obama during election," *Washington Times*, November 10, 2014 washingtontimes.com/news/2014/nov/10/sharyl-attkisson-cbs-hid-benghazi-news-clip-to-hel/. Accessed 29 June 2017.

31 "Bozell Statement: Liberal Media Are Accessories to Benghazi Cover-up," *Newsbusters*, November 1, 2012 newsbusters.org/blogs/nb/nb-staff/2012/11/01/bozell-statement-liberal-media-are-accessories-benghazi-cover. Accessed 29 June 2017.

32 Amber Randall, "Analysis: When Clinton Insinuates Gold Star Mom Is Lying, Media Gives A Pass," *The Daily Caller*, August 6, 2016 dailycaller.com/2016/08/06/analysis-when-clinton-insinuates-gold-star-mom-is-lying-media-gives-a-pass/. Accessed 29 June 2017.

EPA Transparency Scandals Notes

1   Michael Bastasch, "EPA chief's secret 'alias' email account revealed," *The Daily Caller*, November 12, 2012 dailycaller.com/2012/11/12/epa-chiefs-secret-alias-email-account-revealed/. Accessed 27 May 2017.

2   Eliza Krigman, "GOP questions EPA chief's emails," *Politico*, November 16, 2012 politico.com/story/2012/11/gop-questions-epa-chiefs-emails-083990. Accessed 27 May 2017.

3   Joel Gehrke, "EPA's Lisa Jackson resigning as secondary email investigation begins," *Washington Examiner*, December 27, 2012 washingtonexaminer.com/epas-lisa-jackson-resigning-as-secondary-email-investigation-begins/article/2516938. Accessed 27 May 2017.

4   "Board of Directors," Clinton Foundation, n.d. clintonfoundation.org/about/board-directors#CherylMills. Accessed 27 May 2017.

5   Stepen Dinan, "Newly released emails show EPA director's extensive use of fictional alter ego," *Washington Times*, June 2, 2013 washingtontimes.com/news/2013/jun/2/newly-released-emails-show-epa-directors-extensive/. Accessed 27 May 2017.

6   Mark Tapscott, "New mysteries in EPA's Windsorgate scandal," *Washington Examiner*, January 14, 2013 washingtonexaminer.com/new-mysteries-in-epas-windsorgate-scandal/article/2518591. Accessed 27 May 2017.

7   Julian Hattem, "Former EPA chief under fire for new batch of 'Richard Windsor' emails," *The Hill*, May 1, 2013 thehill.com/regulation/energy-environment/297255-former-epa-chief-under-fire-for-new-batch-of-richard-windsor-emails. Accessed 27 May 2017.

8   CJ Ciaramella, "Ex-EPA administrator Lisa Jackson contacted lobbyist from private email," *Washington Times*, August 14, 2013 washingtontimes.com/news/2013/aug/14/ex-epa-administrator-lisa-jackson-contacted-lobbyi/. Accessed 27 May 2017.

9   "EPA IG: 'No Evidence' Lisa Jackson Used Fake Name, Private Emails to Evade Transparency Laws," *CNS News*, October 3, 2013 cnsnews.com/news/article/epa-ig-no-evidence-lisa-jackson-used-fake-name-private-emails-evade-transparency-laws. Accessed 28 May 2017.

10 CJ Ciaramella, "EPA Delays Release of Jackson Emails After White House Review," *The Washington Free Beacon*, November 13, 2013 freebeacon.com/issues/epa-delays-release-of-jackson-emails-after-white-house-review/. Accessed 27 May 2017.

11 Stephen Dinan, "Emails show 'collusion' between Obama's EPA, environmental lobby," *Washington Times*, September 15, 2014 washingtontimes.com/news/2014/sep/15/emails-show-collusion-between-epa-environmental-lo/. Accessed 27 May 2017.

12 Ibid.

13 Michael Bastasch, "EPA Will Take 100 Years To Fulfill Conservative Group's FOIA Request," *The Daily Caller*, March 12, 2015 dailycaller.com/2015/03/12/epa-will-take-100-years-to-fulfill-conservative-groups-foia-request/. Accessed 27 May 2017.

14 Ibid.

15 Susan Ferrechio, "Court slams EPA for destroying emails," *Washington Examiner*, March 2, 2015 washingtonexaminer.com/court-slams-epa-for-destroying-emails/article/2560935. Accessed 27 May 2017.

16 Brittany M. Hughes, "Judge Slams EPA's 'Offensively Unapologetic' Handling of Conservative Group's FOIA," *CNS News*, March 4, 2015 cnsnews.com/news/article/ brittany-m-hughes/judge-slams-epa-s-offensively-unapologetic-handling-conserva- tive. Accessed 22 May 2017.

17 "Is The Obama EPA Running Its Own Black-Ops Program?" *Investor's Business Daily*, November 19, 2012 investors.com/politics/editorials/epa-lisa-jackson-email- ing-as-richard-windsor/. Accessed 27 May 2017.

18 "EPA Gives Info For Free to Big Green Groups 92% of Time; Denies 93% of Fee Waiver Requests from Biggest Conservative Critics," *Competitive Enterprise Institute*, May 14, 2013 cei.org/content/epa-gives-info-free-big-green-groups-92-time-denies- 93-fee-waiver-requests-biggest. Accessed 27 May 2017.

19 Ibid.

20 Ibid.

21 Michael Bastasch, "Vitter: EPA FOIA scandal 'no different than the IRS disaster'," *The Daily Caller*, May 17, 2013 dailycaller.com/2013/05/17/vitter-epa-foia-scandal-no- different-than-the-irs-disaster/. Accessed 27 May 2017.

22 Timothy Cama, "EPA tells court it may have lost text messages," *The Hill*, October 8, 2014 thehill.com/policy/energy-environment/220162-epa-may-have-lost-text-mes- sages. Accessed 27 May 2017.

23 Michael Bastach, "Congress Demands Environmental Protection Agency Hand Over More Emails, Texts," *The Hill*, May 15, 2015 dailycaller.com/2015/05/15/congress-de- mands-environmental-protection-agency-hand-over-more-emails-texts/. Accessed 27 May 2017.

24 CJ Ciaramella, "Senators Question Leak of Private Farmer Info," *The Washington Free Beacon*, June 6, 2013 freebeacon.com/senators-question-epa-leak-of-private-farmer- info/. Accessed 27 May 2017.

25 Tom Blumer, "Press Virtually Ignoring Lisa Jackson's Use of 'Alias' Email Accounts for Official Business," *NewsBusters*, November 20, 2012 newsbusters.org/blogs/nb/ tom-blumer/2012/11/20/press-virtually-ignoring-lisa-jacksons-use-alias-email-ac- counts. Accessed 28 May 2017.

26 Wendy Koch, "EPA chief Lisa Jackson steps down after 4 fiery years," *USA Today*, December 27, 2012 usatoday.com/story/news/nation/2012/12/27/epa-lisa-jack- son-resignation-record/1793979/. Accessed 28 May 2017.

27 John M. Broder, "E.P.A. Chief Set to Leave; Term Fell Shy of Early Hope," *The New York Times*, December 27, 2012 nytimes.com/2012/12/28/science/earth/lisa-p-jack- son-of-epa-to-step-down.html. Accessed 28 May 2017.

28 Curtis Houck, "Networks Skip Judge Ruling EPA Lied and Discriminated Against Conservative Group," *Newsbusters*, March 2, 2015 newsbusters.org/blogs/curtis- houck/2015/03/02/networks-skip-judge-ruling-epa-lied-and-discriminated-against. Accessed 28 May 2017.

The Pigford Scandal Notes

1 Sharon LaFraniere, "U.S. Opens Spigot After Farmers Claim Discrimination," *The New York Times*, April 25, 2013 nytimes.com/2013/04/26/us/farm-loan-bias-claims- often-unsupported-cost-us-millions.html. Accessed 3 June 2017.

2 Ibid.

3 Ibid.

4 Ibid.

5 Zombie, "Pigford v. Glickman: 86,000 claims from 39,697 total farmers?" *PJ Media*, July 27, 2010. pjmedia.com/zombie/2010/7/27/pigford-v-glickman-86000-claims-from-39697-total-farmers/. Accessed 26 June 2017.

6 Zombie, "Pigford v. Glickman: 86,000 claims from 39,697 total farmers?" *PJ Media*, July 27, 2010. pjmedia.com/zombie/2010/7/27/pigford-v-glickman-86000-claims-from-39697-total-farmers/. Accessed 26 June 2017.

7 Sharon LaFraniere, "U.S. Opens Spigot After Farmers Claim Discrimination," *The New York Times*, April 25, 2013 nytimes.com/2013/04/26/us/farm-loan-bias-claims-often-unsupported-cost-us-millions.html. Accessed 3 June 2017.

8 "EDITORIAL: USDA's Pigford fraud," *Washington Times*, February 2, 2011 washingtontimes.com/news/2011/feb/2/usda-s-pigford-fraud/. Accessed 3 June 2017.

The IRS Scandal Notes

1 Zachary A. Goldfarb and Karen Tumulty, "IRS admits targeting conservatives for tax scrutiny in 2012 election," *The Washington Post*, May 10, 2013 washingtonpost.com/business/economy/irs-admits-targeting-conservatives-for-tax-scrutiny-in-2012-election/2013/05/10/3b6a0ada-b987-11e2-92f3-f291801936b8_story.html. Accessed 1 June 2017.

2 Juliet Eilperin and Zachary A. Goldfarb, "Criminal probe of IRS launched as report details targeting of conservative groups," *The Washington Post*, May 14, 2013 washingtonpost.com/business/economy/holder-orders-fbi-justice-probe-of-irs/2013/05/14/7891fde6-bcc0-11e2-9b09-1638acc3942e_story.html. Accessed 1 June 2017.

3 Politico Staff, "Barack Obama's IRS statement (transcript, video)," *Politico*, May 15, 2013. politico.com/story/2013/05/barack-obama-irs-statement-transcript-091445. Accessed 1 June 2017.

4 Sarah Hofmann, "Carney: White House notified of IRS targeting tea party 'several weeks ago'; Obama: I found out Friday. VIDEO," *The Daily Caller*, May 14, 2013 dailycaller.com/2013/05/14/carney-white-house-notified-of-irs-targeting-tea-party-several-weeks-ago-obama-i-found-out-friday-video/. Accessed 1 June 2017.

5 Andrew Stiles, "Five IRS Scandal Myths," *National Review*, June 10, 2013 nationalreview.com/article/350595/five-irs-scandal-myths-andrew-stiles. Accessed 1 June 2017.

6 Patrick Howley, "Twelve different IRS units nationwide targeted conservatives," *The Daily Caller*, June 25, 2013 dailycaller.com/2013/06/25/twelve-different-irs-units-nationwide-targeted-conservatives/. Accessed 1 June 2017.

7 Andrew Stiles, "Five IRS Scandal Myths," *National Review*, June 10, 2013 nationalreview.com/article/350595/five-irs-scandal-myths-andrew-stiles. Accessed 1 June 2017.

8 Stephen Dinan, "IRS officials thought Obama wanted crackdown on tea party groups, worried about negative press," *Washington Times*, September 17, 2013 washingtontimes.com/news/2013/sep/17/report-irs-staff-acutely-aware-tea-party-antipathy/. Accessed 1 June 2017.

9   Vince Coglianese, "IRS's Shulman Had More Public White House Visits Than Any Cabinet Member," *The Daily Caller,* 5/29/2013 dailycaller.com/2013/05/29/irss-shulman-had-more-public-white-house-visits-than-any-cabinet-member. Accessed 1 June 2017.

10 Patrick Howley, "White House, IRS exchanged confidential taxpayer info," *The Daily Caller,* 10/9/2013, dailycaller.com/2013/10/09/white-house-irs-exchanged-confidential-taxpayer-info/[Accessed 1 June 2017.

11 CJ Ciaramella, "Treasury IG Blocking Release of Records on Leaks of Taxpayer Info to White House," *The Washington Free Beacon,* December 3, 2014 freebeacon.com/issues/treasury-ig-blocking-release-of-records-on-leaks-of-taxpayer-info-to-white-house/. Accessed 2 June 2017.

12 Mark Meckler, "IRS Hides Records Revealing White House Collusion As Americans Tire Of Constant Scandals," *The Daily Caller,* July 8, 2016 dailycaller.com/2016/07/08/irs-hides-records-revealing-white-house-collusion-as-americans-tire-of-constant-scandals/. Accessed 2 June 2017.

13 Kaylin Bugos, "Romney Donors Targeted by IRS?" *Spectator,* May 21, 2013 spectator.org/53818_romney-donors-targeted-irs/. Accessed 2 June 2017.

14 "Eric Bolling: I Was Audited After Criticizing Obama," *Fox News,* 5/16/2013 nation.foxnews.com/irs-targeting-tea-party/2013/05/16/eric-bolling-i-was-audited-after-criticizing-obama. Accessed 2 June 2017.

15 Alex Pappas, "Ben Carson: White House Wanted Apology for 'Offending' Obama," *The Daily Caller,* 4/14/2014 dailycaller.com/2014/04/14/ben-carson-white-house-wanted-apology-for-offending-obama/. Accessed 2 June 2017.

16 Jeff Dunetz, "Obamacare Victim Appears On Fox News; Gets IRS Audit," *Truth Revolt,* 11/29/2013 truthrevolt.org/news/obamacare-victim-appears-fox-news-gets-irs-audit. Accessed 2 June 2017.

17 Michael Cieply and Nicholas Confessore, "Leaning Right in Hollywood, Under a Lens," *The New York Times,* 1/22/2014 nytimes.com/2014/01/23/us/politics/leaning-right-in-hollywood-under-a-lens.html. Accessed 2 June 2017.

18 Stephan Dinan, "House Republicans find 10% of tea party donors audited by IRS," *Washington Times,* 5/7/2014 washingtontimes.com/news/2014/may/7/house-republicans-find-10-of-tea-party-donors-audi/. Accessed 2 June 2017.

19 Josh Hicks, "Obama political donor leading Justice Department's IRS investigation," *The Washington Post,* January 9, 2014 washingtonpost.com/news/federal-eye/wp/2014/01/09/obama-political-donor-leading-justice-departments-irs-investigation/?utm_term=.8939564e48c7. Accessed 1 June 2017.

20 Peter Cooney, "FBI doesn't plan charges over IRS scrutiny of Tea Party: WSJ," Reuters, January 13, 2014 reuters.com/article/us-usa-tax-teaparty-idUSBREA0D03420140114. Accessed 1 June 2017.

21 Cleta Mitchell, "What FBI 'investigation' of the IRS scandal?" *Washington Examiner,* January 14, 2014 washingtonexaminer.com/what-fbi-investigation-of-the-irs-scandal/article/2542177. Accessed 2 June 2017.

22 Staff Report, "Lois Lerner's Involvement in the IRS Targeting of Tax-Exempt Organizations," Committee on Oversight and Government Reform, 3/11/14 oversight.house.gov/wp-content/uploads/2014/03/Lerner-Report1.pdf. Accessed 2 June 2017.

23   Katie Pavlich, "BREAKING: New Emails Show Lois Lerner Was in Contact With DOJ About Prosecuting Tax Exempt Groups," *Townhall*, 4/16/2014 townhall.com/tipsheet/katiepavlich/2014/04/16/breaking-new-emails-show-lois-lerner-contacted-doj-about-prosecuting-tax-exempt-groups-n1825292. Accessed 2 June 2017.

24   Gregory Korte, "Households former IRS official Lerner in contempt," *USA Today*, 5/7/2014 usatoday.com/story/news/politics/2014/05/07/lois-lerner-contempt-of-congress/8815051/. Accessed 2 June 2017.

25   Joseph Curl, "CURL: IRS scandal gets Nixonian: The 18½-minute (or 26-month) gap," *Washington Times*, June 15, 2014 washingtontimes.com/news/2014/jun/15/curl-irs-scandal-gets-nixonian-the-18-minute-or-26/. Accessed 2 June 2017.

26   Stephen Dinan, "House to take first vote to censure IRS chief," *Washington Times*, June 13, 2016 washingtontimes.com/news/2016/jun/13/house-take-first-vote-censure-irs-chief-john-koski/. Accessed 2 June 2017.

27   Rich Noyes, "The Burying of a Scandal: TV News Hides the Facts on the IRS's Targeting of Conservatives," *Newsbusters*, May 7, 2014 newsbusters.org/blogs/nb/rich-noyes/2014/05/07/burying-scandal-tv-news-hides-facts-irss-targeting-conservatives. Accessed 2 June 2017.

28   Geoffrey Dickens, "CBS Ends 6-Month Censorship of IRS Scandal to Tell Viewers FBI Won't File Charges," *Newsbusters*, January 14, 2014 mrc.org/biasalerts/cbs-ends-6-month-censorship-irs-scandal-tell-viewers-fbi-wont-file-charges. Accessed 2 June 2017.

29   Stephen Dinan, "Newly recovered Lois Lerner email shows IRS tried to cover up tea party targeting," *Washington Times*, July 28, 2015 washingtontimes.com/news/2015/jul/28/new-irs-lerner-emails-show-block-congress-scrutiny/. Accessed 2 June 2017.

30   Matthew Balan, "Networks Censor Justice Department Ending Probe Into IRS Scandal," *Newsbusters*, October 23, 2015 newsbusters.org/blogs/nb/matthew-balan/2015/10/23/networks-censor-justice-department-ending-probe-irs-scandal. Accessed 2 June 2017.

31   Geoffrey Dickens, "The Seven Most Undercovered Obama Scandals," *Newsbusters*, January 16, 2017 newsbusters.org/blogs/nb/geoffrey-dickens/2017/01/16/seven-most-undercovered-obama-scandals. Accessed 2 June 2017.

Media Spying Scandals Notes

1   Charlie Savage, "Phone Records of Journalists of The Associated Press Seized by U.S.," *The New York Times*, May 13, 2013 nytimes.com/2013/05/14/us/phone-records-of-journalists-of-the-associated-press-seized-by-us.html. Accessed 22 June 2017.

2   Sharyl Attkisson, "8 Times Obama Says He Was Way Out of the Loop," *Sharyl Attkisson*, March 9, 2015 sharylattkisson.com/8-times-obama-says-he-was-way-out-of-the-loop/. Accessed 22 June 2017.

3   S.E. Cupp, "Why the AP scandal is so scary," *New York Daily News*, May 21, 2013 nydailynews.com/opinion/ap-scandal-scary-article-1.1349443. Accessed 22 June 2017.

4   Anne E. Marimow, "A rare peek into a Justice Department leak probe," *The Washington Post*, May 19, 2013 washingtonpost.com/local/a-rare-peek-into-a-justice-department-leak-probe/2013/05/19/0bc473de-be5e-11e2-97d4-a479289a31f9_story.html. Accessed 22 June 2017.

5   Judson Berger, "DOJ invoked Espionage Act in calling Fox News reporter criminal 'co-conspirator," *Fox News*, May 22, 2013 foxnews.com/politics/2013/05/22/doj-invoked-espionage-act-in-calling-fox-news-reporter-criminal-co-conspirator.html. Accessed 22 June 2017.

6   Olivier Knox, "Fox News: Government spying on reporter 'downright chilling," *Yahoo News*, May 20, 2013 yahoo.com/news/blogs/ticket/fox-news-govt-spying-reporter-downright-chilling-182908982.html. Accessed 22 June 2017.

7   "NEW INFO: DOJ May Have Monitored Phone Line of James Rosen's Parents, 30 Others," *Fox News Insider*, May 22, 2013 insider.foxnews.com/2013/05/22/new-info-doj-monitored-30-phone-lines-including-james-rosens-parents. Accessed 22 June 2017.

8   Judson Berger, "DOJ invoked Espionage Act in calling Fox News reporter criminal 'co-conspirator," *Fox News*, May 22, 2013 foxnews.com/politics/2013/05/22/doj-invoked-espionage-act-in-calling-fox-news-reporter-criminal-co-conspirator.html. Accessed 22 June 2017.

9   Jeremy W. Peters, "Justice Department Defends Holder's Testimony," *The New York Times*, June 3, 2013 nytimes.com/2013/06/04/us/politics/justice-department-defends-holders-testimony.html. Accessed 23 June 2017.

10 "Justice Department defends journalist email search," Reuters, May 24, 2013 reuters.com/article/us-usa-justice-warrant-idUSBRE94N0V920130524. Accessed 23 June 2017.

11 Jonathan Easley, "House Judiciary panel launches official probe into whether Holder lied," *The Hill*, May 29, 2013 thehill.com/homenews/house/302337-house-judiciary-panel-opens-probe-of-holder-in-reporter-surveillance-case. Accessed 23 June 2017.

12 "House Judiciary Committee Report: Holder Testimony Deceptive and Misleading," House of Representatives Judiciary Committee, July 31, 2013 judiciary.house.gov/press-release/house-judiciary-committee-report-holder-testimony-deceptive-and-misleading/. Accessed 23 June 2017.

13 "Republican report concludes Holder misled Congress on reporter targeting," *Fox News*, July 31, 2013 foxnews.com/politics/2013/07/31/republican-report-concludes-holder-misled-congress-on-reporter-targeting.html. Accessed 23 June 2017.

14 Jeff Poor, "CBS's Attkisson reports 'some compromising of my computer systems," *The Daily Caller*, May 21, 2013 dailycaller.com/2013/05/21/cbss-attkisson-reports-some-compromising-of-my-computer-systems/. Accessed 25 June 2017.

15 Dylan Byers, "Sharyl Attkisson's computers compromised," *Politico*, May 21, 2013. politico.com/blogs/media/2013/05/sharyl-attkissons-computers-compromised-164456. Accessed 25 June 2017.

16 Erik Wemple, "CBS News confirms multiple breaches of Sharyl Attkisson's computer," *The Washington Post*, June 14, 2013 washingtonpost.com/blogs/erik-wemple/wp/2013/06/14/cbs-news-confirms-multiple-breaches-of-sharyl-attkissons-computer/?utm_term=.29287b56f3c1. Accessed 25 June 2017.

17 Becket Adams, "Sharyl Attkisson: What was left out of reports on hacking," *Washington Examiner*, February 3, 2015 washingtonexaminer.com/sharyl-attkisson-what-was-left-out-of-reports-on-hacking/article/2559748. Accessed 25 June 2017.

18 Kyle Smith and Bruce Golding, "Ex-CBS reporter: Government agency bugged my computer," *New York Post*, October 27, 2014 nypost.com/2014/10/27/

ex-cbs-reporter-government-related-entity-bugged-my-computer/. Accessed 25 June 2017.

19 Howard Kurtz, "Sharyl Attkisson vs. CBS: Reporter first tried to quit a year ago," *Fox News*, March 13, 2014 foxnews.com/politics/2014/03/13/sharyl-attkisson-vs-cbs-reporter-first-tried-to-quit-year-ago.html. Accessed 25 June 2017.

20 Howard Kurtz, "Sharyl Attkisson sues administration over computer hacking," *Fox News*, January 5, 2015 foxnews.com/politics/2015/01/05/sharyl-attkisson-sues-administration-over-computer-hacking.html. Accessed 25 June 2017.

21 Sharyl Attkisson (@SharylAttkisson) "Federal judge recently denied Justice Dept. motion to dismiss my lawsuit and reassigned to Virginia. DOJ still fighting discovery and," Twitter, June 25, 2017, 9:28 PM.

22 Sharyl Attkisson (@SharylAttkisson) "DOJ won't even help us find out who had access to govt IP address found in my computer. Why wouldn't they help with that if we all want," Twitter, June 25, 2017, 9:28 PM

23 Sharyl Attkisson (@SharylAttkisson) "the truth? Here's some info https://sharylattkisson.com/attkisson-v-eric-holder-department-of-justice-et-al/" Twitter, June 25, 2017, 9:29 PM.

24 Larry O'Conner, "NBC News Reporter: AP Scandal Upsets Obama's 'Most Important Constituencies – The Press," *Breitbart*, May 15, 2013 breitbart.com/big-journalism/2013/05/15/ap-scandal-upsets-obamas-most-important-constituencies-the-press/. Accessed 25 June 2017.

25 Kyle Drennen, "ABC and CBS Ignore Obama Administration Investigating FNC's James Rosen," *Newsbusters*, May 21, 2013 newsbusters.org/blogs/nb/kyle-drennen/2013/05/21/abc-and-cbs-ignore-obama-administration-investigating-fncs-james. Accessed 25 June 2017.

26 Dana Milbank, "Dana Milbank: In AP, Rosen investigations, government makes criminals of reporters," *The Washington Post*, May 21, 2013 washingtonpost.com/opinions/dana-milbank-in-ap-rosen-investigations-government-makes-criminals-of-reporters/2013/05/21/377af392-c24e-11e2-914f-a7aba60512a7_story.html. Accessed 25 June 2017.

27 Becket Adams, "Sharyl Attkisson: What was left out of reports on hacking," *Washington Examiner*, February 3, 2015 washingtonexaminer.com/sharyl-attkisson-what-was-left-out-of-reports-on-hacking/article/2559748. Accessed 25 June 2017.

28 "The Obama administration and the Press," Committee to Protect Journalists, October 10, 2013 cpj.org/reports/2013/10/obama-and-the-press-us-leaks-surveillance-post-911.php. Accessed 25 June 2017.

NSA Surveillance Scandals Notes

1 Glenn Kessler, "James Clapper's 'least untruthful' statement to the Senate," *The Washington Post*, June 12, 2013 washingtonpost.com/blogs/fact-checker/post/james-clappers-least-untruthful-statement-to-the-senate/2013/06/11/e50677a8-d2d8-11e2-a73e-826d299ff459_blog.html. Accessed 20 June 2017.

2 Glenn Greenwald, "NSA collecting phone records of millions of Verizon customers daily," *The Guardian*, June 6, 2013 theguardian.com/world/2013/jun/06/nsa-phone-records-verizon-court-order. Accessed 20 June 2017.

3   Barton Gellman, "U.S., British intelligence mining data from nine U.S. Internet companies in broad secret program," *The Washington Post*, June 7, 2013 washingtonpost.com/ investigations/us-intelligence-mining-data-from-nine-us-internet-companies-in-broad-secret-program/2013/06/06/3a0c0da8-cebf-11e2-8845-d970ccb04497_story. html. Accessed 20 June 2017.

4   The Editorial Board, "President Obama's Dragnet," *The New York Times*, June 6, 2013 nytimes.com/2013/06/07/opinion/president-obamas-dragnet.html. Accessed 20 June 2017.

5   Glenn Greenwald and Spencer Ackerman, "How the NSA is still harvesting your online data," *The Guardian*, June 27, 2013 theguardian.com/world/2013/jun/27/ nsa-online-metadata-collection. Accessed 20 June 2017.

6   James Ball and Spencer Ackerman, "NSA loophole allows warrantless search for US citizens' emails and phone calls," *The Guardian*, August 9, 2013 theguardian.com/ world/2013/aug/09/nsa-loophole-warrantless-searches-email-calls. Accessed 20 June 2017.

7   Zeke J. Miller, "President Obama Defends NSA Surveillance Programs As 'Right Balance'," *TIME*, June 7, 2013 swampland.time.com/2013/06/07/president-obama-defends-nsa-surveillance-programs-as-right-balance/. Accessed 20 June 2017.

8   Jeff Poor, "Former AG Eric Holder: Edward Snowden Performed a 'Public Service'," *Breitbart*, May 30, 2016 breitbart.com/video/2016/05/30/former-ag-eric-holder-edward-snowden-performed-public-service/. Accessed 20 June 2017.

9   Michael Isikoff, "NSA program stopped no terror attacks, says White House panel member," *NBC News*, December 20, 2013 nbcnews.com/news/other/nsa-program-stopped-no-terror-attacks-says-white-house-panel-f2D11783588. Accessed 20 June 2017.

10   Charlie Savage and Jonathan Weisman, "N.S.A. Collection of Bulk Call Data Is Ruled Illegal," *The New York Times*, May 7, 2015 nytimes.com/2015/05/08/us/nsa-phone-records-collection-ruled-illegal-by-appeals-court.html. Accessed 20 June 2017.

11   Scott Wilson and Anne Gearan, "Obama didn't know about surveillance of U.S.-allied world leaders until summer, officials say," *The Washington Post*, October 28, 2013 washingtonpost.com/politics/obama-didnt-know-about-surveillance-of-us-allied-world-leaders-until-summer-officials-say/2013/10/28/0cbacefa-4009-11e3-a751-f032898f2dbc_story.html. Accessed 20 June 2017.

12   Ken Dilanian and Janet Stobart, "White House OKd spying on allies, U.S. intelligence officials say," *Los Angeles Times*, October 28, 2013 latimes.com/world/la-fg-spying-phones-20131029-story.html. Accessed 20 June 2017.

13   Adam Entous and Danny Yadron, "U.S. Spy Net on Israel Snares Congress," *The Wall Street Journal*, December 29, 2015 wsj.com/articles/u-s-spy-net-on-israel-snares-congress-1451425210. Accessed 20 June 2017.

14   Ibid.

15   Fred Fleitz, "Did the White House Use the NSA to Spy on Congress about the Iran Deal?" *National Review*, December 30, 2015 nationalreview.com/article/429111/ obama-nsas-congress-spying. Accessed 20 June 2017.

16   Scott Whitlock, "ABC, NBC Morning Shows Ignore Obama in Spying Story; CBS Finds a 'Political Crisis' for President," *NewsBusters*, June 10, 2013 newsbusters.

org/blogs/nb/scott-whitlock/2013/06/10/abc-nbc-morning-shows-ignore-obama
-spying-story-cbs-finds. Accessed 20 June 2017.

17　Claire Cain Miller, "Revelations of N.S.A. Spying Cost U.S. Tech Companies," *The New York Times*, March 22, 2014 nytimes.com/2014/03/22/business/fallout-from-snowden-hurting-bottom-line-of-tech-companies.html. Accessed 20 June 2017.

18　"CREW Calls On DOJ To Investigate DNI Clapper For Lying To Congress," Citizens for Responsibility and Ethics in Washington, July 23, 2013 citizensforethics. org/legal-filing/crew-calls-on-doj-to-investigate-dni-clapper-for-lying-to-congress/. Accessed 22 June 2017.

19　Paul D. Shinkman, "National Intelligence Director Apologizes for Lying to Congress," *U.S. News and World Report*, July 2, 2013 usnews.com/news/articles/2013/07/02/national -intelligence-director-apologizes-for-lying-to-congress. Accessed 22 June 2017.

20　"Wyden Statement Responding to Director Clapper's Statements About Collection on Americans," Ron Wyden: Senator for Oregon, June 11, 2013 wyden.senate. gov/news/press-releases/wyden-statement-responding-to-director-clappers-statements-about-collection-on-americans. Accessed 22 June 2017.

The VA Scandal Notes

1　"Press Release - Obama Campaign Announces National Veterans Advisory Committee," The American Presidency Project, November 12, 2007 presidency.ucsb.edu/ ws/?pid=91891. Accessed 3 June 2017.

2　Matt Cover, "Backlog of Veterans' Disability Claims Increases 179% Under Obama," *CNS News*, October 4, 2012 cnsnews.com/news/article/backlog-veterans-disability-claims-increases-179-under-obama. Accessed 3 June 2017.

3　Aaron Glantz, "Number of veterans who die waiting for benefits claims skyrockets," The Center for Investigative Reporting, December 20,2012 cironline.org/reports/ number-veterans-who-die-waiting-benefits-claims-skyrockets-4074. Accessed　3 June 2017.

4　Matt Cover, "Backlog of Veterans' Disability Claims Increases 179% Under Obama," *CNS News*, October 4, 2012 cnsnews.com/news/article/backlog-veterans-disability-claims-increases-179-under-obama. Accessed 2 June 2017.

5　Scott Bronstein and Drew Griffin, "A fatal wait: Veterans languish and die on a VA hospital's secret list," *CNN*, April 23, 2014 cnn.com/2014/04/23/health/veterans-dying-health-care-delays/. Accessed 3 June 2017.

6　Geoff Dyer, "Veterans scandal risks engulfing Obama," *Financial Times*, May 16, 2014 ft.com/content/328546c0-dd10-11e3-8546-00144feabdc0. Accessed 3 June 2017.

7　Becket Adams, "Eric Holder: No Immediate Plans to Investigate VA Scandal," *The Blaze*, 5/14/2014 theblaze.com/stories/2014/05/14/eric-holder-no-immediate-plans-to-investigate-va-scandal/. Accessed 3 June 2017.

8　Ben Wolfgang, "White House admits Obama knew of VA problems in 2008—blames Bush!," *Washington Times*, May 19, 2014 washingtontimes.com/news/2014/may/19/ white-house-defends-efforts-improve-va-wait-times/. Accessed 3 June 2017.

9　Ed Morrissey, "VA Scandal Exposes Single-Payer Health Care Flaws," *Fiscal Times*, May 29, 2014 thefiscaltimes.com/Columns/2014/05/29/VA-Scandal-Exposes-Single-Payer-Health-Care-Flaws. Accessed 3 June 2017.

10 Richard Simon and Michael Muskal, "Eric Shinseki steps down as VA chief amid wait list scandal," *Los Angeles Times*, May 30, 2014 URL. Accessed 3 June 2017.

11 Josh Hicks, "OSC investigating alleged retaliation against 37 VA whistleblowers," *The Washington Post*, June 5, 2014 washingtonpost.com/news/federal-eye/wp/2014/06/05/osc-investigating-alleged-retaliation-against-37-va-whistleblowers/?utm_term=.7a90c37a7d39. Accessed 3 June 2017.

12 Jill McElhatton, "Whistleblowers flood VA with lawsuits despite apology," *Washington Times*, July 23, 2014 washingtontimes.com/news/2014/jul/23/whistleblowers-flood-va-with-lawsuits-despite-apol/. Accessed 3 June 2017.

13 Ryan Grim and Jennifer Bendery, "Leaked Document: Nearly One-Third Of 847,000 Vets With Pending Applications For VA Health Care Already Died," *Huffington Post*, July 15, 2015 huffingtonpost.com/2015/07/13/veterans-health-care-backlog-died_n_7785920.html?1436821160. Accessed 3 June 2017.

14 Associated Press, "One-Third of Calls to VA Suicide Hotline Don't Get Answered: Ex-Director," *NBC News*, September 26, 2016 nbcnews.com/news/us-news/one-third-calls-va-suicide-hotline-don-t-get-answered-n654741. Accessed 4 June 2017.

15 Scott Whitlock, "In a Month, TV News Gives Less Airtime to VA Scandal Than Christie Controversy Received in Four Days," *Newsbusters*, May 22, 2014 newsbusters.org/blogs/nb/scott-whitlock/2014/05/22/month-tv-news-gives-less-airtime-va-scandal-christie-controversy. Accessed 3 June 2017.

16 "MRC's Brent Bozell Slams Media for Dropping VA Scandal Post-Shinseki Resignation," *Newsbusters*, June 9, 2014 newsbusters.org/blogs/nb/nb-staff/2014/06/09/mrcs-brent-bozell-slams-media-dropping-va-scandal-post-shinseki. Accessed 3 June 2017.

17 Jeffrey Meyer, "ABC, NBC Ignore Report Showing Obama Administration Knew About Ongoing VA Problems," *Newsbusters*, May 19, 2014 newsbusters.org/blogs/nb/jeffrey-meyer/2014/05/19/abc-nbc-ignore-report-showing-obama-administration-knew-about. Accessed 3 June 2017.

18 Michelle Ye Hee Lee, "'Whole bunch' of facts don't support Obama's claim that many VA bosses were fired over scandal," *The Washington Post*, October 12, 2016 washingtonpost.com/news/fact-checker/wp/2016/10/12/obamas-claim-a-whole-bunch-of-people-who-are-in-charge-of-va-facilities-were-fired-over-wait-times/. Accessed 3 June 2017.

19 Dennis Wagner, "Inspectors rip Phoenix VA hospital again for delayed care," *Arizona Republic*, October 4, 2016 azcentral.com/story/news/local/arizona-investigations/2016/10/04/inspector-general-rips-phoenix-va-hospital-again/91554300/. Accessed 3 June 2017.

20 Sarah Westwood, "Trump administration has fired more than 500 VA employees since January," *Washington Examiner*, July 7, 2017 washingtonexaminer.com/trump-administration-has-fired-more-than-500-va-employees-since-january/article/2627988. Accessed 4 August 2017.

21 Meaghan M. McDermott, "Q&A: Veteran suicide hotline now answers 9 of 10 calls in 8 seconds," *USA Today*, June 16, 2017 usatoday.com/story/news/nation-now/2017/06/16/veterans-suicide-hotline/403509001/. Accessed 4 August 2017.

The Bergdahl Swap Notes

1   Byron York, "Outraged by Bergdahl case, fellow soldiers break secrecy pledge to tell story," *Washington Examiner*, June 5, 2014 washingtonexaminer.com/outraged-by-bergdahl-case-fellow-soldiers-break-secrecy-pledge-to-tell-story/article/2549344. Accessed 11 July 2017.

2   Jake Tapper, "Fellow soldiers call Bowe Bergdahl a deserter, not a hero," *CNN*, June 4, 2014 cnn.com/2014/06/01/us/bergdahl-deserter-or-hero/. Accessed 11 July 2017.

3   James Rosen, "EXCLUSIVE: Bergdahl declared jihad in captivity, secret documents show," *Fox News*, June 6, 2014 foxnews.com/politics/2014/06/06/exclusive-bergdahl-declared-jihad-secret-documents-show.html. Accessed 11 July 2017.

4   Jeff Dunetz, "Gen. (Ret.) McChrystal: We Knew Right Away That Bergdahl 'Walked Off Base Intentionally,'" *MRC TV*, May 27, 2015 mrctv.org/blog/general-ret-stanley-mcchrystal-we-knew-right-away-bergdahl-went-awol. Accessed 11 July 2017.

5   Daniel Halper, "Susan Rice: Bergdahl Served With 'Honor and Distinction,'" *The Weekly Standard*, June 2, 2014 weeklystandard.com/susan-rice-bergdahl-served-with-honor-and-distinction/article/794066. Accessed 11 July 2017.

6   "Obama: Bergdahl Scandal A 'Controversy Whipped Up in Washington,'" *The Washington Free Beacon*, June 5, 2014 freebeacon.com/national-security/obama-bergdahl-scandal-a-controversy-whipped-up-in-washington/. Accessed 13 July 2017.

7   Jake Tapper, "Fellow soldiers call Bowe Bergdahl a deserter, not a hero," *CNN*, June 4, 2014 cnn.com/2014/06/01/us/bergdahl-deserter-or-hero/. Accessed 11 July 2017.

8   Justin Sink, "Bergdahl blame shifting to Hagel?" *The Hill*, June 10, 2014 thehill.com/blogs/blog-briefing-room/208803-obama-shifting-blame-for-bergdahl-trade-to-hagel. Accessed 11 July 2017.

9   "Army Charges Bergdahl With Desertion," U.S. Department of Defense, March 25, 2015 defense.gov/News/Article/Article/604348/army-charges-bergdahl-with-desertion/. Accessed 11 July 2017.

10 Jonathan F. Keiler, "Why Obama Did Not Pardon Bergdahl," *American Thinker*, January 28, 2017. americanthinker.com/articles/2017/01/why_obama_did_not_pardon_bergdahl.html. Accessed 11 July 2017.

11 Kristina Wong, "Watchdog: DOD broke law with Bergdahl swap," *The Hill*, August 21, 2014 thehill.com/policy/defense/215699-watchdog-pentagon-broke-law-with-bergdahl-swap. Accessed 11 July 2017.

12 Kristina Wong, "House report: Obama officials misled public on Bergdahl swap," *The Hill*, December 10, 2015 thehill.com/policy/defense/262772-house-report-says-obama-officials-misled-public-on-berghdahl-swap. Accessed 11 July 2017.

13 Jordan Schachtel, "The 'Taliban Five' Freed for Bergdahl Have Resumed 'Threatening Activities,'" *Breitbart*, December 10, 2015 breitbart.com/national-security/2015/12/10/taliban-five-freed-bergdahl-resumed-threatening-activities/. Accessed 11 July 2017.

14 Edwin Mora, "Jihad-Friendly Qatar May Have Inspired Former Gitmo Detainees to Return to Terror," *Breitbart*, June 15, 2017 breitbart.com/national-security/2017/06/15/qatar-influenced-gitmo-detainees-return/. Accessed 11 July 2017.

15 Todd Blumer, "Revised 5 Times, NYT's 'Rush to Demonize Bergdahl' Editorial Attacking GOP 'Operatives' and His Unit Is What Was Rushed," *The New York Times*, June 8, 2014 newsbusters.org/blogs/nb/tom-blumer/2014/06/08/revised-5-times-nyts-rush-demonize-bergdahl-editorial-attacking-gop. Accessed 11 July 2017.

16 Cheri Jacobus, "Is The New York Times Trying to Paint Bergdahl as a Victim/Hero?" *Newsbusters*, June 10, 2014. newsbusters.org/blogs/nb/cheri-jacobus/2014/06/10/new-york-times-trying-paint-bergdahl-victimhero. Accessed 11 July 2017.

17 Tom Blumer, "Daily Beast Writer Partially Blames Bush For Bergdahl," *Newsbusters*, March 31, 2015 newsbusters.org/blogs/tom-blumer/2015/03/31/daily-beast-writer-partially-blames-bush-bergdahl. Accessed 11 July 2017.

18 Matthew Balan, "CNN's Baldwin on Bergdahl's Desertion: Isn't Captivity 'Punishment Enough'?" *Newsbusters*, March 25, 2015 newsbusters.org/blogs/matthew-balan/2015/03/25/cnns-baldwin-bergdahls-desertion-isnt-captivity-punishment-enough. Accessed 11 July 2017.

19 Curtis Houck, "Networks Ignore Susan Rice Praising Bergdahl in 2014 for Serving 'with Honor and Distinction,'" *Newsbusters*, March 25, 2015 newsbusters.org/blogs/curtis-houck/2015/03/25/networks-ignore-clip-susan-rice-praising-bergdahl-2014-serving-honor. Accessed 11 July 2017.

20 Jeffrey Meyer, "ABC and CBS Continue to Omit That Soldier Died While Searching for Sergeant Bowe Bergdahl," *Newsbusters*, March 26, 2015 newsbusters.org/blogs/jeffrey-meyer/2015/03/26/abc-cbs-omit-continue-omit-fact-soldiers-died-while-searching. Accessed 11 July 2017.

21 Tom Blumer, "NY Times Falsely Claims No Soldiers Died Due to Bergdahl's Desertion," *Newsbusters*, December 4, 2016 newsbusters.org/blogs/nb/tom-blumer/2016/12/04/ny-times-falsely-claims-no-soldiers-died-due-bergdahls-desertion. Accessed 11 July 2017.

22 Curtis Houck, "Networks Fail to Cover News Taliban Detainee Swapped for Bergdahl Is Trying to Rejoin Group," *Newsbusters*, January 30, 2015 newsbusters.org/blogs/curtis-houck/2015/01/30/networks-fail-cover-news-taliban-detainee-swapped-bergdahl-trying. Accessed 11 July 2017.

President Stonewall Notes

1 John Solomon, "EXCLUSIVE: FBI blocked in corruption probe involving Sens. Reid, Lee," *Washington Times*, March 13, 2014 washingtontimes.com/news/2014/mar/13/fbi-blocked-in-corruption-probe-involving-sens-rei/. Accessed 4 June 2017.

2 S.A. Miller, "Obama admin blocked FBI probe of Clinton Foundation corruption: Report," *Washington Times*, August 11, 2016 washingtontimes.com/news/2016/aug/11/obama-admin-blocked-fbi-probe-clinton-foundation/. Accessed 4 June 2017.

3 "Inspectors general say Obama aides obstruct investigations: Examiner Editorial," *Washington Examiner*, August 7, 2014 washingtonexaminer.com/inspectors-general-say-obama-aides-obstruct-investigations-examiner-editorial/article/2551805. Accessed 4 June 2017.

4 Melissa Quinn, "Most of Government's Own Watchdogs Say They're Stonewalled," *Daily Signal*, August 7, 2014 dailysignal.com/2014/08/07/governments-watchdogs-say-theyre-stonewalled/. Accessed 4 June 2017.

5 Kelly Riddell, "Obama administration restricts investigative powers of inspectors general," *Washington Times*, July 23, 2015 washingtontimes.com/news/2015/jul/23/obama-restricts-investigative-powers-inspectors-ge/. Accessed 4 June 2017.

6 Eric Lichtblau, "Tighter Lid on Records Threatens to Weaken Government Watch-dogs," *The New York Times*, November 27, 2015 nytimes.com/2015/11/28/us/politics/tighter-lid-on-records-threatens-to-defang-government-watchdogs.html. Accessed 4 June 2017.

7 Andrea Noble, "Congress moves to strengthen authority of inspectors general," *Washington Times*, December 13, 2016 washingtontimes.com/news/2016/dec/13/congress-moves-to-strengthen-authority-of-inspecto/. Accessed 4 June 2017.

8 Office of the Press Secretary, "President Obama Signs the Inspectors General Empowerment Act of 2016," The White House, December 16, 2016 obamawhitehouse.archives.gov/the-press-office/2016/12/16/president-obama-signs-inspectors-general-empowerment-act-2016. Accessed 4 June 2017.

Intelligence Manipulation Scandals Notes

1 Stephen Hayes, "Al Qaeda Wasn't 'on the Run,'" *The Weekly Standard*, September 15, 2014 weeklystandard.com/al-qaeda-wasnt-on-the-run/article/804366 Accessed 27 May 2017.

2 Ibid.

3 Ibid.

4 Ibid.

5 Ibid.

6 Ibid.

7 Marc A. Thiessen, "Defense Intelligence Agency warned Obama about ISIS in 2012," AEIdeas, November 20, 2015 aei.org/publication/defense-intelligence-agency-warned-obama-about-isis-in-2012/ Accessed 26 May 2017.

8 David Remnick, "On And Off The Road With Barack Obama," *The New Yorker*, January 27, 2014 newyorker.com/magazine/2014/01/27/going-the-distance-david-remnick. accessed 26 May 2017.

9 Steve Contorno, "What Obama said about Islamic State as a 'JV' team," *Politifact*, September 7, 2014 politifact.com/truth-o-meter/statements/2014/sep/07/barack-obama/what-obama-said-about-islamic-state-jv-team/. Accessed 26 May 2017.

10 Glenn Kessler, "Spinning Obama's reference to Islamic State as a 'JV' team," *The Washington Post*, September 3, 2014 washingtonpost.com/news/fact-checker/wp/2014/09/03/spinning-obamas-reference-to-isis-as-a-jv-team/. Accessed 26 May 2017.

11 "President Obama: What makes us America," *CBS News*, September 28, 2014 cbsnews.com/news/president-obama-60-minutes/. Accessed 27 May 2017.

12 David Martosko, "Obama has had accurate intelligence about ISIS since BEFORE the 2012 election, says administration insider," *Daily Mail*, September 30, 2014 dailymail.co.uk/news/article-2774122/Obama-accurate-intelligence-ISIS-BEFORE-2012-election-says-administration-insider.html. Accessed 27 May 2017.

13 Eli Lake, "Why Obama Can't Say His Spies Underestimated ISIS," *Daily Beast*, September 28, 2014 thedailybeast.com/articles/2014/09/28/why-obama-can-t-say-his-spies-underestimated-isis. Accessed 27 May 2017.

14 "Obama faces backlash after blaming intel community for missing ISIS," *Fox News*, September 29, 2014 foxnews.com/politics/2014/09/29/obama-faces-backlash-after-blaming-intel-community-for-missing-isis.html. Accessed 27 May 2017.

15 Curtis Houck, "ABC, CBS Ignore News That the Intelligence Community Actually Did Warn Obama About ISIS Threat," *Newsbusters*, September 29, 2014 newsbusters. org/blogs/curtis-houck/2014/09/29/abc-cbs-ignore-news-intelligence-community-did-warn-obama-isis-threat. Accessed 27 May 2017.

16 Mark Mazzetti and Matt Apuzzo, "Inquiry Weighs Whether ISIS Analysis Was Distorted," *The New York Times*, August 25, 2015 nytimes.com/2015/08/26/world/middleeast/pentagon-investigates-allegations-of-skewed-intelligence-reports-on-isis.html. Accessed 26 May 2017.

17 Kyle Drennen, "Only CBS Covers Latest on ISIS Intel Being Altered by Obama Admin.," *Newsbusters*, September 10, 2015 newsbusters.org/blogs/nb/kyle-drennen/2015/09/10/only-cbs-covers-latest-isis-intel-being-altered-obama-admin. Accessed 26 May 2017.

18 Spencer Ackerman, "US spy chief's 'highly unusual' reported contact with military official raises concerns," *The Guardian*, September 11, 2015 theguardian.com/us-news/2015/sep/10/james-clapper-pentagon-military-official. Accessed 26 May 2017.

19 Nancy A. Youssef and Shane Harris, "Republicans and Democrats Agree: CENTCOM Cooked ISIS War Intel," *Daily Beast*, August 11, 2016 thedailybeast.com/articles/2016/08/11/republicans-and-democrats-agree-centcom-cooked-isis-war-intel. Accessed 26 May 2017.

20 Helene Cooper, "Military Officials Distorted ISIS Intelligence, Congressional Panel Says," *The New York Times*, August 11, 2016 nytimes.com/2016/08/12/us/politics/isis-centcom-intelligence.html. Accessed 26 May 2017.

21 Nancy A. Youssef and Shane Harris, "Republicans and Democrats Agree: CENTCOM Cooked ISIS War Intel," *Daily Beast*, August 11, 2016 thedailybeast.com/articles/2016/08/11/republicans-and-democrats-agree-centcom-cooked-isis-war-intel. Accessed 26 May 2017.

22 Rudy Takala, "CIA: Islamic State now bigger than al Qaeda at its height," *Washington Examiner*, June 16, 2016 washingtonexaminer.com/cia-islamic-state-now-bigger-than-al-qaeda-at-its-height/article/2594067. Accessed 26 May 2017.

23 Wikipedia Contributors, "List of terrorist incidents linked to ISIL," *Wikipedia, The Free Encyclopedia*, May 26, 2017 en.wikipedia.org/wiki/List_of_terrorist_incidents_linked_to_ISIL. Accessed 26 May 2017.

Hillary Clinton's Email Scandal Notes

1 Michael S. Schmidt, "Hillary Clinton Used Personal Email Account at State Dept., Possibly Breaking Rules," *The New York Times*, March 2, 2015 nytimes.com/2015/03/03/us/politics/hillary-clintons-use-of-private-email-at-state-department-raises-flags.html. Accessed 16 June 2017.

2 Stephen Dinan, "Hillary Clinton deleted 32,000 'private' emails, refuses to turn over server," *Washington Times*, March 10, 2015 washingtontimes.com/news/2015/mar/10/hillary-clinton-deleted-32000-private-emails-refus/. Accessed 16 June 2017.

3 Chris Frates and Jose Pagliery, "Hillary Clinton's home server hard to trace," *CNN*, March 5, 2015 cnn.com/2015/03/05/politics/hillary-clinton-email-home-server/. Accessed 16 June 2017.

4   Alexandra Jaffe and Dan Merica, "Hillary Clinton: I used one email 'for convenience,'" *CNN*, March 10, 2015 cnn.com/2015/03/10/politics/hillary-clinton-email-scandal-press-conference/. Accessed 16 June 2017.

5   Dan Merica, "Source: Clinton used iPad for personal email at State," *CNN*, March 31, 2015 cnn.com/2015/03/31/politics/hillary-clinton-ipad-e-mail-devices/. Accessed 16 June 2017.

6   Alexandra Jaffe and Dan Merica, "Hillary Clinton: I used one email 'for convenience,'" *CNN*, March 10, 2015 cnn.com/2015/03/10/politics/hillary-clinton-email-scandal-press-conference/. Accessed 16 June 2017.

7   Susan Jones, "FBI 'Unable to Acquire' Any of Clinton's 13 Mobile Devices; Aide Says He Smashed 2 With Hammer," *CNS News*, September 6, 2016 cnsnews.com/news/article/susan-jones/fbi-unable-acquire-any-clintons-13-mobile-devices-aide-says-he-smashed-2. Accessed 16 June 2017.

8   Alex Griswold, "Bob Woodward: Hillary's Emails Remind Me of Nixon Tapes," *Mediaite*, August 17, 2015 mediaite.com/tv/bob-woodward-hillarys-emails-remind-me-of-nixon-tapes/. Accessed 16 June 2017.

9   Rosalind S. Helderman, "State Dept. inspector general report sharply criticizes Clinton's email practices," *The Washington Post*, May 25, 2016 washingtonpost.com/politics/state-dept-inspector-general-report-sharply-criticizes-clintons-email-practices/2016/05/25/fc6f8ebc-2275-11e6-aa84-42391ba52c91_story.html. Accessed 16 June 2017.

10 Ben Wolfgang, "Obama says Hillary Clinton's private server did not endanger national security," *Washington Times*, April 10, 2016 washingtontimes.com/news/2016/apr/10/obama-says-hillary-clinton-emails-did-not-endanger/. Accessed 18 June 2017.

11 Andrew C. McCarthy, "Gee, I'm Starting to Think the Obama DOJ Just Might Be Politicized," *National Review*, January 14, 2017 nationalreview.com/article/443845/obama-justice-department-political-core. Accessed 16 June 2017.

12 Andrew C. McCarthy, "Please Tell Me These FBI/DOJ 'Side Deals' with Clinton E-Mail Suspects Didn't Happen," *National Review*, October 4, 2016 nationalreview.com/article/440697/hillary-clinton-email-scandal-side-deals-fbi-department-justice-politicized. Accessed 16 June 2017.

13 Chuck Ross, "EXCLUSIVE: Clinton Aides Resisted State Department Suggestion That Clinton Use State.gov Account," *The Daily Caller*, January 18, 2016 dailycaller.com/2016/01/18/emails-clinton-aides-resisted-state-department-suggestion-that-clinton-use-state-gov-account/. Accessed 18 June 2017.

14 Patrick Howley, "Hillary Clinton Said She Did Not Want Her Emails to Be 'Accessible,'" *Breitbart*, May 25, 2016 breitbart.com/2016-presidential-race/2016/05/25/hillary-clinton-10/. Accessed 18 June 2017.

15 Julian Hate, "FBI didn't record Clinton interview, did not administer sworn oath," *The Hill*, July 7, 2016 thehill.com/policy/national-security/286849-fbi-didnt-record-clinton-interview-no-sworn-oath. Accessed 16 June 2017.

16 Jake Novak, "The 5 most outrageous things Hillary Clinton said in her FBI interview," *CNBC*, September 2, 2016 politico.com/story/2016/04/barack-obama-hillary-clinton-justice-221770. Accessed 16 June 2017.

17 "Statement by FBI Director James B. Comey on the Investigation of Secretary Hillary Clinton's Use of a Personal E-Mail System," Federal Bureau of Investigation, July 5,

2016   fbi.gov/news/pressrel/press-releases/statement-by-fbi-director-james-b-com-ey-on-the-investigation-of-secretary-hillary-clinton2019s-use-of-a-personal-e-mail-system. Accessed 18 June 2017.

18   Lauren Carroll, "FBI findings tear holes in Hillary Clinton's email defense," *PolitiFact*, July 6, 2016 politifact.com/truth-o-meter/statements/2016/jul/06/hillary-clinton/fbi-findings-tear-holes-hillary-clintons-email-def/. Accessed 18 June 2017.

19   Ben Shapiro, "Hillary Clinton: Too Big To Jail," *Daily Wire*, July 6, 2016 dailywire.com/news/7217/hillary-clinton-too-big-jail-ben-shapiro. Accessed 16 June 2017.

20   Becket Adams, "MSNBC analyst: People have gone to jail over what Clinton did with email," *Washington Examiner*, January 29, 2016 washingtonexaminer.com/msnbc-an-alyst-people-have-gone-to-jail-over-what-clinton-did-with-email/article/2581900. Accessed 16 June 2017.

21   Pamela Brown, Tal Kopan and Dan Merica,, "First on CNN: Bill Clinton says he regrets Lynch meeting," *CNN*, July 3, 2016 cnn.com/2016/07/01/politics/lynch-to-ac-cept-guidance-from-fbi-on-clinton-email-probe/index.html. Accessed 16 June 2017.

22   Jordan Sekulow, "DOJ Document Dump to ACLJ on Clinton Lynch Meeting: Comey FBI Lied, Media Collusion, Spin, and Illegality," American Center for Law and Justice, August 4, 2017 aclj.org/government-corruption/doj-document-dump-to-aclj-on-clinton-lynch-meeting-comey-fbi-lied-media-collusion-spin-and-illegality. Accessed 7 August 2017.

23   Jordan Sekulow, "ACLJ FOIA Unmasks Former Obama Attorney General Loretta Lynch's Secret Email Alias – "Elizabeth Carlisle"," American Center for Law and Justice, August 7, 2017. aclj.org/government-corruption/aclj-foia-unmasks-former-obama-attorney-general-loretta-lynchs-alias-email-account-elizabeth-carlisle. Accessed 7 August 2017.

24   "State Won't Release 18 Emails Between Clinton and Obama That Were on Her Private Server—But Says They Are Not Classified," *CNS News*, January 30, 2016 cnsnews.com/news/article/cnsnewscom-staff/spokesman-says-state-wont-release-18-emails-between-clinton-and-obama. Accessed 16 June 2017.

25   Andrew C. McCarthy, "Obama's Growing Conflict of Interest in the Clinton E-Mail Scandal," *National Review*, February 3, 2016 nationalreview.com/article/430706/obamas-hillary-clinton-e-mail-problem. Accessed 16 June 2017.

26   Blake Neff, "FBI Docs: Obama Used Pseudonym To Email Hillary's Server," *The Daily Caller*, September 23, 2016 dailycaller.com/2016/09/23/fbi-docs-obama-used-pseud-onym-to-email-hillarys-server/. Accessed 16 June 2017.

27   Andrew C. McCarthy, "Obama's Conflict Tanked the Clinton E-mail Investiga-tion — As Predicted," *National Review*, September 26, 2016 nationalreview.com/article/440380/obama-email-alias-clinton-why-fbi-didnt-prosecute-hillary. Accessed 18 June 2017.

28   "Judicial Watch: New State Department Documents Reveal Top Agency Officials Raised Questions about Clinton Emails in Early August 2013," Judicial Watch, September 15, 2016 judicialwatch.org/press-room/press-releases/judicial-watch-new-state-department-documents-reveal-top-agency-officials-raised-questions-clinton-emails-early-august-2013/. Accessed 17 June 2017.

29   "WikiLeaks: The Podesta Emails," WikiLeaks, n.d. wikileaks.org/podesta-emails/emailid/35115. Accessed 18 June 2017.

30 "WikiLeaks: The Podesta Emails," WikiLeaks, n.d. wikileaks.org/podesta-emails/emailid/31077. Accessed 18 June 2017.

31 Lauren French, "Gowdy: Clinton wiped her server clean," *Politico*, March 27, 2015 politico.com/story/2015/03/gowdy-clinton-wiped-her-server-clean-116472. Accessed 18 June 2017.

32 Tamara Chuang, "FBI report: Platte River Network employee used BleachBit to delete old Clinton e-mails," *Denver Post*, September 3, 2015 denverpost.com/2016/09/03/fbi-report-platte-river-network-employee-bleachbit-delete-clinton-e-mails/. Accessed 18 June 2017.

33 "WikiLeaks: The Podesta Emails," WikiLeaks, n.d. wikileaks.org/podesta-emails/emailid/4099. Accessed 18 June 2017.

34 Stephen Dinan, "FBI reopens Clinton email investigation," *Washington Times*, October 28, 2016 washingtontimes.com/news/2016/oct/28/james-comey-fbi-director-reopens-clinton-email-inv/. Accessed 18 June 2017.

35 Fredreka Schouten, Kevin Johnson and Heidi Przybyla, "FBI declares it is finally done investigating Hillary Clinton's email," *USA Today*, November 6, 2016 usatoday.com/story/news/politics/elections/2016/2016/11/06/fbi-not-recommending-charges-over-new-clinton-emails/93395808/. Accessed 18 June 2017.

36 Todd Shephard, "Judicial Watch: New Clinton email shows classified info sent to Clinton Foundation," *Washington Examiner*, June 1, 2017 washingtonexaminer.com/judicial-watch-new-clinton-email-shows-classified-info-sent-to-clinton-foundation/article/2624749. Accessed 18 June 2017.

37 "Full Transcript and Video: James Comey's Testimony on Capitol Hill," *The New York Times*, June 8, 2017 nytimes.com/2017/06/08/us/politics/senate-hearing-transcript.html. Accessed 16 June 2017.

38 "Judicial Watch: Huma Abedin Emails Reveal Transmission of Classified Information and Clinton Foundation Donors Receiving Special Treatment from Clinton State Department," Judicial Watch, August 2, 2017 judicialwatch.org/press-room/press-releases/judicial-watch-huma-abedin-emails-reveal-transmission-classified-information-clinton-foundation-donors-receiving-special-treatment-clinton-state-department/. Accessed 7 August 2017.

39 Peter Hasson, "Bush AG: Lynch 'Betrayal' Made DOJ 'An Arm Of The Clinton Campaign'," *The Daily Caller*, June 9, 2017 dailycaller.com/2017/06/09/bush-ag-lynch-betrayal-made-doj-an-arm-of-the-clinton-campaign/. Accessed 18 June 2017.

40 Julia Limitone, "Obama guilty of real Hillary Clinton obstruction, Fmr. US AG Mukasey says," *Fox Business*, June 13, 2017 foxbusiness.com/politics/2017/06/13/obama-guilty-real-hillary-clinton-obstruction-fmr-us-ag-mukasey-says.html. Accessed 18 June 2017.

41 Debra Heine, "Comey Began Drafting EmailGate 'Exoneration Statement' Before Interviewing 17 Key Witnesses, Including Clinton," PJ Media, August 31, 2017 pjmedia.com/trending/2017/08/31/comey-began-drafting-emailgate-exoneration-statement-interviewing-17-key-witnesses-including-clinton/. Accessed 8 December 2017.

42 Max Kutner, "Comey Drafted Statement Ending Clinton Email Investigation Months Before Interviewing Her, FBI Confirms," *Newsweek*, October 16, 2017 newsweek.

com/james-comey-fbi-clinton-emails-drafted-statement-686140. Accessed 8 December 2017.

43   Jason Le Miere, "Hillary Clinton Calls Email Scandal Fake News and 'Biggest Nothing Burger Ever,'" *Newsweek*, May 31, 2017 newsweek.com/hillary-clinton-emails-fake-news-618557. Accessed 16 June 2017.

44   Geoffrey Dickens, "STUDY: How the Broadcast Networks Have Deleted Hillary's E-Mail Scandal," *Newsbusters*, April 21, 2015 newsbusters.org/blogs/geoffrey-dickens/2015/04/21/study-how-broadcast-networks-have-deleted-hillarys-e-mail-scandal. Accessed 18 June 2017.

45   Matthew Balan, "CNN's Banfield: Hillary E-Mail Scandal 'Not Even a Scandal,'" *Newsbusters*, October 9, 2015 newsbusters.org/blogs/nb/matthew-balan/2015/10/09/cnns-banfield-hillary-e-mail-scandal-not-even-scandal. Accessed 18 June 2017.

46   Rich Noyes, "MRC Study: Documenting TV's Twelve Weeks of Trump Bashing," *Newsbusters*, October 25, 2016 newsbusters.org/blogs/nb/rich-noyes/2016/10/25/mrc-study-documenting-tvs-twelve-weeks-trump-bashing. Accessed 18 June 2017.

47   Mike Ciandella, "Networks Cover for Hillary on Wikileaks, Ignore Mention of Other Journalists," *Newsbusters*, October 12, 2016 newsbusters.org/blogs/nb/mike-ciandella/2016/10/12/networks-cover-hillary-wikileaks-ignore-mention-other-journalists. Accessed 18 June 2017.

48   Nicholas Fondacaro, "ABC Ignores Revelation that Obama Knew About Clinton's Private Server," *Newsbusters*, October 25, 2016 newsbusters.org/blogs/nb/nicholas-fondacaro/2016/10/25/abc-ignores-revelation-obama-knew-about-clintons-private. Accessed 18 June 2017.

49   Tom Blumer, "AP Buries, Notes Nothing Unusual in Obama E-Mailing Hillary's Private Server Using Pseudonym," *Newsbusters*, September 26, 2016 newsbusters.org/blogs/nb/tom-blumer/2016/09/26/obama-emailed-hillarys-private-server-using-pseudonym-ap-buries-notes. Accessed 18 June 2017.

50   Jordan Sekulow, "DOJ Document Dump to ACLJ on Clinton Lynch Meeting: Comey FBI Lied, Media Collusion, Spin, and Illegality," American Center for Law and Justice, August 4, 2017 aclj.org/government-corruption/doj-document-dump-to-aclj-on-clinton-lynch-meeting-comey-fbi-lied-media-collusion-spin-and-illegality. Accessed 7 August 2017.

51   Scott Whitlock, "Nets Censor Bombshell That Comey Didn't Wait for Facts to Rescue Hillary," *Newsbusters*, September 1, 2017 newsbusters.org/blogs/nb/scott-whitlock/2017/09/01/nets-censor-bombshell-comey-didnt-wait-facts-rescue-hillary. Accessed 8 December 2017.

The OPM Hacking Scandal Notes

1   CQ Transcripts Wire , "Obama Remarks On Confronting Terrorist Threats," *The Washington Post*, July 16, 2008 washingtonpost.com/wp-dyn/content/article/2008/07/16/AR2008071601474.html. Accessed 15 June 2017.

2   Devlin Barrett, Danny Yadron and Damian Paletta, "U.S. Suspects Hackers in China Breached About 4 Million People's Records, Officials Say," *The Wall Street Journal*, June 5, 2015 wsj.com/articles/u-s-suspects-hackers-in-china-behind-government-data-breach-sources-say-1433451888. Accessed 14 June 2017.

3 Devlin Barrett and Damian Paletta, "Officials Masked Severity Of Hack," *The Wall Street Journal*, June 24, 2015 wsj.com/articles/hack-defined-as-two-distinct-breaches-1435158334. Accessed 14 June 2017.

4 Mike Levine, "OPM Hack Far Deeper Than Publicly Acknowledged, Went Undetected For More Than A Year, Sources Say," *ABC News*, June 11, 2015 abcnews.go.com/Politics/opm-hack-deeper-publicly-acknowledged-undetected-year-sources/story?id=31689059. Accessed 14 June 2017.

5 Cory Bennett, "GOP chairman: Breach could affect 32 million," *The Hill*, June 24, 2015 thehill.com/policy/cybersecurity/245964-gop-chair-thinks-breach-could-reach-32-million. Accessed 14 June 2017.

6 Paul Barrett, "When Spotting a Hack Doesn't Help You," *Bloomberg*, October 28, 2016 bloomberg.com/news/articles/2016-10-28/when-spotting-a-hack-doesn-t-help-you. Accessed 14 June 2017.

7 Shane Harris, "Spies Warned Feds About OPM Mega-Hack Danger," *The Daily Beast*, June 30, 2015 thedailybeast.com/spies-warned-feds-about-opm-mega-hack-danger. Accessed 14 June 2017.

8 Paul Conway, "How Obama's Poor Judgment Led to the Chinese Hack of OPM," *The Daily Signal*, 7/27/2015 dailysignal.com/2015/07/27/how-obamas-poor-judgment-led-to-the-chinese-hack-of-opm/. Accessed 14 June 2017.

9 Jim Geraghty, "The OPM Hack and Obama's Politicization of the Federal Bureacracy," *National Review*, June 29, 2015 nationalreview.com/article/420449/opm-hack-and-obamas-politicization-federal-bureacracy-jim-geraghty. Accessed 14 June 2017.

10 Dave Boyer, "Obama still backs OPM chief despite massive data breach," *Washington Times*, June 17, 2015 washingtontimes.com/news/2015/jun/17/obama-still-backs-opm-chief-despite-data-breach/. Accessed 14 June 2017.

11 Julie Hirschfeld Davis, "Katherine Archuleta, Director of Personnel Agency, Resigns," *The New York Times*, July 10, 2015 nytimes.com/2015/07/11/us/katherine-archuleta-director-of-office-of-personnel-management-resigns.html. Accessed 14 June 2017.

12 Aaron Boyd, "Contractor breach gave hackers keys to OPM data," *Federal Times*, June 23, 2015 federaltimes.com/smr/opm-data-breach/2015/06/23/contractor-breach-gave-hackers-keys-to-opm-data/. Accessed 15 June 2017.

13 Zack Whittaker, "The company linked to the OPM hack just got hired by the government again," *ZDNet*, October 3, 2016 zdnet.com/article/the-company-linked-to-opm-hack-just-got-hired-by-the-government-again/. Accessed 15 June 2017.

14 Joseph Rossell, "Networks Ignore Obama's Broken Promises on Cybersecurity in 90 Percent of Cyber Stories," *Newsbusters*, August 13, 2015 newsbusters.org/blogs/business/joseph-rossell/2015/08/13/networks-ignore-obamas-broken-promises-cybersecurity-90. Accessed 15 June 2017.

15 Editorial Board, "The cyber defense crisis," *The Washington Post*, July 11, 2015 washingtonpost.com/opinions/the-cyber-defense-crisis/2015/07/11/2fb8a500-2732-11e5-aae2-6c4f59b050aa_story.html. Accessed 15 June 2017.

EPA Environmental Scandals Notes

1 Jesse Paul, "EPA: Waste pressure evidently never checked before Colorado mine spill," *Denver Post*, August 26, 2015 denverpost.com/2015/08/26/epa-waste-pressure-evidently-never-checked-before-colorado-mine-spill/. Accessed 11 June 2017.

2 John M. Glionna and Matt Pearce, "States downstream from contaminated river upset that EPA didn't alert them," *Los Angeles Times*, August 11, 2015 latimes.com/nation/la-na-colorado-river-spill-20150811-story.html. Accessed 11 June 2017.

3 Julie Turkewitz, "Environmental Agency Uncorks Its Own Toxic Water Spill at Colorado Mine," *The New York Times*, August 10, 2015. Accessed 11 June 2017.

4 City Enders, "Confusion plagues EPA response to toxic Colorado mining spill it caused," *The Guardian*, August 11, 2015 theguardian.com/us-news/2015/aug/11/colorado-animas-river-spill-mine-toxic-waste-epa. Accessed 11 June 2017.

5 Richard Pérez-Peña, "Study Faults E.P.A. for Toxic Wastewater Spill in Colorado Rockies," *The New York Times*, October 22, 2015 nytimes.com/2015/10/23/us/study-faults-epa-for-toxic-wastewater-spill-in-colorado-rockies.html. Accessed 11 June 2017.

6 Elizabeth Chuck, "EPA Chief on Toxic Colorado Spill: 'This River Is Restoring Itself," *NBC News*, August 13, 2015 nbcnews.com/news/us-news/epa-chief-toxic-colorado-spill-river-restoring-itself-n409336. Accessed 11 June 2017.

7 Bruce Finley, "Gold King one year later: Colorado's mustard-yellow disaster spurs plans for leaking mine," *Denver Post*, July 24, 2016 denverpost.com/2016/07/24/gold-king-mine-spill-animas-river-one-year-later/. Accessed 11 June 2017.

8 Ethan Barton, "DOJ WON'T Charge EPA Employee Who Caused Gold King Mine Disaster," *The Daily Caller*, October 13, 2016 dailycaller.com/2016/10/13/doj-wont-charge-epa-employee-who-caused-gold-king-mine-disaster/. Accessed 12 June 2017.

9 Michael Biesecker, "Documents Show EPA Officials Knew Of Potential For Mine 'Blowout," *Talking Points Memo*, August 22, 2015 talkingpointsmemo.com/news/epa-mine-leak-documents. Accessed 13 June 2017.

10 Valerie Richardson, "Outraged Westerners look to Trump after Obama's EPA refuses to pay claims from Gold King Mine spill," *Washington Times*, January 18, 2017 washingtontimes.com/news/2017/jan/19/obamas-epa-refuses-pay-claims-gold-king-mine-spill/. Accessed 11 June 2017.

11 Bruce Finley, "Inspector general clears EPA in investigation of Gold King Mine disaster," *Denver Post*, June 12, 2017 denverpost.com/2017/06/12/gold-king-mine-inspector-general-clears-epa/. Accessed 16 June 2017.

12 Wikipedia Contributors, "Flint water crisis," *Wikipedia, The Free Encyclopedia*, June 12, 2017. en.wikipedia.org/wiki/Flint_water_crisis#Condensed_timeline_of_the_crisis. Accessed 12 June 2017.

13 Ashley Southall, "State of Emergency Declared Over Man-Made Water Disaster in Michigan City," *The New York Times*, January 18, 2016 nytimes.com/2016/01/18/us/obama-flint-michigan-water-fema-emergency-disaster.html. Accessed 13 June 2017.

14 Devin Henry, "Obama: 'I would be beside myself' if I were a parent in Flint," *The Hill*, 1/20/2016 thehill.com/policy/energy-environment/266494-obama-i-would-be-beside-myself-to-be-a-parent-in-flint. Accessed 11 June 2017.

15 David French, "Can the Truth Survive the Left's Onslaught in Flint?" *National Review,* January 25, 2016 nationalreview.com/article/430279/flint-water-scandal-democrats-try-pin-blame-republicans. Accessed 11 June 2017.

16 Josh Sunburn, "Why the EPA is Party to Blame for the Flint Water Crisis," *TIME,* January 22, 2016 time.com/4190643/flint-water-crisis-susan-hedman-epa/. Accessed 13 June 2017.

17 Ben Mathis-Lilley, "The EPA *Also* Knew Flint's Water Might Be Poisoned Last Year But Didn't Tell Anyone," *Slate,* January 14, 2016 slate.com/blogs/the_slatest/2016/01/14/epa_knew_about_flint_water_problems_in_april_2015.html. Accessed 11 June 2017.

18 Kyle Keldscher, "EPA memo: Flint not worth going 'out on a limb for," *Washington Examiner,* March 15, 2016 washingtonexaminer.com/epa-memo-flint-community-not-worth-going-out-on-a-limb-for/article/2585831. Accessed 13 June 2017.

19 "Management Alert: Drinking Water Contamination in Flint, Michigan, Demonstrates a Need to Clarify EPA Authority to Issue Emergency Orders to Protect the Public," U.S. Environmental Protection Agency, October 20, 2016 epa.gov/sites/production/files/2016-10/documents/_epaoig_20161020-17-p-0004.pdf. Accessed 13 June 2017.

20 Kate Abbey-Lambertz, "Obama Declared An Emergency In Flint One Year Ago. The Crisis Isn't Over," *Huffington Post,* January 16, 2017 huffingtonpost.com/entry/flint-water-crisis-continues_us_587c7f05e4b0b3c7a7b2026a. Accessed 13 June 2017.

21 Todd Blumer, "Press Downplays, Hides EPA's Responsibility for Western River Contamination," *Newsbusters,* August 9, 2015. newsbusters.org/blogs/nb/tom-blumer/2015/08/09/press-downplays-epas-responsibility-colorado-river-contamination. Accessed 13 June 2017.

22 Kyle Drennen, "MSNBC Tries to Blame 'Locals,' Not EPA, for River Pollution," *Newsbusters,* August 10, 2015 newsbusters.org/blogs/nb/kyle-drennen/2015/08/10/msnbc-tries-blame-locals-not-epa-river-pollution. Accessed 11 June 2017.

23 Spencer Riley, "Activist On MSNBC Compares EPA Disaster To Defusing 'A Bomb In A Crowded Market', Blames Local Mines," *Newsbusters,* August 12, 2015 newsbusters.org/blogs/nb/spencer-raley/2015/08/12/activist-msnbc-compares-epa-disaster-diffusing-bomb-crowded-market. Accessed 13 June 2017.

24 Becket Adams, "CNN ignores EPA's role in story on Flint water crisis," *Washington Examiner,* January 19, 2016 washingtonexaminer.com/cnn-ignores-epas-role-in-story-on-flint-water-crisis/article/2580908. Accessed 13 June 2017.

The Iran Ransom Scandal Notes

1 James Phillips, Luke Coffey and Michaela Dodge, "The Iran Nuclear Agreement: Yes, There Is a Better Alternative," Heritage Foundation, July 24, 2015 heritage.org/middleeast/report/the-iran-nuclear-agreement-yes-there-better-alternative. Accessed 8 July 2017.

2 Alex Griswold, "John Kerry Thanks Iran For Releasing Captured U.S. Soldiers," *Mediaite,* January 13, 2016 mediaite.com/tv/john-kerry-thanks-iran-for-releasing-captured-u-s-soldiers/. Accessed 8 July 2017.

3 Laura Koran, "U.S. to pay Iran $1.7 billion in legal settlement," *CNN,* January 17, 2016 cnn.com/2016/01/17/politics/us-pays-iran-1-7-billion/. Accessed 8 July 2017.

4   Laura Koran, "U.S. to pay Iran $1.7 billion in legal settlement," *CNN*, January 17, 2016 cnn.com/2016/01/17/politics/us-pays-iran-1-7-billion/index.html. Accessed 8 July 2017.

5   Elise Labor, "John Kerry: Some sanctions relief money for Iran will go to terrorism," *CNN*, January 21, 2016 cnn.com/2016/01/21/politics/john-kerry-money-iran-sanctions-terrorism/index.html. Accessed 8 July 2017.

6   Jay Solomon and Carol E. Lee, "U.S. Sent Cash to Iran as Americans Were Freed," *The Wall Street Journal*, August 3, 2016 wsj.com/articles/u-s-sent-cash-to-iran-as-americans-were-freed-1470181874. Accessed 8 July 2017.

7   Andrew C. McCarthy, "If the $400 Million to Iran Was Legit, Why Won't the Administration Answer Basic Questions?" *National Review*, August 9, 2016 nationalreview.com/article/438804/iran-ransom-payment-barack-obama-tried-be-sneaky. Accessed 8 July 2017.

8   Stephen Collinson, Elise Labott and Kevin Liptak, "Obama on Iran payment: 'We do not pay ransom,'" *CNN*, August 5, 2016 cnn.com/2016/08/04/politics/iran-400-million-kerry-rejects-ransom/index.html. Accessed 8 July 2017.

9   Jay Solomon and Carol E. Lee, "U.S. Sent Cash to Iran as Americans Were Freed," *The Wall Street Journal*, August 3, 2016 wsj.com/articles/u-s-sent-cash-to-iran-as-americans-were-freed-1470181874. Accessed 8 July 2017.

10 Stephen Collinson, Elise Labott and Kevin Liptak, "Obama on Iran payment: 'We do not pay ransom,'" *CNN*, August 5, 2016 cnn.com/2016/08/04/politics/iran-400-million-kerry-rejects-ransom/index.html. Accessed 8 July 2017.

11 Jay Solomon and Carol E. Lee, "U.S. Held Cash Until Iran Freed Prisoners," *The Wall Street Journal*, August 18, 2016 wsj.com/articles/u-s-held-cash-until-iran-freed-prisoners-1471469256. Accessed 8 July 2017.

12 Daniel Halper, "State Dept.: $400M to Iran was contingent on US prisoners' release," *New York Post*, August 18, 2016 nypost.com/2016/08/18/state-department-400m-cash-to-iran-was-contingent-on-us-prisoners-release/. Accessed 8 July 2017.

13 Jonathan Broder, "Exclusive: U.S. Taxpayers, Not Tehran, Compensated Victims Of Iranian Attacks Against Americans," *Newsweek*, January 22, 2016 newsweek.com/iran-nuclear-deal-terrorism-victims-families-stephen-flatow-barack-obama-418770. Accessed 8 July 2017.

14 Joe Tacopino, "Hostage: We couldn't leave until second plane landed in Iran," *New York Post*, August 5, 2016 nypost.com/2016/08/05/hostage-we-waited-for-2nd-plane-to-land-in-iran-before-leaving/. Accessed 8 July 2017.

15 Marisa Schultz and Bob Fredericks, "GOP blasts Obama's $400M 'secret ransom' paid to Iran," *New York Post*, August 3, 2016 nypost.com/2016/08/03/gop-blasts-obamas-400m-secret-ransom-paid-to-iran/. Accessed 8 July 2017.

16 Bradley Klapper, "Obama lied 'openly and blatantly' about cash payment to Iran, Trump says," *CTV News*, August 19, 2016 ctvnews.ca/world/obama-lied-openly-and-blatantly-about-cash-payment-to-iran-trump-says-1.3035464. Accessed 8 July 2017.

17 Jonathan Broder, "Exclusive: U.S. Taxpayers, Not Tehran, Compensated Victims Of Iranian Attacks Against Americans," *Newsweek*, January 22, 2016 newsweek.com/iran-nuclear-deal-terrorism-victims-families-stephen-flatow-barack-obama-418770. Accessed 8 July 2017.

18 Louis Nelson, "U.S. wire payments to Iran undercut Obama," *Politico*, September 18, 2016 politico.com/story/2016/09/us-iran-payments-wire-transfer-228324. Accessed 8 July 2017.

19 "Hensarling Statement on State Department Admission That Payment to Iran Was Contingent on Release of Hostages," Financial Services Committee, August 18, 2016 financialservices.house.gov/news/documentsingle.aspx?DocumentID=400963. Accessed 8 July 2017.

20 Andrew C. McCarthy, "President Obama Violated the Law with His Ransom Payment to Iran," *National Review*, August 6, 2016 nationalreview.com/article/438744/iran-ransom-payment-president-obama-broke-law-sending-cash-iran. Accessed 8 July 2017.

21 McCarthy, "President Obama Violated the Law.".

22 Adam Kredo, "Obama Admin Hiding Secret Hostage Docs Signed With Iranian Intel Officials," *The Washington Free Beacon*, October 5, 2016 freebeacon.com/national-security/obama-admin-hiding-secret-hostage-docs-signed-iran-spymasters/. Accessed 8 July 2017.

23 Adam Kredo, "Congress: Attorney General Lynch 'Pleads Fifth' on Secret Iran 'Ransom' Payment," *The Washington Free Beacon*, October 28, 2016 freebeacon.com/national-security/attorney-general-lynch-pleads-fifth-secret-iran-ransom-payments/. Accessed 8 July 2017.

24 Geoffrey Dickens, "The Seven Most Undercovered Obama Scandals," *Newsbusters*, January 17, 2017 newsbusters.org/blogs/nb/geoffrey-dickens/2017/01/16/seven-most-undercovered-obama-scandals. Accessed 8 July 2017.

25 "The Fake $400 Million Iran 'Ransom' Story," *The New York Times*, August 23, 2016 nytimes.com/2016/08/23/opinion/the-fake-400-million-iran-ransom-story.html. Accessed 8 July 2017.

26 Allen S. Weiner and Duncan Pickard, "The $400 million payment to Iran was American diplomacy at its finest," *The Washington Post*, August 11, 2016 washingtonpost.com/opinions/global-opinions/the-400-million-payment-to-iran-was-american-diplomacy-at-its-finest/2016/08/11/2d1e6d5a-5f3c-11e6-af8e-54aa2e849447_story.html. Accessed 8 July 2017.

27 Kristine Marsh, "PolitiFact Laughably Rates Trump's Claim $400 Million to Iran Was 'Ransom' as 'Mostly False'," *Newsbusters*, August 25, 2016 newsbusters.org/blogs/nb/kristine-marsh/2016/08/25/politifact-laughably-rates-trumps-claim-400-million-iran-was. Accessed 8 July 2017.

28 Tim Graham, "WashPost Buries Iran-Ransom Admission in Middle of Page A-10 -- Despite Ransom Paid for Post Reporter!," *Newsbusters*, August 19, 2016 newsbusters.org/blogs/nb/tim-graham/2016/08/19/washpost-buries-iran-ransom-admission-middle-page-10-despite-ransom. Accessed 10 July 2017.

29 Carol Morello, "Post reporter Jason Rezaian and his family file federal lawsuit against Iranian government," *The Washington Post*, October 3, 2016 washingtonpost.com/world/national-security/post-reporter-jason-rezaian-and-his-family-file-federal-lawsuit-against-iranian-government/2016/10/03/a36fa8a2-8962-11e6-bff0-d53f592f176e_story.html. Accessed 10 July 2017.

30 Ibid.

31 Marc A. Thiessen, "Jason Rezaian files suit saying Iran held him as a hostage to 'extort' $1.7 billion payment," American Enterprise Institute, October 4, 2016 aei.org/publication/jason-rezaian-iran-hostage-1-7-million-payment/. Accessed 10 July 2017.
32 Ibid.

The Trump Surveillance Scandal Notes

1 Jeremy Diamond, Jeff Zeleny and Shimon Prokupecz, "Trump's baseless wiretap claim," *CNN*, March 5, 2017 cnn.com/2017/03/04/politics/trump-obama-wiretap-tweet/index.html. Accessed 14 July 2017.

2 Pierre Thomas, Jack Date, Rhonda Schwartz, and Erin Dooley, "FBI director James Comey asked Justice Department to refute Trump's wiretapping claims, sources say," *ABC News*, March 5, 2017 abcnews.go.com/Politics/fbi-director-james-comey-asked-justice-department-refute/story?id=45927629. Accessed 14 July 2017.

3 Matthew Boyle, "Non-Denial 'Denial': Obama Response to Trump 'Wiretap' Claim Raises More Questions," *Breitbart*, March 4, 2017. breitbart.com/big-government/2017/03/04/non-denial-denial-obama-response-trump-wiretap-claim-raises-questions/. Accessed 14 July 2017.

4 Eddie Scarry, "New York Times downplays 'wiretapped data' in online story of Trump investigation," *Washington Examiner*, March 9, 2017 washingtonexaminer.com/new-york-times-downplays-wiretapped-data-in-online-story-of-trump-investigation/article/2616939. Accessed 14 July 2017.

5 Maggie Haberman, Matthew Rosenberg, Matt Apuzzo and Glenn Thrush, "Michael Flynn Resigns as National Security Adviser," *The New York Times*, February 13, 2017 nytimes.com/2017/02/13/us/politics/donald-trump-national-security-adviser-michael-flynn.html. Accessed 14 July 2017.

6 Ellen Nakashima and Greg Miller, "FBI reviewed Flynn's calls with Russian ambassador but found nothing illicit," *The Washington Post*, January 23, 2017 washingtonpost.com/world/national-security/fbi-reviewed-flynns-calls-with-russian-ambassador-but-found-nothing-illicit/2017/01/23/aa83879a-e1ae-11e6-a547-5fb9411d332c_story.html. Accessed 14 July 2017.

7 Andrew C. McCarthy, "The Obama Camp's Disingenuous Denials on FISA," *National Review*, March 5, 2017 nationalreview.com/corner/445504/obama-camps-fisa-surveillance-trump-denials. Accessed 14 July 2017.

8 Gage Cohen, "FISA Surveillance Requests Are Almost Never Rejected," *The Daily Caller*, March 6, 2017 dailycaller.com/2017/03/06/fisa-surveillance-requests-are-almost-never-rejected/. Accessed 14 July 2017.

9 Andrew C. McCarthy, "The Obama Camp's Disingenuous Denials on FISA Surveillance of Trump," *National Review*, March 5, 2017 nationalreview.com/corner/445504/obama-camp-disingenuous-denials-fisa-surveillance-trump. Accessed 14 July 2017.

10 Andrew C. McCarthy, "The Obama Camp's Disingenuous Denials on FISA Surveillance of Trump," *National Review*, March 5, 2017 nationalreview.com/corner/445504/obama-camp-disingenuous-denials-fisa-surveillance-trump. Accessed 14 July 2017.

11 Karoun Demirjian, "House Intelligence Chairman Devin Nunes recuses himself from Russia probe," *The Washington Post*, April 6, 2017 washingtonpost.com/powerpost/house-intelligence-chairman-devin-nunes-recuses-himself-from-russia-

probe/2017/04/06/8122b5bc-1ad2-11e7-855e-4824bbb5d748_story.html. Accessed 14 July 2017.

12   Eli Lake, "Susan Rice Sought Names of Trump Associates in Intel," *Bloomberg*, April 3, 2017 bloomberg.com/view/articles/2017-04-03/top-obama-adviser-sought-names-of-trump-associates-in-intel. Accessed 14 July 2017.

13   Eli Lake, "Susan Rice Sought Names of Trump Associates in Intel," *Bloomberg*, April 3, 2017 bloomberg.com/view/articles/2017-04-03/top-obama-adviser-sought-names-of-trump-associates-in-intel. Accessed 14 July 2017.

14   Richard Pollock, "Former US Attorney: Susan Rice Ordered Spy Agencies To Produce 'Detailed Spreadsheets' Involving Trump," *The Daily Caller*, April 3, 2017 dailycaller. com/2017/04/03/susan-rice-ordered-spy-agencies-to-produce-detailed-spread-sheets-involving-trump/. Accessed 14 July 2017.

15   Adam Housley, "Susan Rice requested to unmask names of Trump transition officials, sources say," *Fox News*, April 3, 2017 foxnews.com/politics/2017/04/03/susan-rice-requested-to-unmask-names-trump-transition-officials-sources-say.html. Accessed 14 July 2017.

16   "CNN Goes On Rampage Against Susan Rice Bombshell, Instructs Viewers to Ignore Story," *Grabien News*, April 4, 2017 news.grabien.com/story-cnn-goes-rampage-against-susan-rice-bombshell-instructs-view. Accessed 14 July 2017.

17   Andrew C. McCarthy, "Susan Rice's White House Unmasking: A Watergate-style Scandal," *National Review*, April 4, 2017 nationalreview.com/article/446415/susan-rice-unmasking-trump-campaign-members-obama-administration-fbi-cia-nsa. Accessed 14 July 2017.

18   "Fresh evidence the Russia 'scandal' is a Team Obama operation," *New York Post*, April 3, 2017 nypost.com/2017/04/03/fresh-evidence-the-russia-scandal-is-a-team-obama-operation/. Accessed 14 July 2017.

19   Dan Boylan and Guy Taylor, "Congress issues subpoenas in push for more info on 'unmasking' by Obama-era officials," *Washington Times*, June 1, 2017 washingtontimes. com/news/2017/jun/1/congress-pushes-more-alleged-unmasking-trump-campa/. Accessed 14 July 2017.

20   Jack Crowe, "Former Obama Aide Ben Rhodes Named In House Unmasking Investigation," *The Daily Caller*, August 8, 2017 dailycaller.com/2017/08/02/former-obama-aide-ben-rhodes-named-in-house-unmasking-investigation/. Accessed 8 August 2017.

21   Adam Kredo, "Former U.N. Amb. Power Unmasked 'Hundreds' In Final Year Of Obama Admin," *The Washington Free Beacon*, August 2, 2017 freebeacon.com/ national-security/former-u-n-amb-power-unmasked-hundreds-last-year-obama-admin/. Accessed 8 August 2017.

22   Michael W. Chapman, "Judicial Watch Sues for Records on Obama White House Unmasking Trump Associates," *CNS News*, May 26, 2017 cnsnews.com/news/article/ michael-w-chapman/judicial-watch-sues-records-obama-white-house-unmasking-trump. Accessed 14 July 2017.

23   "Judicial Watch: Obama NSC Advisor Susan Rice's Unmasking Material is at Obama Library," Judicial Watch, June 19, 2017 judicialwatch.org/press-room/press-releases/ judicial-watch-obama-nsc-advisor-susan-rices-unmasking-material-obama-library/. Accessed 14 July 2017.

24 Dan Boylan and Guy Taylor, "Sealing and transfer of Susan Rice records angers House committee investigating 'unmasking," *Washington Times*, June 22, 2017 washington-times.com/news/2017/jun/22/susan-rice-records-intelligence-committee-wants-ar/. Accessed 14 July 2017.

25 Evan Perez, Shimon Prokupecz and Manu Raju, "FBI used dossier allegations to bolster Trump-Russia investigation," *CNN*, April 18, 2017 cnn.com/2017/04/18/politics/fbi-dossier-carter-page-donald-trump-russia-investigation/index.html. Accessed December 10, 2017

26 Kenneth P. Vogel, "The Trump Dossier: What We Know and Who Paid for It," *The New York Times*, October 25, 2017 nytimes.com/2017/10/25/us/politics/steele-dossier-trump-expained.html. Accessed 10 December 2017.

27 Tom Hamburger and Rosalind S. Helderman, "FBI once planned to pay former British spy who authored controversial Trump dossier," *The Washington Post*, February 28, 2017. washingtonpost.com/politics/fbi-once-planned-to-pay-former-british-spy-who-authored-controversial-trump-dossier/2017/02/28/896ab470-facc-11e6-9845-576c69081518_story.html. Accessed 10 December 2017.

28 Mark Hosenball and Jonathan Landay, "U.S. congressional panels spar over 'Trump dossier' on Russia contacts," *Reuters*, October 10, 2017 reuters.com/article/us-usa-trump-russia-dossier/u-s-congressional-panels-spar-over-trump-dossier-on-russia-contacts-idUSKBN1CG02L. Accessed 10 December 2017.

29 "READ: James Comey's prepared testimony," *CNN*, June 8, 2017 cnn.com/2017/06/07/politics/james-comey-memos-testimony/index.html. Accessed 10 December 2017.

30 Adam Entous, Devlin Barrett and Rosalind S. Helderman, "Clinton campaign, DNC paid for research that led to Russia dossier," *The Washington Post*, October 24, 2017 cnn.com/2017/06/07/politics/james-comey-memos-testimony/index.html. Accessed 10 December 2017.

31 Byron York, "After Trump dossier revelation, FBI is next," *Washington Examiner*, October 25, 2017 washingtonexaminer.com/byron-york-after-trump-dossier-revelation-fbi-is-next/article/2638540. Accessed 10 December 2017.

32 James Rosen and Jake Gibson, "Top DOJ official demoted amid probe of contacts with Trump dossier firm," *Fox News*, December 7, 2017 foxnews.com/politics/2017/12/07/top-doj-official-demoted-amid-probe-contacts-with-trump-dossier-firm.html. Accessed 10 December 2017.

33 "CNN Goes On Rampage Against Susan Rice Bombshell, Instructs Viewers to Ignore Story," *Grabien News*, April 4, 2017 news.grabien.com/story-cnn-goes-rampage-against-susan-rice-bombshell-instructs-view. Accessed 14 July 2017.

34 Nicholas Fondacaro, "ABC, NBC Cover-Up Revelation Susan Rice Ordered Trump Aides Unmasked, CBS Defends," *Newsbusters*, April 3, 2017 newsbusters.org/blogs/nb/nicholas-fondacaro/2017/04/03/abc-nbc-cover-revelation-susan-rice-ordered-trump-aides. Accessed 14 July 2017.

35 Bradford Richardson, "Susan Rice's critics are sexist and racist: MSNBC," *Washington Times*, April 5, 2017 washingtontimes.com/news/2017/apr/5/msnbc-susan-rice-critics-are-sexist-racist/. Accessed 14 July 2017.

36 Brenden Kirby, "Media Forced to Cover Dossier Bombshell," *LifeZette*, October 25, 2017 lifezette.com/polizette/media-cant-ignore-trump-dossier-revelation/. Accessed 10 December 2017.

NSA/FISA Scandal Notes

1 Sara A. Carter, "Obama intel agency secretly conducted illegal searches on Americans for years," *Circa*, May 23, 2017 circa.com/story/2017/05/23/politics/obama-intel-agency-secretly-conducted-illegal-searches-on-americans-for-years. Accessed 14 July 2017.

2 Ibid.

3 Ibid.

4 Ibid.

5 Sara A. Carter, "Declassified memos show FBI illegally shared spy data on Americans with private parties," *Circa*, May 23, 2017 circa.com/politics/declassified-memos-show-fbi-illegally-shared-spy-data-on-americans-with-private-parties. Accessed 14 July 2017.

6 Andrew C. McCarthy, "Explosive Revelation of Obama Administration Illegal Surveillance of Americans," *National Review*, May 25, 2017 nationalreview.com/article/447973/nsa-illegal-surveillance-americans-obama-administration-abuse-fisa-court-response. Accessed 14 July 2017.

7 Glenn Harlan Reynolds, "Was Obama administration illegal spying worse than Watergate?" *USA Today*, May 30, 2017 usatoday.com/story/opinion/2017/05/30/obama-admin-illegal-spying-worse-than-watergate-glenn-reynolds-column/102284058/. Accessed 14 July 2017.

8 Nicholas C. Fondacaro, "Nets Blackout Massive Constitutional Violations by Obama's NSA," *Newsbusters*, May 25, 2017 newsbusters.org/blogs/nb/nicholas-fondacaro/2017/05/25/nets-blackout-massive-constitutional-violations-obamas-nsa. Accessed 14 July 2017.

Uranium One Scandal Notes

1 Fred Lucas, "6 Key Elements in Understanding the Tangled Uranium One Scandal," *The Daily Signal*, November 16, 2017 dailysignal.com/2017/11/16/6-key-elements-to-understanding-the-tangled-uranium-one-scandal/. Accessed 20 December 2017.

2 Jo Becker and Mike McIntire, "Cash Flowed to Clinton Foundation Amid Russian Uranium Deal" *The New York Times,* April 23, 2015 nytimes.com/2015/04/24/us/cash-flowed-to-clinton-foundation-as-russians-pressed-for-control-of-uranium-company.html. Accessed 20 December 2017.

3 Becker and McIntire, "Cash Flowed to Clinton Foundation."

4 John Solomon and Alison Spann, "FBI uncovered Russian bribery plot before Obama administration approved controversial nuclear deal with Moscow," *The Hill*, October 17, 2017 thehill.com/policy/national-security/355749-fbi-uncovered-russian-bribery-plot-before-obama-administration. Accessed 20 December 2017.

5 Solomon and Spann,. FBI uncovered Russian bribery plot.".

6 Fred Lucas, "6 Key Elements in Understanding the Tangled Uranium One Scandal," *The Daily Signal*, November 16, 2017 dailysignal.com/2017/11/16/6-key-elements-to-understanding-the-tangled-uranium-one-scandal/. Accessed 20 December 2017.

7 Chuck Ross, "FBI Informant's Lawyer — Obama Admin 'Threatened' My Client And His Career," *The Daily Caller*, October 26, 2017 dailycaller.com/2017/10/26/fbi-informants-lawyer-obama-admin-threatened-my-client-and-his-career/. Accessed 20 December 2017.

8 Ibid.

9 "Grassley wants 'gag order' lifted for FBI informant allegedly 'threatened' by Obama DOJ," *Fox News*, October 19, 2017 foxnews.com/politics/2017/10/19/grassley-wants-gag-order-lifted-for-fbi-informant-allegedly-threatened-by-obama-doj.html. Accessed 20 December 2017.

10 Brooke Singman, "Sessions directs prosecutors to 'evaluate certain issues' involving Uranium One and Clinton, leaves door open on special counsel," *Fox News*, November 13, 2017 foxnews.com/politics/2017/11/13/sessions-directs-prosecutors-to-evaluate-certain-issues-involving-uranium-one-and-clinton-leaves-door-open-on-special-counsel.html. Accessed 20 December 2017.

11 Geoffrey Dickens, "Networks Censor Latest Bombshell on Russia/Uranium/Clinton Scandal," *NewsBusters*, October 18, 2017 newsbusters.org/blogs/nb/geoffrey-dickens/2017/10/18/networks-censor-latest-bombshell-russiauraniumclinton-scandal. Accessed 20 December 2017.

12 Dan Gainor, "Media won't touch Russian uranium story tied to Hillary, and other epic journalism disasters," *Fox News*, October 21, 2017 foxnews.com/opinion/2017/10/21/dan-gainor-media-wont-touch-russian-uranium-story-tied-to-hillary-and-other-epic-journalism-disasters.html. Accessed 20 December 2017.

Project Cassandra Scandal Notes

1 Josh Meyer, "The Secret Backstory of How Obama let Hezbollah Off The Hook," *Politico*, December 17, 2017 politico.com/interactives/2017/obama-hezbollah-drug-trafficking-investigation/. Accessed 19 December 2017.

2 Ibid.

3 Ibid.

4 Ibid.

5 Ibid.

6 Ibid.

7 Ibid.

8 Lahav Harkov and Tovah Lazaroff, "Lapid: If Obama Protected Hezbollah Over Iran Deal, He Should Give Back Nobel" *Jerusalem Post*, December 18, 2017 jpost.com/American-Politics/Did-Obama-block-Hezbollah-drug-investigation-over-Iran-deal-518430. Accessed 20 December 2017.

9 Harkov and Lazaroff, "Lapid: If Obama Protected Hezbollah.".

10 Joseph A. Wulfsohn, "Politico Reporter Hits Former Obama Officials For Denying Hezbollah Bombshell: It's 'Ridiculous'" *Mediaite*, December 20, 2017 mediaite.com/online/politico-reporter-hits-former-obama-officials-for-denying-hezbollah-bombshell-its-ridiculous/. Accessed 20 December 2017.

11 Jonathan S. Tobin, "Now, this is presidential obstruction" *New York Post*, December 18, 2017 nypost.com/2017/12/18/now-this-is-presidential-obstruction/. Accessed 19 December 2017.

12 Nicholas Fondacaro, "Nets Cover for Obama, Omit 'Sabotage' of Anti-Terror Efforts for Iran Deal" *Newsbusters*, December 18, 2017 newsbusters.org/blogs/nb/nicholas-fondacaro/2017/12/18/nets-cover-obama-omit-sabotage-anti-terror-efforts-iran-deal. Accessed 19 December 2017.

Conclusion Notes

1 "Adams' Argument for the Defense: 3–4 December 1770," Founders Online, n.d. founders.archives.gov/documents/Adams/05-03-02-0001-0004-0016. Accessed 22 July 2017.

2 "Hillary and Barack Prepare for Texas Debate; McCain Defends Integrity," *CNN*, February 21, 2008 transcripts.cnn.com/TRANSCRIPTS/0802/21/sitroom.03.html. Accessed 28 July 2017.

3 Kyle Smith, "Why comedians and 'SNL' are shielding President Obama," *New York Post*, August 24, 2014 nypost.com/2014/08/24/why-comedians-and-snl-are-shielding-president-obama/. Accessed 9 August 2017.

4 Billy Baldwin (@BillyBaldwin) "I don't like wasting money but if you'd send me a copy I gladly use the pages for kindling or to wipe my ass. #Indivisible #TheResistance," Twitter, April 25, 2017, 8:42 AM.

5 Tim Worstall, "Fascinating Number: Google Is Now 40% Of The Internet," *Forbes*, August 17 2013 forbes.com/sites/timworstall/2013/08/17/fascinating-number-google-is-now-40-of-the-internet/#7400266227c7. Accessed 9 August 2017.

6 Matthew A. Cherry (@MatthewACherry) "I miss the days when the biggest presidential scandal was that time Obama wore a tan suit," Twitter May 9, 2017, 9:09 AM.

7 Karol Markowicz, "Sorry: Trump's excesses don't normalize Obama's," *New York Post*, July 31, 2017 nypost.com/2017/07/31/sorry-trumps-excesses-dont-normalize-obamas/. Accessed 1 August 2017.

8 Glenn Kessler, "Has the Obama White House been 'historically free of scandal'?" *The Washington Post*, January 19, 2017 washingtonpost.com/news/fact-checker/wp/2017/01/19/has-the-obama-white-house-been-historically-free-of-scandal/. Accessed 1 August 2017.

9 Hugh Hewitt, "Democrats demanding a special prosecutor should be careful what they wish for," *The Washington Post*, March 7, 2017 washingtonpost.com/opinions/democrats-demanding-a-special-prosecutor-should-be-careful-what-they-wish-for/2017/03/07/dd5c6730-02ca-11e7-ad5b-d22680e18d10_story.html. Accessed 4 June 2017.

10 Kerry Picket, "Illinois Establishes 'Barack Obama Day'," *The Daily Caller*, August 4, 2017 dailycaller.com/2017/08/04/illinois-establishes-barack-obama-day/. Accessed 9 August 2017.

11 "Thomas Jefferson to Charles Yancey, 6 January 1816," Founders Online, n.d. founders.archives.gov/documents/Jefferson/03-09-02-0209. Accessed 22 July 2017.